Shepherding the Church into the 21st Century

Shepherding the Church into the 21st Century

JOSEPH M. STOWELL

Unless otherwise indicated, all Scripture references are from the *New American Standard Bible*, © the Lockman Foundation 1960, 1962, 1963, 1968, 1971, 1972, 1973, 1975, 1977; other references are from the *Authorized (King James) Version* (KJV).

Copyediting: Barbara Williams
Cover Design: Scott Rattray
Cover Photo: Comstock

ISBN: 1-56476-240-8

Suggested Subject Heading: CHRISTIAN MINISTRIES

1 2 3 4 5 6 7 8 9 10 Printing/Year 98 97 96 95 94

Dedication

To my parents,
Dr. & Mrs. Joseph M. Stowell,
who having ministered for over sixty years
continue to be role models for me
of effectiveness, faithfulness, and balance.

To my grandfather,
Rev. J.J. Pease,
whose exemplary life as a pastor continues to stimulate my ministry.

Contents

Acknowledgments

With Gratitude to:

Our Lord, for calling me to the privilege of ministry and graciously equipping my life for the task.

My wife Martie, for sharing those years of ministry with me as my friend, lover, helper, teacher, and co-laborer in the cause.

Three churches, who welcomed me as their shepherd and patiently sheltered me in their midst.

Lori Imhof, whose skills as my executive secretary have enabled me to be free of many details and demands so that this manuscript could be completed.

Beth Longjohn, whose skillful typing and editing have left a positive impact on this work.

Tim Ostrander, for his insightful recommendations regarding the manuscript.

The good people at Victor Books. My longtime friend, Mark Sweeney, along with Greg Clouse and Barbara Williams, have exercised an unusual measure of patience as they encouraged me through this project.

All who open their hearts to the ministry of this book. May it enable us to be increasingly usable for the glory of our Lord and the gain of His kingdom.

Introduction

If you're looking for a book that deals with methodology, managerial paradigms, and leading-edge concepts for numerical church growth, then this is not the book you're looking for.

This book is about the core of ministry. It is about those who shepherd the flock. It is about the shepherd's call and capacity to cultivate within himself not only a commitment to the fundamental, biblical functions of ministry, but also to the personhood, proclamation, and proficiency that is required if a shepherd is to be effective in an increasingly pagan environment.

When ministries fail, it is most often not because we have failed to understand or even apply the best techniques and programmatic advances with the flock. We most often fail because we have either forgotten or have not known that the key to every ministry is the quality of the shepherd who leads. This book is about qualitative issues that emanate from the life of the leader that enable him to be effective, to be most capable and usable in the hand of the Lord, and about what it takes to develop these core qualities in a rapidly changing, secularized environment.

This extended exposition of 1 Timothy 4:12-17 is about targets. About biblical bull's-eyes that must preoccupy the focus and attention of a spiritual leader who has a passion for effectiveness. And like all target shooting, it's about what it takes to move from the outer rings to a more consistent alignment of our efforts with the center of God's expectations.

Unfortunately, hitting the mark these days is tougher than it's ever been. The dramatic shift of our society has tended to blur vision and divide our focus. The shift has disoriented and discounted the quality of the flock as well. Some have assumed that this new environment demands new targets. Targets more related to programmatic configurations that address the cultural change, and therapeutic perspectives that address the fallout in personal lives. Our fault is not that we are asking how to do church in this new and challenging context or that we are wrestling with how we heal the phenomenal brokenness that increases around us. Our fault is that we are tempted to assume that this new environment changes the target, while our new environment has simply changed the direction and velocity of the wind.

An effective shepherd keeps his finger to the wind, adjusts his technique, but never takes his eyes off the center of the target by which his life and divinely prescribed ministry will be measured.

This book is intended to encourage those who lead toward progress, not perfection.

This book is for leaders who have a passion to succeed, to hear on the other side, "Well done, good and faithful servant."

Section One

PERSPECTIVE:
Perplexities, Priorities, and Platforms

"Our generation is lost to the truth of God, to the reality of divine revelation, to the content of God's will, to the power of His redemption, and to the authority of His Word. For this loss it is paying dearly in a swift relapse to paganism. The savages are stirring again; you can hear them rumbling and rustling in the tempo of our times."

—Carl F.H. Henry

Chapter One

The Best Things in the Worst Times

Triumph in a Tough Environment

In the mid seventeenth century, the rule of Oliver Cromwell in Great Britain began with the execution of Charles I and continued with a ruthless agenda to divest England of any vestige of the monarchy. Targeted in the aftermath of the Cromwellian civil war were the Anglicans who were tied closely to the king who had served as the head of the church. Cromwell emptied the monasteries, removed baptismal fonts from the churches, defamed the clergy, and did everything in his power to disengage their place and influence in the culture. If you were an Anglican pastor, these were tough times to be in the religion business.

In the face of such times there were some who were undaunted. An inspiring but little known inscription hidden away in Harold Church, Staunton, England reads like this: "In the year of 1653, when all things sacred were throughout the nation destroyed or profaned, this church was built to the glory of God by Sir Robert Shirley, whose singular praise it was to have done the best things in the worst times."

I recently spent four days outside of Minsk, Belarus, where I met with 260 godly shepherds of what we used to know as the Soviet Union. I must admit I felt unworthy to stand in their midst. For seventy years the church in the Soviet republics did the work of Christ fearlessly under great oppression. Pastors who would not cooperate with the KGB were often imprisoned or forced to live in a peasant status far from the honor that was due their calling. And yet in these, the toughest of times, they endured and remained faithful until the light broke through and their ministries began to flourish as statues of Lenin, Stalin, and Marx were dismantled throughout the land.

I thought of the inscription on a stone marker behind the bust of Marx directly across the street from the Bolshoi Theater just a few blocks from Red Square in Moscow. They are the words of Lenin inscribed in stone concerning Marx: "His words will last forever, because his words are true." These men who sat before me with legacy-laden faces had never believed that. They never conceded to the prevailing attitudes of their day nor folded under the pressure of their pagan society. They knew they served One whose Word, indeed, will last forever, because *it* is true. And they served with dignity. These were men who did the best things in the worst times.

As we met outside of Minsk where the temperature rarely rose above 15 degrees in the warmest part of the day, we gathered in an auditorium where there was no heat and stayed in hotel rooms where there was no hot water. Most of these pastors crowded into small rooms at night where three of them shared an accommodation. We gathered for lunch in a crowded dining room where we ate meals that were subsistence level at best. We taught in multiple sweaters and coats. Yet, none of it seemed to phase these heroes. They sat, listened, and wrote intently hour after hour as we lectured on matters pertaining to the ministry, theology, apologetics, and the Word of God. It was clear to me that long ago they had made up their minds that life for them would not be a matter of comfort and convenience, but rather commitment to a calling that would in the long run render them pleasing to God and keep the Gospel flame burning during the worst of times.

Not unlike the Cromwell era when Anglicans were disenfranchised, and not unlike our colleagues who battled through seventy years of oppression in the USSR, we are now in the process of being underclassed and forced into a subculture that faces the challenge of affirming truth in an intensely nontruth environment. Our calling is increasingly defamed, Christianity has ceased to be fashionable, and we are often the object of ridicule. We now must proclaim that there are absolutes in a world where relativism rules. It is our task to call people to something beyond themselves in a day where self-fulfillment has been elevated as the ultimate god. We must be willing to stand unintimidated for biblical correctness when it crosses swords with political correctness. It is into a culture where tolerance is the ultimate value that we are called to clearly and compassionately proclaim righteousness in a way that delineates the difference between right and wrong and communicates by its very articulation an intolerance of that which is evil.

THE WORST TIMES

In the last four decades there has been a shift in our culture in terms of its assumptions regarding God. The rise of relativism as a fundamental societal creed has eliminated the God of Scripture, the God of the universe, from any consideration in or over the affairs of society. A culture that wants to do what it wants to do must somehow dethrone a God who rightfully calls men to live under His authority—a God who holds us accountable for embracing what is right and eschewing what is wrong.

Relativism provides the philosophical excuse for life on our own terms. And so in forty short years the God whose laws had provided societal stability has become an outcast. Now, if there is to be a god at all, he will be created by us after our own imagination or after Eastern, New Age formations. But he will not be the God who is truly there, whose wisdom and ways are right and who not only holds man accountable but ultimately reigns over the affairs of men.

Like Rip Van Winkle, we have in large measure slept through these last four decades, and as the alarm clock rings to usher in the twenty-first century, we wake to notice how dramatically different our world is now that God has been relegated to the private compartments of a few lives and the churches they inhabit.

This macro move of society makes our task as spiritual leaders far more complicated.

For reasons best known to God, I have been given the advantage of being a third-generation minister. My grandfather, a 1913 graduate of the Moody Bible Institute, ministered well into the 1970s, first as an evangelist, then as a pastor (in fact, as a pastor in one church for thirty years). My father, who just celebrated his sixtieth year of ministry, has labored faithfully through several strategic pastorates, a stint of denominational leadership, and now, at 83, continues to keep a busy schedule of both preaching and serving on the boards of a major mission agency as well as a Bible college and seminary. Growing up in that kind of context gives one a sixth sense about ministry. It also gives one a long-view perspective of ministry spanning decades of commitment to the cause of Christ. I have read with interest my grandfather's papers, class notes from Moody, and sermon notes as well. And I have recalled a hundred dozen productive memories of my dad's dedication to the Lord's work. Although I am incurably optimistic, I have to admit that trying to tackle spiritual leadership in this season of world history creates challenges and difficulties that neither my grandfather nor father were called to face.

As we seek to effectively manage ministry in this new era, it is imperative that we understand the nature of the change and the elements of our task that are in flux. When it comes to ministry, ignorance about the context in which we minister is not bliss. There are at least twelve ways in which the landscape of ministry has changed. These changes force the issue of getting serious about how we must configure ministry in our day to enable us to be effectively usable in His hand.

The Parson's Prestige

A brief look at American history reminds us that in the early days of our country, it was the local minister who held the highest level of prestige. He not only pastored the church, but also served as teacher of the school, and as such was looked at as the prime authority in the community. We no longer hold that status. The secularization of our culture has devalued the position of spiritual leadership to that of a civil servant for marriages and funerals, to be little more than the local holy man who basically deals in nonessentials and irrelevancies. Just watch the surveys of the most prestigious positions in America, and you'll note that clergy never even make the list. Add to this the growing cynicism toward our kind from our self-inflicted wounds of public failure and you begin to understand why we are so marginalized in terms of influence.

Not only is our status diminished on the outside, but those within may not be as impressed as they once were.

The Parishioner's Perspective

If a shepherd-feeder in our day went to the mirror and said, "Mirror, mirror, on the wall, who's the greatest of them all?" and our people were standing on the other side of the mirror, they'd probably answer, "Swindoll!" But it hasn't always been this way. There was a time when our people would have responded, "You, O blessed pastor," primarily because they never heard anyone else. If they wanted to hear one of the superstars they had to take a chunk of time, drive a long way to a conference, experience his stellar gifts, and bring home their written notes.

Technology has changed everything. The best preachers today are piped into our homes, cars, and heads via our Walkman as we jog. Most of us preach our hearts out, hoping to be affirmed by our flock as shepherd-feeder superior, only to walk through the foyer and hear our flock talking about the terrific series that Stanley is doing on the radio this week. Now that's discouraging! However, if we are committed to the feeding of the saints regardless of who the feeder is, we will be able to celebrate their growth even though it may not be happening directly and immediately through us.

Of course, pleasing church people today is more difficult in more ways than just preaching.

The Great Divide

When my grandparents passed the torch of their generation on to my parents, and when my parents passed the torch of their generation to me, there were some differences, but nothing major. We sang the same hymns, worshiped in the same forms, lived in a similar societal setting, and basically affirmed the same perspectives regarding lifestyle and mind-set. As I am passing the torch of my generation on to my children, I am very much aware (sometimes painfully so) of what a phenomenal difference there is between my generation and theirs. The gap, or should we say the "gulf," is measured in musical styles and preferences, perceptions of truth, perspectives on material goods, purity, commitment, and a host of other issues. This makes doing church in our day a far more difficult task. Take, for instance, the phenomenal upheaval in terms of ministering to people through music. The continuum is broad from people who are comfortable worshiping through the forms of traditional church music to others who have no identity with that form but whose cultural context is more in tune with contemporary styles of worship—idioms resembling the music that they have been brought up with and have learned to relate to. If you're a pastor I don't have to convince you about the struggle.

Churches are full of older folks, middle folks, boomers, busters, and teenagers. Teenagers and young adults who have grown up in a fractured, video-oriented society where there is little tolerance for cognitive contemplation. A world where deep-seated needs for experience, involvement, and sound bites drive the nature of both their existence and expectations.

And then there are the older folks who just want it the way it's always been.

Part of this generational transition is reflected in our shift from an industrialized society where the work ethic was in place, to what is now a service-oriented society where consumerism and specialization are valued.

What's in It for Me?

While pastoring in Detroit, the specific needs of the growing singles population in our ministry led most of us to conclude that we needed to hire a singles pastor. As we processed the vision, we ran into some resistance from the long-timers or, as we affectionately called them, "the lifers," in our congregation. Their question was rather insightful and, quite frankly, one that was difficult to field. According to their memory, in the late '30s and early '40s, the church was running 1,500 in Sunday School, and they only had two pastors. "Why," they asked, "do we need so many pastors today?"

The reality of it was that the church was planted in a time when the work ethic was valued in America. In fact, it was planted in the heart of Detroit where immigrants from the old country had come to work in the automobile factories with a sense of the importance of work and contribution. When they went to the factory, they planned to participate and give of themselves as much as they could. When they came to church, they came the same way—walking in with that "what-can-I-do-to-help" attitude.

As you're aware, all of that has changed. We now live in a consumer-oriented society where we no longer ask "What can I do to help?" but "What will this job (or this church) do for me?" People come to our churches asking "Do I like this pastor? Do I like this choir? Do I like this youth program? Do I like these people?" And asking most of all, "Will this church meet my needs?" It rarely crosses our minds anymore to wonder whether or not we can contribute something or be used to meet the needs of the kingdom in the context of our local church.

Not only are we a consumer-oriented society, but we're a service-oriented society that provides specialists who serve every part and parcel of our lives. This has given rise to an expectation that employers and organizations like government and the church should be specialists in regard to meeting individual needs. Add to this the fragmentization of our societal structures with the resultant deep and crying needs in so many segments, and you have people looking to the church to help meet their specific personal needs in specific ways. There are more singles in our churches than in previous times. More divorcees. More single parents. More who have been abused. More alcoholics. More who are addicted to drugs, pornography, and to a host of other disorders. Since we claim that Christ is sufficient to meet us where we are and bring us consolation, healing, and growth, you can't fault people for expecting and hoping to find that at church. But most of us as spiritual leaders find ourselves unable to meet such a variety of specified challenges.

Thankfully, there are a host of helpful books, video- and audiotapes that can aid us in this process of bringing specified healing to a myriad of needs. Yet the pressure on shepherds to be effective in these areas does bring additional stress, particularly in smaller churches that minister in proximity to mega-churches which offer high-profile programs to these specific needs and drain sheep from our fold into the allure of their long list of tailormade offerings for healing and help.

Not only are we caught in the web of consumerism and the high expectations of specialization, but this new generation is becoming increasingly illiterate.

Dumbing Down

Our culture as a whole is becoming illiterate in terms of its skills of analysis, reason, logic, and other basic cognitive capacities, and the church often reflects the same propensity. According to studies, biblical literacy is at an all-time low in evangelical churches. This dumbing of the church makes it difficult for a shepherd to lead his congregation in a thoughtful analysis of truth and its integration into life. Since they too may lack skills for analysis and integration and in actuality know little about Scripture, George Barna says that the job of the pastor

> . . . is made even more difficult by the biblical illiteracy of the flock. It seems that no amount of Bible-based preaching, scriptural teaching, or small group meetings moves the congregation to a higher plane of Bible knowledge.
>
> For most of the people sitting in the church on a given morning, the pastor knows that his Scripture readings and references will be the only ones to which they will be exposed during the week. Only four out of every ten adults will read any portion of the Bible outside the church during the week.
>
> Those people who do read will commit about one hour to Bible reading during the week. Those people will actually spend more time showering, commuting to and from work, watching television, reading the newspaper, eating meals, or talking on the telephone. Obviously, the Bible is not a high priority in the lives of most people.
>
> And what kind of base of knowledge can the minister realistically hope to build upon through his teaching efforts? Lay members are abysmally ignorant of the basics of the Bible. Most cannot name half of the Ten Commandments. Most people do not know that it was Jesus Christ who preached the Sermon on the Mount. Asked about the book of Thomas, nearly half of all adults will be unaware that such a book is not in the Bible.
>
> The names of the gospels—the first four books in the New Testament—are not known to most people. In fact, probably the most quoted verse is, "God helps those who help themselves." Unfortunately, though people think that verse is in the Bible, Ben Franklin wrote that line two hundred years ago.[1]

And then Barna asks the penetrating question: "Where do you start with this type of audience?"

Our culture is oriented to video experiences, discussions of serious issues in sound bite formats, more storytelling than substantive dialogue, and all of these have impacted the mental formations of Americans.

Not too many decades ago even the non-Christians in our society had a fairly decent grasp on basic biblical stories and content. In today's society, Christians who are fairly regular adherents to the faith may know less than the non-Christian did in the days when the Bible was held in high esteem in our society.

This dumbing of the Christian mind creates fresh challenges in preaching, discipleship, and the educational programming of our ministries which already suffer from a long season of neglect in regard to doctrine.

The Demise of Doctrine

Because of the disintegration of values and societal stability, we have, for the most part, shifted from preaching on doctrinal themes to focusing on pragmatic applications of Scripture. The majority of our pulpit, seminar, workshop, and writing emphases now focuses on families, sexuality, identity, relationships, bitterness, forgiveness, cultural conflicts, and a host of other valid ministry concerns. Noting this trend, *U.S. News & World Report* observes, "Many congregations have multiplied their membership by going light on theology and offering worshipers a steady diet of sermons and support groups that emphasize personal fulfillment."[2]

Dealing with contemporary issues is not the problem. Our fault has been that we have dealt with them without grounding them in the basic doctrinal realities which undergird them. Much of what we hear today is perceived by the average listener as being true because it is better than the alternative, because it works, because it will make life better, because they will be happier. And while that may be true, that is not the reason that we are committed to biblical formulas for living. Biblical principles are imperative because they are applications of the authoritative Word of God and grounded in fundamental doctrine. They are practiced by a true follower whether they work or not. Whether they make us happy or not.

I fear that in the press of the felt needs that have surfaced in our degraded environment, we have bred an intolerance in our listeners for proclamation that focuses on the foundations of our faith. Foundations-doctrine seem to be less relevant, less thrilling, and less oriented to our needs. Admittedly, this is partially the fault of us, the preachers/teachers. In Scripture, doctrinal teaching is accompanied by specific values and life-related applications that are inherently linked to the substance of the doctrine. For instance, family instructions, which have become so popular through the last several decades, are intrinsically grounded in doctrines dealing with the Holy Spirit (Eph. 5:18-21), ecclesiology (vv. 22-24), Christology (vv. 25-33), and the nature of God (6:1-4). Morality is biblically rooted in the doctrine of redemption (1 Cor. 6:15-20). Servanthood is built on the foundation of the Incarnation (Phil. 2:3-11).

The jeopardy for us is not so much that those of us who grew up with stronger doctrinal roots will be swayed; it's that the next generation will know a form of existential Christianity that will be easily jeopardized by its rootlessness.

Of course, focusing on foundations would be easier if our people weren't so distracted.

Stepping Up the Pace

There is no doubt about the fact that the busyness of our society has made us more distracted than we have been in the past. With all of our conveniences, appliances, and advanced equipment, you'd think we'd have more time. Strange, isn't it, that instead we've become busier? Busy with community activities, Little League, civic responsibilities, jobs, family commitments, vacations, travel, and a dozen other things that give us a life not unlike the gerbil who spends most of his time running that weird wire wheel in his cage.

Busyness makes it difficult for us to recruit workers and to program successful special emphases in our churches. Some of us remember when you could hold a missionary conference for a week from Sunday to Sunday (in earlier days for two weeks) and fill the church every night. In the days of D.L. Moody and Billy Sunday, people would crowd halls that were built especially for the crusades, and night after night for four to five weeks, thousands of people would come to hear God's Word proclaimed. Before we get too covetous about those days we need to remember that in those days the only exciting things that ever happened in town were the circus and the revival meetings.

We, on the other hand, struggle to have a missions *emphasis*. We kick it off Friday night with a great banquet, have a youth emphasis on Saturday, and a great closing meeting on Sunday morning.

Sunday evenings are scarcely populated . . . to say nothing of Wednesday night. People are just busier than they've ever been before.

In addition to these changes that challenge the effectiveness of the contemporary church, there are a group of changes that directly relate to the philosophical shift in our culture.

Relatively Pluralistic

Ministering in a pluralistic culture requires that we understand that it is not a true pluralism, but rather a pluralism that is grounded in and tainted by our deep-rooted relativism. Actually, Christianity could flourish in a pure pluralistic setting. Pluralism fundamentally says that everyone has the right to their own truth conclusions. As a result there is a basic respect for a multiplicity of belief systems. Relativism, on the other hand, says that there is no truth and while it encourages us to spend our lives seeking the truth, those who claim to have found it are held in contempt and considered to be naive, intolerant, bigoted, and otherwise unintellectual.

Relativism has groomed a culture that no longer believes in the absolutes of right and wrong but believes in a pluralism that tolerates everything except those of us who claim to know the truth.

In the ministries of my grandfather and father, there was basic cultural assent to the principles that they proclaimed. Divorce was not encouraged. Homosexual acts were clearly wrong. Adultery, pornography, and a host of other social evils were out of bounds. People were not less evil in those days, it's just that they admitted that what they were doing was wrong. This made preaching about righteousness and godliness far more palatable to even the casual hearer. Today, to attempt clear and nonnegotiated teaching regarding principles of right and wrong, sin and righteousness is often greeted by both saint and sinner alike as something that is "too negative," or too "culturally insensitive" to be dealing with in public forums.

While waiting for my shirts at the dry cleaners recently, a highly respected scholar was delivering a lecture on fundamentalism over the radio. He stated that the one thing that was true about fundamentalists is that they believe in absolutes. And then in a cynical aside said, "and to top that, they believe they know what the absolutes are." While this pluralistic perspective characterizes us as being arrogant and foolish, the truth is we do not claim to arbitrarily choose which absolutes we will promote, nor do we have a corner on knowing what all the absolutes are. It goes far deeper than that. It's that we believe in a God who is absolute and true. Since there is a God who is true, who has revealed His truth to us, we humbly affirm what is already grounded in the nature of His existence. Our affirmation of absolutes is sourced in the very essence of the God we serve. We affirm as well that these absolutes are standards to which we will be held accountable. But very few people, even some who have been around the kingdom for a while, will either understand or feel comfortable when we get dogmatic about absolutes.

A recent study reveals how deeply entrenched this relativistic pluralism is even within the new generation to which we minister. Josh McDowell notes, ". . . seventy percent (70%) of today's generation (both churched and nonchurched youth) claim that absolute truth does not exist, that all truth is relative. Most of them say that everything in life is negotiable, and that 'nothing can be known for certain except the things that you experience in your own life.' . . . Our society has so emphasized personal choice and tolerance that practically an entire generation of young people has rejected an absolute standard for right and wrong. And this thinking has greatly affected your children and mine."[3]

Alan Bloom of the University of Chicago notes, "There is one thing a professor can be absolutely certain of: almost every student entering the university believes, or says he believes, that truth is relative. . . . Some are religious, some atheists; some are to the left, some to the right. . . . They are unified only in their relativism. . . ."[4]

Our predicament is complicated by the reality that this shift from theism to relativism has taken the issue of moral authority and vested it in the individual.

I'll Do It My Way

There was a time when just the fact that you were the pastor gave you a big head start in terms of people's respect for your authoritative statements about God and life. But the relativistic mind-set has given us permission to play God and determine what is best, what is right and not right for us, quite apart from any external authority. People today, regardless of what is said, listen for the most part with the arms of their hearts folded.

They assume they have the right to decide for themselves. The failure of public figures hasn't helped us in this arena, nor have educational systems that teach students to make up their own mind regardless of what authority figures like God may have said.

This would not be a particular problem for the shepherd if it weren't for the fact that we speak not in our own authority, but in the authority of the Word of God. When our constituents distance themselves and maintain their autonomy, it is the authority of Christ in their lives that is victimized.

Relativism's birth of the autonomy of the individual in regard to moral authority is spawning a society not unlike the Old Testament times when everyone did what was right in their own eyes.

Princeton University sociologist Robert Wuthnow, in his book *The Restructuring of American Religion*, observes, "We are becoming less theologically and institutionally grounded and more inclined to make up our own faiths as we go along." Jeffrey Sheler describes it as the "design-your-own approach to spirituality. . . ."[5]

The challenge of individuals who believe that moral authority has no external source is encouraged by our culture's commitment to the value of privacy.

Behind Closed Doors

Privacy in American society has been elevated to constitutional status. Many of today's social agendas are grounded in the assumption that our constitution guarantees the right of privacy to all citizens; meaning that we all have a private sphere into which no one has a right to intrude. Abortion is grounded in the issue of privacy, as are alternate sexual preferences. Recent Senate confirmation hearings on Supreme Court nominees have centered on the candidate's view of privacy. This has been a veiled way to ask the candidate about his or her views on the hot topics of abortion and gay rights.

The cascading effect of this is that Americans are increasingly coming to believe that there are certain arenas in their lives into which no one else has the right to intervene. As this attitude seeps into the sphere of the exercise of our faith, it jeopardizes fundamental issues like *total* surrender, submission, and lordship. Privatism leads to religious lives that become compartmentalized, in which God occupies several unrelated and often isolated compartments of our lives. It gives us permission to manage other compartments where no one, including God, has the right to enter. Harvard professor Stephen Carter points out in *The Culture of Disbelief* that society finds it easy to tolerate ". . . people whose religion consists of nothing but a few private sessions of worship and prayer, but who are too secularized to let their faiths influence the rest of their week. This attitude exerts pressure to treat religion as a hobby. . . ."[6]

Privatism works against the nature of the church as a community and mitigates against the functions of discipline and accountability.

The Psalmist David was aware that there were no private sectors in his life when it came to God's right to enter and morally cleanse his life. He prayed, "Search me, O God, and know my heart; try me and know my anxious thoughts; and see if there be any hurtful way in me, and lead me in the everlasting way" (Ps. 139:23-24). Anything short of inviting our Lord's full involvement in every area of our lives is something less than authentic Christianity.

Given the loss of a moral reference point due to the impact of relativism, we are now given to constructing our own sense of right.

When our society establishes something that it affirms to be correct, it becomes the standard for measurement and accountability. These cultural conclusions about right and wrong are "politically correct."

Correctly Incorrect

It's tougher today to preach into a context that ascribes personal, sociological, and moral meaning to certain perspectives, concepts, phrases, and words. On the lighter side, it keeps us on our toes to stay current. People who help on planes are no longer stewardesses, they are "flight attendants," and the handicapped are, at this writing, "challenged." The slightest nuances that violate perceived cultural correctness disenfranchise sensitive hearers. On a recent ministry assignment in Boston, I included in my message an illustration about a husband who came home from work and failed to notice the hard work his wife had been doing that day to straighten the home. I then reversed the illustration and told about a disappointed husband whose wife had failed to notice the stellar job he had done to clean the garage and get the yard in shape.

While the illustrations fit well into applying the principle of the message, they did not fit well into the grid of a couple of university coeds. Afterward they graciously thanked me for being there and then asked why I had so carelessly undone what they had worked so hard to rectify. In their minds I had affirmed stereotypical roles of men and women that they felt needed to be changed. They had evidently given themselves to the liberation of both men and women from these roles that they perceived to be restrictive. I had said nothing that indicated that all women should be at home or all men ought to work in the yard, but my applications, in the grid of their perspective, were culturally incorrect.

More seriously, when political correctness contradicts that which is biblically correct, by and large the relativistic American will reject that which is biblical. It is *correct* to be tolerant. The Bible disagrees if we are talking about sin. It is *correct* to reject absolutes. The Bible disagrees. It is *correct* to affirm our right to alternate sex preferences. The Bible says this is not correct.

It's not surprising, since Christians have refused to shift and chosen rather to fight the drift, that we are often maligned and marginalized in secular America.

The Maligned Minority

Christianity at best has become undervalued. We have been forced into a subculture that runs counter to the prevailing paganism of our day. As we have noted, during the last forty years we have finally made up our mind in America that we really don't want God telling us what to do, what not to do, what is right, or what is wrong. In fact, as we have decided to do the things we want to do, those of us who have tried to put the brakes on have been viewed as impediments to social progress. What Francis Schaeffer predicted has come true. There is now a backlash against Christians and Christianity because we are perceived to be against those things that are "good for us," that make us a more progressive, enlightened community of people. As a result, Christians are ridiculed in sitcoms and the movies and are discounted in terms of what we say, what we believe, and what is important to us.

Our truth claims and calls to repentance are a threat to the godless power base of this new paganism. The word "Christian" did not resonate with tones of honor and respect in the early history of the church, and increasingly it is the same today. In the past those who resisted the flow were tagged as "fundamentalists," then the "radical right," then the "religious right," and now more and more the public references are simply to "Christians" who create trouble by opposing agendas that have been deemed as politically correct. It's hard for a secular society to tolerate those of us who cannot tolerate that which is an offense to God.

We live in a world that, for the most part, no longer wants to hear what we have to say. And it is possible that the churches we shepherd in the decades to come, if we remain authentically committed to Christ and His truth, may indeed suffer persecution beyond the social and media intimidation that we now face.

Add to this rather long list of perplexing dilemmas and differences the stress we heap on ourselves as we compare ourselves to fast-growing, stellarly gifted ministries whose leaders have unusual capacities to accomplish great things in short periods of time; the pressures of working with volunteers; and the reality of finding ourselves in the midst of increased spiritual warfare.

It's just plain tougher to stay committed, encouraged, and unflinching in our call than it has ever been before.

COURAGE AND CONFIDENCE

But then God has not called us to a kingdom cakewalk. Biblical metaphors for being productive in the work of His kingdom all reflect the reality of a tough task. Scripture says that we are like *athletes* in training to win the prize, and that we are to run with focus and discipline lest we ourselves should be disqualified in the process. We are like *farmers* who faithfully carry out our responsibilities in the face of heat, cold, drought, flood. Regardless of the environmental elements, we do our work of planting and watering, and trust God to bring the harvest. We are like *soldiers.* It is clear that soldiering is a difficult task. It requires a commitment to a cause greater than ourselves, worth being wounded for, worth dying for, worth giving up comfort and convenience for if necessary. A commitment that roots itself in total allegiance to the will of a Commander-in-Chief, in whose wisdom we trust and in whose strategy we believe, and on whose field we are willing to spend our lives. Ministry has always been tough.

It was tough for John G. Payton when he, with his young wife, left the British Isles for the New Hebrides Islands where no missionary had ever gone before. It was tough to hear the captain of the ship that took them ashore tell them they were foolish. Tough to land on that shore with no support network, no friends, no manuals on proven missiological principles for reaching cannibal-infested islands where no white man has ever been. It was tough to live in a camp on the beach wondering how they would ever penetrate the jungle, the villages, the hearts of these natives. It was tough when his wife gave birth to their child and died in childbirth along with the baby. It was tough to sleep on their graves every night lest the cannibals come and dig them up. In time God began His move as an expelled native from the tribe found his way to the beach and made friends with Payton, taught him the language, and then led him back into the village. And while it had not been easy, he left thirty years later writing in his journal that he had come to the sound of cannibal drums and left to the sound of church bells.

It was tough for five brilliant, committed, savvy, and adventuresome young men to walk away from their wives and children and land on that Ecuadorian jungle beach on the Curaray River, trying to build friendship bridges with the Auca Indians, knowing full well that they might never see their wives and children again. And they didn't.

It is tough for pastors in small American villages or struggling urban ministries where no one knows their name, who are never asked to speak at conferences, who never know the limelight. It's tough to be unaffirmed and criticized to boot. It's tough to be rejected, compared, and taken advantage of. It's tough to be confused, to be weary, to be spent, and to have to spend again. It's just plain tough. And it's tougher now than it has been before. Yet the call comes for us to be faithful. To do our best. To do the best things, even in the worst times. To keep singing to ourselves the words of the Isaac Watts hymn:

> Am I a soldier of the cross, a follower of the Lamb?
> And shall I fear to own His cause or blush to speak His name?

Must I be carried to the skies on flowery beds of ease,
While others fought to win the prize and sailed through bloody seas?

Are there no foes for me to face? Must I not stem the tide?
Is this vile world a friend to grace to help me on to God?

Sure I must fight if I would reign; increase my courage, Lord.
I'll bear the toil, endure the pain, supported by thy Word.

My mind reflects on the first three centuries of the church, when Christians did the best things in the worst times. In times not unlike our times. In fact, times far more brutal, more violent, more oppressive toward Christianity than we will ever fear to face. They were burned at the stake, used by Nero as pitch-coated torches to light the streets of Rome, and fed to lions to the cheers of packed arenas. Yet they neither recoiled nor recanted. They were faithful from the very core of their beings and, ultimately, their faithfulness empowered by the Spirit made the difference. A difference so dramatic that after 300 years of blood spent nonnegotiated perseverance, the godless empire declared Christianity the religion of the land.

Charles Dickens opened his classic *The Tale of Two Cities* with the now familiar line, "It was the best of times, it was the worst of times. . . ." Nothing could be more true for us as we move into the twenty-first century.

While they are for us the worst of times, they hold a strategic opportunity to present the clarity of the Gospel to a world that more than ever has an increasing awareness of the needs and emptiness of life. As paganism matures, the despair, disorientation, and disenfranchisement will deepen as life gets worse and solutions prove ineffective. It will be the opportunity to stand by the side of early Christians whose pagan environment gave them the privilege of impacting their world with the biblical strategy spoken of by Christ who said, "You are the light of the world. A city set on a hill cannot be hidden. Nor do men light a lamp, and put it under the peck-measure, but on the lampstand; and it gives light to all who are in the house. Let your light shine before men in such a way that they may see your good works, and glorify your Father who is in heaven" (Matt. 5:14-16). It was to a persecuted and displaced church whose lot would get worse before it got better that Peter wrote, "But you are a chosen race, a royal priesthood, a holy nation, a people for God's own possession, that you may proclaim the excellencies of Him who has called you out of darkness into His marvelous light; for you once were not a people, but now you are the people of God; you had not received mercy, but now you have received mercy. Beloved, I urge you as aliens and strangers to abstain from fleshly lusts, which wage war against the soul. Keep your behavior excellent among the Gentiles, so that in the thing in which they slander you as evildoers, they may on account of your good deeds, as they observe them, glorify God in the day of visitation" (1 Peter 2:9-12).

Even a casual review of church history notes that the worst of times environmentally were the best of times for the church. When the pressure comes, a generation rises with clear and unflinching convictions, understanding their identity in Christ and the unsurpassed value of His eternal cause, and willing to be rejected, misunderstood, and underclassed for Christ if necessary. A generation that has such an undaunted and tenacious grasp on truth and righteousness that they produce lives, families, and actions that are noticeably different in terms of stability, peace, success, productivity, and an undaunted sense of hope and confidence. This noticeable difference then becomes a compelling beam of light that a dark and despairing world cannot ignore.

If we do ministry well in these times that are for us increasingly the worst times, they may indeed prove to be, in the hand of God, the best times for the Gospel and the advance of His kingdom.

Will Durant, who is often contemptuous of or amused by Christianity, writing of the rise of the church in the days of Caesar, draws this relevant and timely observation:

> All in all, no more attractive religion has ever been presented to mankind. . . . It offered itself without restrictions to all individuals, classes, and nations; it was not limited to one people, like Judaism, nor to the freemen of one state, like the official cults of Greece and Rome. By making all men heirs of Christ's victory over death, Christianity announced the basic equality of men, and made transiently trivial all differences of earthly degree. To the miserable, maimed, bereaved, disheartened, and humiliated it brought the new virtue of compassion, and an ennobling dignity; it gave them the inspiring figure, story, and ethic of Christ; it brightened their lives with the hope of the coming Kingdom, and of endless happiness beyond the grave. To even the greatest sinners it promised forgiveness, and their full acceptance into the community of the saved. To minds harassed with the insoluble problems of origin and destiny, evil and suffering, it brought a system of divinely revealed doctrine in which the simplest soul could find mental rest. To men and women imprisoned in the prose of poverty and toil it

> brought the poetry of the sacraments. . . . Into the moral vacuum of a dying paganism, into the coldness of Stoicism and the corruption of Epicureanism, into a world sick of brutality, cruelty, oppression, and sexual chaos, into a pacified empire that seemed no longer to need the masculine virtues of the gods of war, it brought a new morality of brotherhood, kindliness, decency, and peace. So molded to men's wants, the new faith spread with fluid readiness. Nearly every convert, with the ardor of a revolutionary, made himself an office of propaganda. . . .[7]

If we are to be empowered like the early church, then we as spiritual leaders must know and be committed to the best things. Whether pastor, leader of a Christian organization, deacon, elder, youth worker, Sunday School teacher, parent, spouse, or marketplace person; our capacity to turn the downsides of these days to His advantage will begin with those of us who want to be impact players and by the very nature of our position are leaders committed to the nonnegotiated elements of ministry that are indeed the best things.

Thankfully, the essentials are basic and not difficult to grasp. It begins with affirming the divinely prescribed tasks of the church through the lives of shepherds who process ministry in a way that is worthy of respect as we become credible in our personhood, proclamation, and the proficient outworking of our ministry.

Effectiveness into the coming century will be measured by knowing and doing the *best things.* May it be said of us, like it was said of Sir Robert Shirley, that the "church was built to the glory of God . . ." by shepherds "whose singular praise it was to have done the best things in the worst times."

Chapter Two

The Best Things: Defining the Task

The Function

If you want to start a good old-fashioned donnybrook at the next pastor's fellowship meeting, bring up the subject of ministry methodology, particularly in the context of modern church growth movements that are attempting to contextualize ministry into the current cultural environment. All you have to do is introduce the word "seekers" into the conversation and throw in a couple of names like MacArthur and Hybels, and there will be enough tension to take up the rest of the morning. But if at some point the discussion does not deal with the preservation and promotion of the fundamental functions of a biblical church then we have lost our focus. Too often biblical functions get lost in the discussion of the forms through which the functions flow. Yet, the specific tasks, not the stages on which they're played out, are the critically strategic issues of ministry. They are in our day, as in every era, the "best things."

The "best things" requires some definition. And Scripture helps with clear definitions of what these fundamental functions of ministry are. In fact, there are three basic functions that cannot be compromised if we are to be effective in building flocks that glorify Him and contribute to the gain of His kingdom: evangelism, identification, and discipleship. Interestingly enough, these are the tasks that were delineated for the early church in an environment far more pagan than ours. It was the early church leaders' adherence to a biblically defined focus of ministry functions that brought power, effectiveness, and unusual success to their endeavors.

It should be unnecessary to reiterate the fundamentals of the task, except for the fact that in our day we have been so pressed by the rapid change of society that, in our scurrying to do something relevant, productive, and significant, we have kicked up the dust of ministry and, I fear, often obscured our focus and compromised fundamental function.

Os Guinness, speaking of these specific tasks as "traditional marks," reflects his concern when he writes, "Today theology is really more than marginal in the church growth movement at the popular level. Discussion of the traditional marks of the church is virtually nonexistent. Instead, methodology is at the center and in control. The result is a methodology only occasionally in search of a theology. After all, church growth . . . is a self-professed 'science,' not a theology."[1] He goes on to register his extended concern that this naiveté and resistance to the traditional marks of the church and the theology that undergirds them has led to the subordination of worship and discipleship to evangelism, and has given rise as well to the overarching presentation of the church as a place of entertainment.

Kent Hughes, pastor of the College Church in Wheaton, Illinois, in a recent vision statement wrote to his church of the tension today that has risen in regard to how we should do church in today's dramatically changed society. He says that our tendency is to drift toward what he calls a *man-focused model* and observes the inherent dangers in a sloppy contextualization of the ministry to culture:

> Preaching, for example, is often shortened to a 15- or 20-minute homily. Bible exposition is jettisoned as "too heavy" in favor of a lighter topical homily. And since the average TV-sotted American has a shrinking attention span, "sermons" become story-laden and sometimes a string of vignettes loosely related to a scriptural pretext.
>
> Moreover, there is often such a strained attempt to be "relevant" that anything that has not come out of the last 20 years is consciously avoided. The great hymns of the church are shelved. A reverse elitism is instilled which is proudly cast. The end effect of this approach is to produce the unfortunate illusion that the evangelical church has come out of nowhere—without heritage or roots!
>
> The great danger of the man-focused worship approach is, of

> course, pragmatism, and when pragmatism becomes the conductor, the audience increasingly becomes man rather than God. And when we play to man first, when what he wants becomes the determining factor, it can corrupt not only our worship, but our theology. Given enough time, the inevitable end of man-centered worship and ministry is heresy.[2]

On the other hand, we must realize that those of us who are unwilling to wrestle with the issues of a radically changed society and who assume that the old forms are the best and only forms will soon be presiding over ministries that are passing from the scene with the passing of the last generation that understands those forms. In light of our changing society, the reevaluation of and reconfiguration of forms within a proper theological context, without compromising biblical functions, may no longer be a preference but a necessity given the fact that the thought paradigms and cultural languages of the modern American have radically changed. Reaching them and discipling them demands a clear understanding of the appropriate and effective passageways to both their head and their heart.

Sorting through all of this really begins, however, with a proper prioritizing of the issues that relate to form and function.

FORM AND FUNCTION

There is a basic maxim in architecture. It is that "form follows function." An architect could have a dream of developing a tall building with tiers of stairs leading to its pillared porch, whose large brass doors would provide entry to a massive marbled foyer graced by great staircases that flow from one floor to the other. While the building may be a stunning statement, enhance the landscape, bring great credit and glory to the architect, and be hailed by both media and masses as a great technological advance, if the primary function of the building is to be a center for the physically challenged, then no matter how glorious the form is, it has worked against the function.

We as shepherds are inundated with the pressure to construct our ministries according to *forms* that offer stunning opportunity for growth, that keep us at the leading edge of our profession, that prevent us from feeling and appearing old and stodgy, and that reflect well on our own glory. In fact, the vast majority of books, seminars, workshops, and conferences for shepherds today deal primarily in the realm of forms.

This is not to say that forms are not critical. The functions that God divinely prescribed need to have well-constructed forms through which to flow; passageways that reflect an understanding of the mind-set of the culture into which ministry is making its way. However, forms must honor and support biblical tenets. We must always be on guard lest *changing* forms eclipse or erode *changeless* function. Forms can never become an end in themselves, nor can any one form become the fashionable and final statement of authentic ministry. Our culture is far too diverse to have one form dictate the pattern by which all ministries must be managed. Those who do not follow trendy forms are not necessarily less significant because their form is perceived by some to be out-of-vogue. On the other hand, radical and avant-garde forms should not always be eschewed without careful evaluation.

Scripture speaks very little to form and almost exclusively to function. In fact, when form is modeled it is never as a static entity, but fluid, given the environment. Christ's formation of ministry flexed to place His message in a compatible context for the woman at the well (John 4), the rich young ruler (Matt. 19), the Pharisees, and the tax collector. Paul's forms cut a variety of passageways on Mars Hill, with Jews, with Gentiles, with commoners, and with lofty political bureaucrats. The common thread is not the form but the purpose of the form: to effect a means by which the message uncompromised can have impact given the context of the recipients' world, mind-set, understanding, and common experience.

I find it interesting that some churches and pastors who resist and in fact speak with intensity against changing forms would not consider supporting a missionary who didn't take time to understand the context, culture, and language of the people and then fashion an appropriate form through which to effectively minister.

While form remains fluid, function is clearly defined in Scripture and, unlike form, is never fluid. And, importantly, we must remind each other that the power in ministry lies in its biblically prescribed functions. Form is merely the passage through which the power flows. If all the emphasis is on form, particularly forms that erode our function, we will have the form of godliness without the power. Too often we are led to believe that if we had the right forms we'd have the power. Ministry was never intended to be managed that way. The Spirit is poised to empower biblical functions (Acts 1:8; Matt. 28:18-20).

It is also critical to remind ourselves that we will be held accountable for the function of our ministry and not the form. Unless, of course, the form violates biblical principle. Given that reality, we need to reclaim a clear understanding and commitment to the functions that God has prescribed. Functions—biblical functions—are the best things in the worst times. When godly shepherds figure out how to do ministry in a pagan environment by structuring creative and effective forms through which to carry out uncompromised function, they will be well positioned to be used of God regardless of the times in which they minister.

Christ sharpens our focus regarding the fundamental function of the church. His statement of function has defined and driven the work of the church through every generation and every season of both good times and bad. Known as the Great Commission, it is articulated in Matthew 28 and wrapped in the empowerment of the unchallenged authority of Jesus Christ and the assurance of His presence as we carry out His clearly defined task. He stated, "All authority has been given to Me in heaven and on earth. Go therefore and *make disciples of all nations, baptizing them in the name of the Father and the Son and the Holy Spirit, teaching them to observe all that I commanded you;* and lo, I am with you always, even to the end of the age" (vv. 18-20, italics added).

These are the three distinct functions of the church. All we do is measured by them. **Evangelism** . . . *Go therefore and make disciples of all nations;* **Identification** . . . *Baptizing them in the name of the Father and the Son and the Holy Spirit;* and **Discipleship** . . . *Teaching them to observe all that I commanded you.* The true effectiveness of our ministry is measured in the context of these three compelling tasks. It is to this standard that we will be held accountable.

At the risk of being perceived as naive and simplistic, we need to focus on these three functional realities of Christ's work in light of a dramatically changed ministry environment. Keeping them uncompromised and central will not be as easy as it has been in the past. Quite frankly, both the changing times and our familiarity with these functions have threatened not only our understanding of their importance but also their primary place in ministry.

EVANGELISM

We cannot forget that the fundamental mission of Jesus Christ was to "seek and to save that which was lost." There was only one compelling interest in the heart of Jesus Christ, and that was to fulfill His Father's pleasure by reclaiming a lost human race, hopelessly and helplessly unable to rescue itself. Christ's singular passion was people, all kinds of people, and their need to know Christ. He took His redemptive message to the worst kind of people—tax collectors and sinners (Luke 15:1-2). He crossed racial, political, and gender boundaries to seek to rescue the Samaritan woman at the well (John 4). And, though His strongest words of reproof were reserved for the religious systems of His day, He nevertheless had a heart for people of the system as individuals, such as Nicodemus the Pharisee (John 3). The people on which He focused His seeking passion were rich young rulers, blind beggars, prostitutes, and white collar thieves like Zaccheus.

We should not ignore the fact that at the close of His ministry, Jesus Christ said, "As the Father has sent Me, I also send you" . . . not only to our towns and our cities, but to "all nations." Christ reconfirmed this after His resurrection and before His ascension, commissioning us to be Spirit-empowered witnesses for Him both in Jerusalem and Judea, and Samaria, and unto the uttermost parts of the earth.

Unfortunately, the purpose, purity, priority, and potential of the Gospel is threatened by a multiplicity of pressures both from the culture at large and from the community of belief.

Estrangement

The new paganism in America has placed the Gospel in a strenuous tension between the modern man and its fundamental character. As we have noted, when my father and grandfather proclaimed the Gospel, its fundamental tenets of heaven, hell, sin, and the Savior were not foreign concepts to the masses of people in our culture. And while those in past decades were not necessarily more righteous, they at least gave assent to the basic tenets of the Gospel so that the proclaimer of the Good News found common ground upon which to build his call to heaven.

All of that has changed.

Philosophically. Politically. Practically.

Chuck Colson tells of having dinner with a media personality, and trying to talk with him about Christianity. When Colson shared his testimony, his friend replied, "Obviously Jesus worked for you," and then went on to tell Chuck about someone he knew whose life had been turned around by New Age spirituality: "Crystals, channeling—it worked for her just like your Jesus." Gene Veith in his book, *Postmodern Times*, relates that "Colson tried to explain the difference, but got nowhere. He raised the issue of death and the afterlife, but his friend did not believe in heaven or hell and was not particularly bothered by the prospect of dying. Colson explained what the Bible said, but his friend did not believe in the Bible or any other spiritual authority."

Veith goes on to relate that Colson finally was able to move into the mind and heart of this listener, but not in ways that would have been effective through most of the history of the church in America.[3]

The philosophical alienation of the postmodern man is a tremendous challenge to the communication of the Gospel. Today's American mind has been immersed in heavy doses with our culture's relativism and pluralism. How does one proclaim the Gospel into a mind-set that does not believe in absolutes and therefore has no awareness of or consciousness regarding sin? Whose pluralistic base of thinking tells him that everyone is entitled to their own truth conclusions, but that no one ever really finally knows truth? To proclaim, "I am the way, the truth, and the life; no man comes to the Father but by Me" (John 14:6) is an untenable thought in our new society.

Not only have relativism and pluralism created a worldview in which the Gospel is incomprehensible, but the outworking of these two fundamental cultural dogmas has further complicated the task of the Gospel. The relatively new movements of deconstructionism and revisionism have successfully created an environment in which reason and logic aren't objectively disciplined or even regarded as being important. We are led to deconstruct normal flows of logic and reason in order to build our own social constructs, mental frameworks that will endorse, excuse, and enable us to do all those things that would have, in other generations, been thought of as irrational and immoral. Revisionism fundamentally states that all of history is unreliable because it has been written through the eyes and perspectives of those who brought their own prejudices to the recording of history. Therefore, since history is unreliable, we have the right to rewrite it from our own perspectives, giving us the ability to recast history in ways that support politically correct views.

How then does one communicate the Gospel into mind-sets that no longer value reason, logic, or history, given the fact that the Gospel is a reasoned progression of logical thought from sin to a Savior, a logical, historical proclamation rooted in the real history of the life of a real Man who died on a real cross and left a real grave empty after three days?

This past Easter season I had the privilege of proclaiming the good news of a risen Lord in three different churches in large American cities. Given the contexts I found myself in, I was immediately aware of the fact that there would be many who, though they may not be philosophically sophisticated, would receive my message through relativistic, pluralistic, deconstructivist, and revisionist mind-sets. Many who would find what I was saying to be unintelligible and in fact foreign to their whole mental frame of reference. It's not that those who have been steeped in the prevalent philosophies of postmodernism are unwilling to listen to us. It's that their philosophical presuppositions make them unable to hear what we have to say.

Not only is there philosophical estrangement, but there is political estrangement as well. The moral majority of the past has now become the maligned minority of the present. Those of us who are committed to being biblically correct will often not be politically correct and, as we noted earlier, our passion to advance the Gospel and its attendant moral principles poses a threat to this new progressive secular society. As a result, the power brokers and social engineers of our culture have taken it on themselves to paint Christians as superstitious relics from the past. Our profile has been downgraded from being significant contributors to a culture whose values we affirmed and upheld, to a marginalized non-mainstream group of no account because of our lack of intellectual or social consciousness, our bigoted intolerance, or our basic ineptness in life. These portrayals are projected on a regular basis in sitcoms, movies, and the literature of society.

More recently in the political arena, Christians are taking a direct hit from those who resist our interest in checking the drift of an increasingly decadent society. Representative Vic Fazio, head of the Democratic Congressional Campaign Committee, recently condemned those that he called the "religious right." Within the same few days, President Clinton attacked certain evangelical Christians. Mr. Fazio went on to describe Christian activists as a "peril" and "what the American people fear the most." A *New York Times* editorial accused a Christian group of spreading "homophobic panic," and the present Surgeon General, Jocelyn Elders, recently publicly castigated those that she described as the "unchristian" religious right.[4]

The accumulative result of this is that to be known today as a Christian by those who are subscribing to the public portrayal of Christianity makes it difficult to walk up to people, claim to represent Christ, and share the Gospel with them. Chances are, their first impulse is not to want to be one of our kind.

And, as though the cultural resistance to the Gospel weren't enough in the arenas of philosophical estrangement and political distortion, the practical realities of proclaiming a Gospel that calls some pleasure sin and calls for a measure of self-control in our lives is an unwelcome thought to a society that is committed to pleasure at all costs. Indeed we live in a day when men prefer to be lovers of pleasure rather than lovers of God, and where personal discipline and the practice of righteousness as higher priorities than self-fulfillment is increasingly unattractive.

In light of this, the Gospel is in tension with a world that, in one sense, is not able to hear our proclamation because of a dramatic distance in terms of philosophical mind-set, and in another sense unwilling to hear what we have to say because of their perceptions of who we are as Christians and their aversion to anything that speaks to the discounting of the pleasure potential in their lives.

How then do we promote the Gospel in a world that cannot and does not want to hear what we have to say? It's interesting to note a variety of responses that seem to be prevalent in the church today; from white-knuckled protests and taunts from the sidelines against well-placed and powerful opponents to the cause of Christ, to those who withdraw, faces lifted to the sky, looking for Christ's soon return; those who are erecting polling booths hoping to somehow shift this culture toward sanctification through political gain; those who have dropped their Bibles to appear more relevant; those who have their ratchet sets out and are dismantling the Gospel to remove any offense and to recast it in terms of a "let me make you feel better" theology; those who have decided to leave their distinctives behind and dabble in the drift . . . all of which, at best, are less than effective responses and, at worst, compromise the very Gospel we hope to proclaim.

There is a biblical way.

In fact, we must remember how well the Gospel thrived in a culture far worse than ours, where Christians were more severely marginalized than we are. Theirs too was a highly relativistic and pluralistic environment. The New Testament strategy in this context is simply that we are to be committed to living out the principles of righteousness in such a way that the results of righteous living—our good works—become such compelling evidence of the reality of our faith that those in a world whose unrighteousness brings disintegration and despair will notice the dramatic contrast and in time come to inquire what it is that has made such a dramatic difference between us and them. This biblical strategy brought ultimate victory over the powerful Roman Empire as succeeding generations practiced it with an unintimidated tenacity even in the face of great peril. Both Christ and the Apostle Peter articulate this perspective. As we noted in chapter 1, Christ outlined the strategy when He said, "You are the light of the world. A city set on a hill cannot be hidden. Nor do men light a lamp, and put it under the peck-measure, but on the lampstand; and it gives light to all who are in the house. Let your light shine before men in such a way that they may see your good works, and glorify your Father who is in heaven" (Matt. 5:14-16). Note that the key element of our effectiveness is not so much what *we say*, but what *they see* in our lives. When they are no longer willing or able to hear what we have to say, you can count on it that they will still be watching how we live.

Realizing that they had been castigated as the evil elements of society, not unlike our society today, Peter wrote to a persecuted and maligned church that they should, "Keep your behavior excellent among the Gentiles, so that in the thing in which they slander you as evildoers, they may on account of your good deeds, as they observe them, glorify God in the day of visitation" (1 Peter 2:12). I take the "day of visitation" in this text to mean the visitation of God's judgment on sinful practices through the debilitating consequences of their self-styled lifestyles.

What God is calling us to and what drove the early church was a commitment to create, through their unflinching submission to the lordship of Christ and His righteousness, compelling stories that the world could not ignore. God seeks to create *lives so well lived* that the effects of relativism and all the slanderous rancor and rumors thrown against us melt and dissipate in the light of what is clearly observed in our lives.

This strategy will be effective in terms of both melting down the resistance to us and effecting the *miracle* of redemption in observers' lives. Rahab, the Jericho harlot, told the spies that Jericho's resistance had indeed dissipated and that her heart was ready to receive the God of Israel because of the compelling stories that God had spun through His people at the Red Sea and during the course of their amazing military conquests. For her this strategy effected a meltdown of resistance and a miracle of redemption. Scripture records her words,

> I know that the Lord has given you the land, and that the terror of you has fallen on us, and that all the inhabitants of the land have melted away before you. For we have heard how the Lord dried up the water of the Red Sea before you when you came out of Egypt, and what you did to the two kings of the Amorites who were beyond the Jordan, to Sihon and Og, whom you utterly destroyed. And when we heard it, our hearts melted and no courage remained in any man any longer because of you; for the Lord your God, He is God in heaven above and on earth beneath (Josh. 2:9-11).

Another dramatic example of the power of the compelling story of righteousness to melt down cultural resistance took place recently in Chicago. It was the national pro-choice "Night of Resistance" marking the anniversary of the murder of abortion doctor David Gunn. Here in Chicago the protest was focused against one of our fine inner-city churches, the Armitage Baptist Church. Demonstrators were to gather in front of the church during their midweek prayer service to disrupt the church and make their point for all of the Chicago and national press to see.

Demonstrators were asked to bring whistles and other noisemakers to drown out the services. Fliers were posted around town urging the demonstrators to "dress to shock and/or impress; come in costume and show your rage." The sponsors included Queer Nation (an anarchist youth group), Sister Serpents (an underground women's collective), and a terrorist group was thrown in to boot. A few demonstrators wore patches that said, "Feminine Witch" and "Support Vaginal Pride." Needless to say, the church was expecting trouble.

I had been in their Sunday evening service the Sunday before this demonstration was to take place. There was much prayer for the coming Wednesday evening, yet an unusual sense of stillness and confidence was evident in the believers' hearts in spite of the fact that they had good reason to be concerned. A couple of years ago a dozen members of Queer Nation were invited to attend the church's Easter services. They interrupted the sermon, blew whistles, and threw condoms in the collection plate. Six were arrested. The church has often been a victim of vandalism—slashed car tires, and pro-gay and pro-abortion graffiti sprayed on the church's walls.

A couple of weeks after the demonstration I picked up a copy of *U.S. News & World Report,* and while casually perusing the magazine I noticed John Leo's "On Society" column. He had entitled this week's editorial "An Anti-Anti Abortion Rally." I was interested. I began reading, and to my surprise he was reporting on the demonstration at the Armitage Baptist Church. He observed,

> The most common chant was "Racist, sexist, anti-gay/Born-again bigots go away!" The "racist" charge is particularly weird: the Armitage congregation is roughly 30% black, 30% Hispanic, and 40% white. The security force on the steps seemed about half Hispanic. The church is located in the Logan Square area, a neighborhood mixed by class and race, maybe 60% Hispanic, 25% white, and 15% black. For "born-again bigots," the congregation has made an unusually successful effort to cut across racial lines.
>
> While the crowd chanted about racism, a group of young black men showed up wearing long red jackets that said, "SHS Security." They were from a southside black Baptist church, The Sweet Holy Spirit, and had come to protect a fellow evangelical church.
>
> Somewhat confused, the woman with the bullhorn tried to lead the crowd in singing, "Little Boxes"—a song about suburban conformity popularized by Pete Seger in the 1960s. It was, without a

> doubt, the least appropriate song anyone could have sung about this diverse urban congregation.
>
> Next, five yellow buses rolled up, and a seemingly endless stream of people poured out. "They're bringing in the homeless," said one demonstrator in dismay. But no, they were evangelicals from a second southside church, most black families, showing up for the service. More than 1,000 people were now in the church.
>
> The security men had been singing all along, picking fast-paced music that almost matched the volume of the demonstrators. Now, they gave way to a choir of black kids. The demonstrators were done for. The kids were too good and too loud.[5]

I felt like standing up and shouting "Glory!"

Later, talking with Chuck Lyons, the pastor of the church, he related that for weeks these demonstrators had canvassed the neighborhood seeking to get the neighbors to come and demonstrate against the church. He went on to say, however, that none of the neighbors had shown up. When I asked why, he said there were probably many reasons, though the neighborhood has little sympathy for the church's stand against the cultural agendas of abortion and gay rights. He observed that when the Chicago school board kept the schools closed in the fall of 1993 because of a budget crisis, through those weeks the teachers in their church opened an alternate school in the church building where they taught and ministered to the neighborhood children. "The neighbors," he said, "know that our church cares about them."

The long-term submission of this community of believers to the righteous principles of embracing all types of people at the cross, reaching out to fellow believers across the city regardless of race or class, and of seeking to compassionately minister to the needs of their neighbors, created such a compelling story that when the stage was set the voices of the most hostile elements of our society were not able to overcome the power of Christ through their lives. It was a story that the secular press could not ignore as they took note and heralded this conquering story of good works.

Granted, the stage is not always so dramatically set. Sometimes it's just the routine faithfulness of believers that sets the stage for the melting of resistance on a personal level. On a recent vacation Martie and I decided to take an afternoon to do some sightseeing. We signed up for a tour and ended up sitting next to a couple who were complete strangers. To my surprise, I found out that he was from the town where I grew up in New Jersey. As we compared notes, we found that we had gone to the same high school, graduated in the same class, had many mutual friends, and lots of interesting memories about teachers and coaches that we had had in common. In the course of the conversation this Jewish attorney asked me, "Did you say your name was Stillwell?" I told him that my name was "Stowell," and he replied, "Oh. I have a client whose name is Stillwell." I asked him if his name was Art Stillwell, and he responded with surprise that it was. Art Stillwell was a member of my dad's church where I grew up and is the owner of a large car dealership in north Jersey.

"Art is different than any other client I have," the attorney noted. When I asked why, he replied, "Most of my clients who have a problem want me to do whatever is necessary to guarantee an outcome that favors them, regardless of the ethics involved. But when Art has a problem and I ask him what he wants me to do, he always responds, 'Do whatever is right.' "

Art's routine faithfulness in a watching world caught the attention of this attorney. No miracle of redemption yet. Just the meltdown of resistance. If the attorney ever gets to heaven, it will largely be because of the compelling story that Art's life told. A story that was unable to be ignored. The power of its impression opened a crack in the door of this attorney's heart.

There will be times that the compelling stories of our good works move from the meltdown stage to a miraculous moment of redemption. In my first pastorate, a woman and then later her husband had come to remedy the tension in their marriage. Over time, they worked to understand the biblical principles of what it meant to build a godly home and committed themselves to the process.

One evening their neighbors came over, and as they stood on their front lawn talking together, the neighbors said, "We've noticed that your home is different than ours. What is it that makes the difference?" They took them inside, opened the Bible, and told them that it was Jesus Christ. That night their neighbors received Christ as their personal Savior. I had the joy of baptizing them.

This strategy is far different than the more immediate impact of a five-day crusade or an evangelistic rally on a given night. More and more our culture will be leery of these kinds of Gospel formats, and more and more we will be called back to the strategy of the New Testament church, to live lives so well-lived that the culture can no longer ignore the truth claims of our belief system. The strategy takes time. It requires perseverance in righteousness, and the patience to wait for God to bring His outcomes in His time. For the faithful believers under seventy years of Russian oppression, it took that long for God to use the power of their witness to kick open the doors of the Gospel into that former bastion of brutal atheism. And as we have noted, it took the early church 300 years of routine righteousness to finally bring the Roman Empire to its knees.

As we shift our strategy to this New Testament paradigm that was practiced so well by the early church, the effective shepherd needs to note that one of the ways a congregation is stimulated to good works is through the example of the shepherd's life and the faithful preaching of the Word of God. Paul tells Timothy to be an example of good works to the flock (1 Tim. 4) and in regard to the power of the Word proclaimed. He wrote, "All Scripture is inspired by God and profitable for teaching, for reproof, for correction, for training in righteousness; that the man of God may be adequate, equipped for every good work. I solemnly charge you in the presence of God and of Christ Jesus, who is to judge the living and the dead, and by His appearing and His kingdom: preach the word; be ready in season and out of season; reprove, rebuke, exhort, with great patience and instruction" (2 Tim. 3:16–4:2).

The patient modeling and proclamation of Scripture in effective ways enables our flock to become "adequate, equipped for every good work." Equipped for good works that create stories that the world cannot ignore.

The Gospel is not only challenged by the tremendous distance between its claims and our cultural mind-set, but it is also caught in the debate over the forms and formats for the staging of the Gospel in terms of the church gathered.

Forms and Formats

As we have alluded, one of our great debates today is between those who hold to traditional church forms and those who are launching into new and sometimes risky contextualization to attempt to make the gathered church both compatible with and understandable to the lost in this new generation.

In the conflict regarding church forms, it is held in some circles that the church gathered is not appropriate for evangelism. And while the in-house functions of the church are indeed biblically focused toward believers, it is hard to find a prohibition in Scripture about believers gathering together to effectively bring unbelievers to encounter either a pre-evangelistic or direct evangelistic message. Throughout the history of the church, and particularly during the great revival movements, Christians gathered to hear the Gospel clearly and forcefully proclaimed, praying that their unsaved friends who were there would respond. Celebrated sermons such as "Sinners in the Hands of an Angry

God" were preached in church as an attempt to communicate the Gospel to the unsaved listener. In England, ardent Calvinists were so committed to the doctrine of election that it is reported that in some of their churches the elect sat on one side and the unelect sat on another side. It is said that John Gill, the British preacher who would preach only to the elect would often sprinkle into his sermons phrases such as: "If these people over here only knew what Jesus Christ can do to save a life, they would want to come and receive it like you have." Charles Haddon Spurgeon claimed that in his sermons he always headed ultimately to the cross and its redemptive work.

It should not go unnoticed that all of the Great Commission is the responsibility of the church. In light of that it seems legitimate for a church to program evangelistic activities into its structure.

Throughout most of American history, church services were used to reach the lost. When I was growing up, believers were encouraged to bring their unsaved friends to the Sunday evening Gospel services where both the music and the message were geared to the proclamation of the Gospel to the unsaved in the audience. So in reality, "seeker services" are not all that new. What is new is that our culture has moved so far away from the ideals and values of the church culture that sinners are no longer interested in coming into the church to hear the Gospel. In fact, they find that its tradition, language, and patterns of worship are not only uncomfortable, but in many respects, unintelligible. Hence there have arisen those in our midst who are asking the question, "How can we take away everything but the offense of the cross and restructure a church setting to reach sinners who need to know the liberating truth of the Gospel?" Doing so, they take the traditional time of "church" and transition it into a totally new form that in reality is not biblical church. It's really the old Sunday evening evangelistic service tailored to the modern mind-set on Sunday morning. These churches then shift the church gathered to a midweek setting where worship and exposition takes place.

Churches that choose to fulfill the function of evangelism in this way need to be careful that they do not assume that the masses who come on Sunday comprise the church. The scope, depth, and breadth of the church in their situation is really measured by what happens when "church" happens at the midweek point. And churches that opt for this form to fulfill the function of evangelism need to be sure that, if their seeker services are pre-evangelistic, there is a way in which they can clearly communicate the Gospel at some point to those who come. And if the gathering is to evangelize, then we cannot neglect to speak of sin—intrinsic and committed guilt before God, the work of the Savior as the only means of forgiveness, and the necessity of a personal faith step toward the Savior.

Our children often tried to give me what they thought was a realistic view of Christian contemporary music so that I would not lapse into irrational rages when they played their tapes. When Petra, a contemporary Christian band, was coming to town, needless to say, our kids wanted to go. I wasn't real comfortable with the prospect, but thought it might be a good idea if we all went together. That way I could critique it honestly and their observations and mine could be used to come to *my conclusions* about the evening! Well, after an evening of rather exotic special effects, lots of music, and lots of noise, the band leader asked the packed theater to be seated so that they could talk about something very important. I thought to myself, "Here comes the message; I bet it will be some 'If you want peace, find Jesus' approach to the Gospel," and I settled in for what I anticipated to be a rather existential view of Christianity.

To my shock and delight, the band-member-turned-preacher began to speak to the teenagers about the reality of sin, its guilt, resulting alienation from God, and judgment. And while that was surprising in and of itself, he went on in the course of the message to say, "And it's not really the sins that you've committed that have left you guilty before God; it is that you have been born with an Adamic nature." He went on to explain that we are all born in sin, and having the sin nature in and of itself is enough to condemn us to an eternity in hell, let alone the things that we've done on top of that. He then spoke clearly of the cross, of its meaning, and of its liberating power from not only the practice of sins but our fallen nature that gives rise to the practice of sin. He invited those who would like to deal with their sin problem to come forward, that someone might show them from God's Word how they could know this Christ who was the only hope of their liberation. Not much fluff. Not much allure. Just the solid stuff of the Gospel. Better stuff than I had heard at a lot of evangelistic meetings where long-term Christian adults gather to listen to seasoned evangelists who themselves had become seduced into appealing to people on the basis of lesser things on behalf of Christ.

I was reminded afresh of the importance of the clear presentation of the Gospel when, on one occasion, I asked Billy Graham what he thought needed to be changed in how we preach to people in the '90s in comparison to the way we preached to people in the '50s. I thought it was a rather important question and expected some profound analysis of our culture and the contextualization of our preaching in the face of the societal shift. He replied simply and straightforwardly, "Nothing has really changed in terms of the needs of people. Wherever or whatever you preach, you must remind people of their sin, speak to them of heaven and hell, show them to the cross, and urge them to come to the Savior." What a refreshing response.

The Gospel speaks to real needs. And whereas we can enter the door of the real needs by speaking to people's felt needs, ultimately a clear and compassionate presentation of the Gospel is not only necessary but will ring true in the hearts of those whom God is leading to Himself. And to those who are offended, is it not this which Scripture speaks to when it speaks of the offense of the cross? We should never be offensive in terms of the communication of the cross, but if the *clear* and *compassionate* communication of Christ does offend, then that is a price that must be borne as a privilege by the teller of the Gospel.

In fact, those who hold that the gathered church should not be seeker-oriented need to guard that this more restrictive view of the function of the church gathered does not communicate to our adherents that the Gospel is not really all that important. The cocooning of Christianity, encasing Christians into houses of comfort, was never what Christ intended the mission of the church to be. Evangelism is the function of the church. And if it's not done by bringing sinners in, then it must be done by sending believers out.

And while we're talking about forms and formats, a church that will remain viable not only in today's culture but for generations to come must understand that Christians who are coming to know Christ in our day are coming with a totally different cultural mix; not a bad mix, just a different mix than our forefathers brought when they came to Christ from the world. We must tackle the very difficult agenda of seeking somehow to do church in a way that enables committed and concentrated Christians who are living into the twenty-first century to identify with and grow within the church. Some of our old traditions and forms are there because they worked so well in our forefathers' days. We must make sure that our forms today work well for God's flock in this day. There is nothing sacred about that which is old if it is not intrinsically biblical. And there is nothing sacred about the contemporary, particularly if it erodes changeless, age-worn, biblical truth.

Not only does the Gospel face the challenge of philosophical estrangement from without and the issue of forms and formats within; it also is in tension with the context in which it's proclaimed.

Context

The Gospel needs to be presented in a broader context than just seeking to achieve the function of punctiliar justification, i.e., identity with the body of Christ and discipleship into the likeness of Christ. We must guard that the function of our witness does not jeopardize the Gospel's larger context, or that the Gospel is not eroded by an external context that compromises its essence. Both of these contexts are in jeopardy when we realize that our societal shift has made the Gospel more urgent but at the same time culturally less compelling.

As always, there are some who carry out notch-belt evangelism by seeking to save as many as possible, and like knocking down ducks with a pistol at the county fair, go about sharing the Gospel, sometimes in distorted ways, to attract more converts. In this context there is little thought of integrating them into the body of Christ and discipling them to do all the things that He has commanded us. Some churches in particular are guilty of building their ministry around the message of John 3:16, seeking to create an evangelistic center that can become "the fastest growing church in town." As soon as the hundreds come on decision day, it is tempting to forget the importance of emphasizing the legitimate patterns of discipleship that will take their converts past a simple yet helpful understanding of the Gospel. Driven by the urgency of evangelism, their sense of urgency tends to short-circuit the important context of the long-term nature of wooing, winning, and then weaning their converts into a whole life experience with Jesus Christ.

Unfortunately, some parachurch organizations have isolated themselves from the context of the local church and have thus relegated themselves to sequestering their accumulated converts into nonchurch-related Bible studies, sending the distinct message that identity with and growth in the context of a local church are not important parts of our function as believers.

Our sense of urgency which is legitimately fanned by the paganization of our culture, the reality of judgment, and the unpredictability of our life span, has led some to elevate the Gospel above other essential elements of our faith, as though in order to catch the attention of as broad a spectrum as possible we should ignore vital truth distinctions in regard to those whom we endorse and identify with in the course of our evangelistic endeavors. The reality of it is that fundamental truth about the deity of Christ, His finished work on the cross, His resurrection, second coming, and virgin birth all are intrinsically linked to the very essence of the Gospel. In fact, they are foundational to the Gospel. The Gospel is driven by grace and by a grace that stands by itself, apart from the works of man. Too often, we have been willing to place the Gospel in alliance with nontruth systems in order to reach as many as possible, when in effect we have tipped our hat and condoned by association systems of belief that are antithetical to the Gospel and in so doing have eroded the perceived importance of the truth base upon which the Gospel itself stands.

Our sense of urgency may also entice us to use cultural contexts in the presentation of the Gospel that ultimately and finally erode not only the essentials of the Gospel, but the ensuing principles of righteousness to which converts are called in order to grow through the process of discipleship. The Gospel really can take no endorsement outside of that which is fully and completely consistent with the Gospel. We dare not threaten its theology or its ensuing impact on discipleship no matter how tempting and alluring endorsements from broader constituencies, whether theological or cultural, may seem in effecting the breadth of the message.

I'm reminded of the time in Philippi when Paul and his evangelistic entourage were followed in the streets by a demoniac slave girl who had a high profile in town as the local psychic and brought her masters high profits by the practice of divination. She shouted, "These men are bond-servants of the most high God, who are proclaiming to you the way of salvation" (Acts 16:17). Having just arrived into this ancient pagan environment, this endorsement provided an enticing opportunity to serve as a local affirmation of the Gospel. With an endorsement like this by someone of high community profile who was sought after and respected, one would assume that Paul would have valued the help. Paul, unwilling to have the truth endorsed from a nontruth source, lest in so doing he endorse that which was antithetical to the Gospel, turned and cast the demon out of her, and instead of having the Gospel advanced in the streets through his ministry, he and Silas were thrown in jail. Their effectiveness was reduced to one jailer who came to know Christ because of the powerful hand of God who intervened in his life. But in the end, though their results were limited, the theology of what they preached had not been compromised. Evidently God wanted to reach a jailer, not a city, and wanted that small band of converts to know early on that the focus of nontruth in this city was not compatible or even co-existed with the Gospel.

The proclamation of the Gospel must always be tempered by an understanding that the Gospel was never intended to be only a fixed point in history, but the beginning of a life built on truth and righteousness. The foundations of both truth and righteousness must be preserved as we proclaim the Gospel if we hope to be effective in discipling people's lives after the Gospel is proclaimed.

That is not to say that the Gospel should not be understood as being highly urgent. After proclaiming the Gospel of Jesus Christ to a crowded hall in Chicago, D.L. Moody closed his message by encouraging the attendees to go home, consider the claims of the Gospel, and return the next week to settle the matter in their lives. But that night Chicago heard the ringing of the fire bells and the clatter of horse-drawn water wagons being hurried through their streets. Mrs. O'Leary's cow had kicked the lantern, and the Great Chicago Fire swept the city and hundreds of lives were lost. D.L. Moody committed himself that night to a new sense of urgency in the proclamation of the Gospel. But it would be fair to say that the Bible calls us to an urgency within the context of preserving its long-range impact and an environment where truth and righteousness are preeminent.

Politicization

Through the last three decades, the evangelical church in America has become increasingly politicized. In fact, at times our churches look more like political action groups than spiritual way stations. If we are not careful, our political activism will blur the potential, distinctiveness, and clarity of the Gospel.

This politicization of the church has more often than not distracted us from an unhindered expression of the priority of the Gospel. As elections draw near, our lobbies become full of material supporting various candidates that affirm our biblical values. We have to ask ourselves if this doesn't erode our capacity to reach out with the good news of Jesus Christ to those who are on the other side of the political spectrum.

I fear as well that our emphasis on political causes may distract us from the dramatic spiritual needs that are all around us, particularly in terms of reaching the lost with the Gospel. For instance, if we were to announce that next Saturday the church was going to have a pro-life rally or march against the local abortion clinic because babies are dying, and if we were to throw an early morning pancake breakfast and promise transportation to and from, chances are we would get a major crowd out on Saturday morning. If the following Sunday we thank everybody for coming and then announce that the next Saturday we are going to have another early morning pancake breakfast and afterward go into the community to rescue adults who, though living, are dead in sin and on their way to a Christless eternity; promise transportation to and from along with a convenient prepackaged program of evangelism that will make it easy for them to get the job done . . . my guess is that the numbers compared to the week before will be minimal.

In the values crisis of our culture we are called, and I think rightly so, to promote political endeavors that are often done hand-in-hand with other moralists and religious cobeligerents who do not share our belief in Christ's ability to save by grace alone apart from sacraments or human effort. If we're not careful we can become numb to the reality that, though having common political convictions, those we march arm-in-arm with may still need to know the saving truth of Jesus Christ.

And, I fear that our anger at the political shifts in our culture has robbed us of the fundamental compassion of Christianity, compassion for *all* the lost. We have become selectively interested in lost souls. If they are "our kind" then let's win them. If they are a part of the other side of the political spectrum, then it's judgment that they deserve. When is the last time we heard people praying for the lost soul of the doctor who runs the abortion clinic or the executive director of the local gay rights alliance? How many of our churches have ministries to AIDS victims seeking to effect a last-minute rescue of a life for eternal gain? Given our political frenzy, it seems that the church today is much more interested in "search and destroy" than "seek and to save." We are prone to be too long on mad and too short on mercy.

The Gospel lives today in tension with secular philosophy, forms and formats, its contexts, and our politic. If we are not watchful these tensions will tempt us to compromise the Gospel by seeking to popularize the Gospel.

Popularization

We must resist as well the temptation in the face of the disdain of our culture to popularize the Gospel and in so doing trivialize the depth and power of the Gospel. Gospel presentations that speak merely of finding peace in Jesus, that claim that the Gospel is about thinking positively or that we're really here to help people recover and feel good about themselves, leave the essence and issue of the Gospel in jeopardy. Attempts to entertain people into the kingdom and to put only the foot forward that is going to be accepted and applauded by the culture without putting the essence of the Gospel forward creates an environment in which we discount and, in effect, destroy the very heart of Christianity.

MacArthur, who has a wonderful way of keeping us in the tension of truth, writes,

> the overriding goal is becoming church attendance and worldly acceptability rather than a transformed life. Preaching the Word and boldly confronting sin are seen as archaic ineffectual means of winning the world. After all, those things actually drive most peo-

> ple away. Why not entice people into the fold by offering what they want, creating a friendly, comfortable environment, and catering to the very desires that constitute their strongest urges? As if we might get them to accept Jesus by somehow making Him more likable or making His message less offensive. . . . That kind of thinking badly skews the mission of the church. . . . It is the Word of God, not an earthly enticement, that plants the seed for a new birth (1 Peter 1:23). We gain nothing but God's displeasure if we seek to remove the offense of the Cross (see further Gal. 5:11).[6]

Temporalism

We must consider one other observation regarding the function of evangelism in what has become a hurting and despairing society. We hear so much emphasis today on meeting the *felt* needs of people, that we can easily forget that their greatest *real* need is for a Savior. Filling stomachs, mending the broken, comforting the hurting, fixing homes, and a host of other vitally important ministries cannot ignore the ultimate need of eternity. As Christ said, "What is a man profited if he gains the whole world, and loses or forfeits himself?" (Luke 9:25)

Ray Ortlund, Jr., of Trinity Seminary, in his book *A Passion for God,* issues a clear call for the Gospel to be unclouded by modernity and contemporary contextualization. He states,

> A wave of authentic revival sweeps over the church when three things happen together: teaching the great truths of the gospel with clarity, applying those truths to people's lives with spiritual power, and extending that experience to large numbers of people. We Evangelicals urgently need such an awakening today. We need to rediscover the gospel.

He goes on to say,

> Imagine the Evangelical church without the gospel. . . . What might our Evangelicalism, without the evangel, look like? We would have to replace the centrality of the gospel with something else, naturally. So what might take the place of the gospel in our sermons and books and cassette tapes and Sunday School classes and home Bible studies, and above all, in our hearts? A number of things, conceivably. An introspective absorption with recovery from past emotional traumas, for example. Or a passionate devotion to the pro-life cause. Or a confident manipulation of modern

> managerial techniques. Or a drive toward church growth and "success." Or a deep concern for the institution of the family. Or a fascination with the more unusual gifts of the Spirit. Or a clever appeal to consumerism by offering a sort of cost-free Christianity Lite. Or a sympathetic, empathetic, thickly honeyed cultivation of interpersonal relationships. Or a determination to take America back to its Christian roots through political power. Or a warm affirmation of self-esteem. The Evangelical movement, stripped of the gospel, might fix upon any or several of such concerns to define itself and drive energy for its mission. In other words, Evangelicals could marginalize or even lose the gospel and still potter on their way, perhaps even oblivious to their loss.

He concludes,

> We should not think, "Well, of course we have the gospel. The Reformation recovered it for us." Such complacency will cost us dearly. Every generation of Christians must be retaught afresh the basic truths of our faith. The church is always one generation away from total ignorance of the gospel, and we today are making rapid progress toward that ruinous goal. Rather than carefully assume the gospel, we must aggressively, deliberately, fully, and passionately teach and preach the gospel. . . . In fact, pastors and church leaders in particular are under enormous pressure today to satisfy the immediate demands of the marketplace at the cost of the gospel. People want what they want when they want it, or they will drive down the street to the First Church of Where It's At to get it. . . . What we really need is not to be pandered to, but to be re-educated in reality, as it is interpreted for us by the gospel. We need to know who God really is. We need to find out who we really are. We need to understand what our root problem really is and what God's merciful answer really is. And we need that new perception of reality to percolate deep down into our affections and desires, re-arranging us radically and joyfully to a whole new way of life. But if we frankly feel that the plain old gospel offers very little for people's real needs, then we have never really known it at all.[7]

Calvin Miller astutely observed in a recent conversation, "If we are talking about relevance then we need to talk about truth. Truth is relevant. It speaks beyond felt needs to real needs."

The function of evangelism appropriately executed in the context of our culture with clarity, compassion, and purity builds the stage for the second aspect of Christ's vision for the church.

IDENTIFICATION

The second indispensable function of ministry is *identity.* In His commission to us Christ went on to say, "Baptizing them in the name of the Father, the Son, and the Holy Spirit." In the early church, baptism was a public identity with Jesus Christ, His message, and His people. For many in the early church, it meant immediate ostracization from family, friends, and sometimes employment. While the ordinance of baptism today is usually done within the four walls of the church (losing some of its public statement) and for most is not the cause for persecution, it continues to be an important step in terms of identifying with Christ, His finished work on the cross, and His people, the body of Christ. A casual reading of the New Testament makes it clear that baptism, though not a means of grace, is a distinct and important act of public commitment for the believer. It introduces us to and identifies us with the larger body of Christ not only in our day, but it integrates us into and gives us a sense of belonging to a whole legion of people who throughout history have taken this step of obedience. In a sense, it is an outward rite of passage into the context of the believing community. That is not to say that those who are not baptized are not a part of the body of Christ, but it is to say that in the definition of early Christianity, it was an important identity statement not to be ignored or minimized.

Needless to say, there have been fewer issues in the church throughout the centuries that have caused more debate and division than the issue of baptism in terms of timing, mode, and meaning. No doubt many of us would have differing perspectives on these issues. What is critical at this point is not a conformity to one person's view on baptism, but an understanding of the principle and purpose behind baptism. Baptism in the early church was a clear statement of and step toward identity with Christ and the community of believers. If believer's baptism is not clearly understood by our people, then it is our task as leaders in the church to develop emphases toward means of identity with Christ and His community.

In the New Testament, baptism speaks to the issue of being joined publicly without shame to the heritage and belief structures of the church of Christ. Our task is to take those who have come to know Christ through authentic evangelism and bear them into the context of the community of our Lord. How does this happen? Some might say through church membership. But it's interesting that membership forms, though there was certainly a sense of organization in the New Testament, are not delineated for us in terms of the New Testament church. The public point of identity and association was not walking down an aisle, signing a membership card, or showing up in the pictorial directory. The intended point of identification was baptism. And being done in the context of the local assemblies, it meant an identity with an established body of believers who functioned under exemplary leadership, authority, discipline, and programs that ministered effectively to the needs of the community of followers and reached out effectively to the lost. While some would not believe that baptism is a requirement for official entry into a local body of believers, it is, on the other hand, clearly a public statement that identifies one with those who follow Christ.

As we reflect on identifying believers with the community of His followers, there are several things that should be noted. Some may initially object to the priority of baptism, or resist the principle because of some particular aversion to the ordinance. While some of us may bring reasons to the table as to why we would feel this way, we must recognize that God did establish this as a public statement and a post-conversion commitment that has held great significance in the ongoing work of Christ. Throughout the centuries it has been a high priority within the context of the church, and in fact, only in recent generations has it lost some of its sense of visibility and viability. Whatever the reasons for this may be, they have to be measured with the place that the authority of Scripture gives baptism in the New Testament. If for some reason there is an aversion to the act of baptism, then one would have to ask what public statement—what other right of passage, would be more consistent with the meaning of salvation and would identify us more closely with those who have carried the torch of the faith through all generations, passing it sequentially into ours?

There is a foreboding sense of rootlessness and disregard for the significance of history and heritage in our culture, and I fear that this has slipped into the mind-set of many modern Christians. We have a great legacy through the centuries of people who bravely followed Christ's example of baptism as an initial commitment that set the pace for courage and perseverance through the rest of their lives.

Perhaps the damage to the place and priority of baptism is self-inflicted. I don't think we've done a good job of helping people to understand the high priority of baptism in terms of its public statement of our identity with Christ and His community. We say it is an act of obedience, which it is. We make it, in some groups, a requirement for membership. We bury it in a Sunday night service, in the least noticeable context possible. We sometimes trivialize it by running adherents through the ordinance like doughnuts that are routinely dipped to glaze them for sale. We tend to marginalize it by encouraging children to take this step who perhaps are too young to understand its full impact and who are so vulnerable to wanting to do it because everyone else in the Sunday School class is doing it.

We should call the church to understand that baptism is a public post-conversion rite of passage into the context of the community of Christ and a public declaration of the person's commitment to Christ, His message, His ministry, His mission, and His people through all the ages. As it was in the New Testament, we should revive it as a central point not only in a believer's life but in the life of the church as well. Some reeducation and relocation of this rite might help restore it to the original function intended.

Moving beyond the biblical and historical significance of baptism and its relevance to today, something must be said about false identity points that are often established. Integrating new believers into the community of Christ through baptism is a public affirmation of faith and personal identity with Christ through His death, burial, and resurrection. In a sense it is an initial outward step toward bonding our lives with Christ. Unfortunately, even for those of us who have started out like that, the identity soon shifts in the community of faith to a litany of lesser points of identification. If we are not careful we soon view the gathering of God's people not as a mutual gathering to celebrate our identity with the person, work, and ongoing cause of Christ, but a place that primarily provides an identity with others in terms of friendships, fellowship, and even therapy. A place where I can establish my own identity through performance, position, and power. A place where I can bond my identity to a particular shepherd. A place where I can enhance my identity by having my needs met, or establish my identity through service in fulfilling experiences like music or other types of satisfying ministry. The point is that as we initially identify with Christ, we must hold Him as our singular and all-compelling point of identity through all the activities, functions, and focus of the ongoing community. When Paul reveled in the marvelous reality of Christ, he concluded his ecstatic exposition of the Savior by saying, "So that He Himself might come to have first place in everything" (Col. 1:18).

We as shepherds must work to make that true in our own lives and in the lives of our flock. When they are done seeing us, counseling with us, hearing us preach, praying with us, or socializing with us, it is important that they have been drawn closer to and shown more clearly the person of Jesus Christ. One problem in many of our churches today is that while we have encouraged believers to publicly identify with Christ at the outset, we have then given them opportunities to shift that point of identity to a host of good but lesser things.

As we will note in a subsequent chapter, Christ reproved the church at Ephesus, after affirming them for doing a list of good things, for having "lost their first love" (Rev. 2:1-7). He called them to repentance; to do the right things for the right reason. And the right reason was their personal, primary identification with Christ as Savior and Lord, whom they loved enough to serve completely. He went on to say that if there wasn't repentance, that if the church wished to do the right things for all the wrong reasons, then He would remove their capacity to be effective. Or, as He said it, He would "remove the lampstand out of its place."

Another challenge to the function of *identification* is that "boomers are not joiners." It is true that we live in a culture that shuns the ensuing commitments that come from a consecrated allegiance to a group of any kind. One church has tried to deal with the problem by establishing a tiered membership plan where the first level of membership is made up of those who are fully committed to the church, its doctrine, and its ongoing ministry; a second level of membership is for those who do not seek in-depth involvement but want a measure of identity; and a third class of membership is for those who want to be identified with but are not yet ready to fully commit themselves to Jesus Christ and in fact may not even be Christians. This effort to satisfy different levels of interest in identity may work well in a generation full of noncommitters, but somehow it must be managed in a way that doesn't contradict the essence of what it means to belong to the body of Christ. Since local assemblies are reflections of the larger body of Christ, then certainly commitment, conformity, discipline, and dedication to advancing the cause of Christ together should be the point of identification with Christ and His church.

In fact, the whole sense of being a loner is a contradiction of the reality of what the community of believers is all about. We are His body. He is our head. And as His body we all play a different part in the function. Scripture knows of no place for loners, wallflowers, bench-sitters, or marginalized participants in the body of Christ. For those in the early church, to identify with the cause of Christ meant that the rite of passage known as baptism was just the beginning of what would necessarily be a life of courageous consecration to Christ and His community that sometimes held consequences that were less than appealing but well worth it in light of the One that we are called to serve. Throughout history God's people have loved His church and have marshaled to Christ's rally cry when He said, "I will build My church; and the gates of Hades shall not overpower it" (Matt. 16:18). Throughout history our forefathers believed that identifying with Christ and Christ's people was identifying with a cause worth living for; indeed, dying for if necessary.

DISCIPLESHIP

The third function of the church, according to Christ, is that we be about the business of "teaching them to observe all that I have commanded you." This task of transitioning people from the mind-set of their fallen past to the knowledge of the truth of Christ and the subsequent conformity to living out these truths is the ongoing long-term function of the faithful shepherd. Evangelism in a person's life is punctiliar, as the act of baptism. But the meaning of baptism flows into this third function and seems a natural transition from evangelism to discipleship. Discipleship, our teaching, training, and grooming ministries consume the vast remaining segment of our function as shepherds.

Needless to say, this becomes a more difficult task, given the fact that the culture is now so diametrically opposed to "all the things that He has commanded us." New believers need massive doses over long periods of time of spiritual stimulants that will transition them to the kinds of thoughts, habits, responses, and patterns of living that will make them truly unique in Jesus Christ. New believers today come into the kingdom literally saturated with mental and lifestyle addictions to nontruth values such as relativism, pluralism, hedonism, sensualism, materialism, temporalism, and existentialism. All are counter to the teachings of Christ. As we shall learn in the unfolding principles of what it takes to do the best things in the worst times, it will first of all require that we as spiritual leaders are examples in terms of our personhood, are effective in terms of our proclamation, and are proficient in the exercise of our ministries according to the gifts that God has given to us. Without that there is little hope for these newborn babes to grow into the wonderful privilege of being true adherents to all that is involved in the kingdom of Christ.

We should note that the point of this third function is to lead them to a life that is characterized by the *observance* of that which is taught. It is difficult to believe that we have truly been successful in our ministries if people are not demonstrating changed behavior patterns that accumulate not only to the common good of the community of believers and to the glory of Christ but also to the meltdown of resistance and the miracle of redemption replicated in the lives of others.

Ministry is about transformation. Transformation that is far more radical today than in previous generations.

There are several elements within a shepherd's ministry that facilitate and fortify a progressive behavioral conformity to the principles of Christ. The most powerful is the example of the shepherd. Everyone else can consistently fail, but if the shepherd projects a positive, real, and consistent example of what it means to be a believer conforming to the image of Christ, then there will be a powerful compulsion within the body to grow as the shepherd is growing. As shepherds we will either be their example or their excuse. I don't know about you, but when I'm around people who are genuinely, authentically growing in Christ, I am stimulated to want to grow with them. In fact, I try to make it a habit to be in the presence of people whose responses to life are exemplary and admirable. I find myself saying, "I want to be like that." That is the power base of an effective transformational shepherd. Long before they go to school on our words, they will go to school on our behavior and be motivated to follow the leadership of our lifestyle.

Along with the shepherd's example is the valuable contribution of righteous peer pressure within a community of believers. When righteousness becomes the prevailing attitude of a body of believers, it establishes a peer pressure that stimulates all believers to the truly good life in Jesus Christ. A church full of persons who love the lost; husbands who love their wives; people who willingly serve; lips that are slow to criticize, slander, and gossip, but rather are dedicated to healing, helping, and encouraging; finances that are focused on glorifying God; and Christians who are passionately addicted to acts of compassion develop an environment that stimulates others to make a similar contribution to the group.

Another element that enhances this discipleship function of Christ's commission is the clear communication of standards of righteousness, bolstered by a church that is willing to exercise redemptive, remedial, biblical church discipline. When our adherents know that we mean business about observing the things that Christ commanded us and upholding the testimony of His name through our church, there is a certain seriousness that envelops the issue of our behavior. Churches that never back up their beliefs with balanced discipline find that quite often believers take lightly the issues of our conformity to Christ.

The clear, effective, relevant communication of God's Word from the pulpit, from lecterns in Sunday School rooms and leaders' lips in small group Bible studies provides both clarification and application regarding fundamental principles and codes of Christian behavior. In fact, shouldn't it be the goal of our preaching not to inform or to impress, but to stimulate believers to conformity to the image of Christ through obedience to His principles in their lives? We will deal with what comprises effective transformational preaching later in the book, but for now it needs to be said that the effectiveness of our preaching is not measured by how enamored they are with our preaching or how stellar we are in our capacity to communicate, but rather in whether or not their lives are more like Christ today than they were six months ago. And while very few lives will be changed in a sermon, it is the effective teaching and preaching of the Word of God over the long haul that slowly but surely enables our people to process and actualize a commitment to observing all the things that He has commanded us.

In fact, if we say we have growing, vibrant, healthy churches, then let's not look at programs, plans, popularity, or position; rather, let's look at our people. Not the quantity but the quality. They are the ultimate barometer of how well we have carried out the three foundational functions of ministry. Of whether or not we have done the best things in these, the worst times.

Christ commissioned us to evangelize people who will identify themselves openly with Christ, His church, and His cause, and who are in the process of transforming their lives to reflect the glory of His likeness. But with our oftentimes perceived inadequacies and insecurities, and in light of our times one has to wonder, "Is it even possible for *me* in *this day* to do the best things?" If I didn't know better, I'd be tempted toward pessimism and feelings of inadequacy given the fact that our society is so polarized against the very essence of each of them.

Our struggle is reflected in a recent *Doonesbury* comic strip. The parish rector of the Little Church of Walden is discussing the focus of his church with a prospective couple. The pastor asks, "So what would you like to know about Little Church of Walden, folks? Don't hold back—I know how difficult it can be to choose a church."

The interested husband responds, "Well, what's your basic approach here, Reverend? Is it traditional gospel?"

"In a way, I like to describe it as a 12-step Christianity. . . . Basically, I believe that we're all recovering sinners. My ministry is about overcoming denial, it's about re-commitment, about redemption. It's all in the brochure there."

The pastor's response stimulates the wife's interest, and she queries, "Wait a minute—sinners? Redemption? Doesn't all that imply . . . guilt?"

To which the pastor responds, "Well, yes, I do rely on the occasional disincentive to keep the flock from going astray. Guilt's part of that!"

The husband responds, "I dunno. There's so much negativity in the world as it is." And his wife chimes in, "That's right. We're looking for a church that's supportive, a place where we can feel good about ourselves. I'm not sure this guilt thing works for us."

The husband observes, "On the other hand, you do offer racquetball . . ." To which his wife responds, "So did the Unitarians, honey. Let's shop around some more."[8]

Lest discouragement prevail, we must remember that we are about God's business. That God is the supernatural Overcomer, who, in many generations and in a variety of hostile contexts, through faithful leaders and a faithful church empowered these functions that in the very beginning the church overcame the power of the pagan Roman Empire. That this is the God who in surprising and dramatic ways has delivered people from darkness into the kingdom of His dear Son. A God who has done it through those who believed that "greater is He who is in you than he that is in the world" (1 John 4:4).

Chapter Three

Who, Me?
Adequacy and Success
The Facilitator

Wondering why her son hadn't gotten up for church, Mrs. Smith went up to his bedroom and insisted that he get up. He said he wasn't planning to go to church, to which she replied, "Bob, you're thirty-eight years old! Now get out of bed and go to church!"

"I don't like that church," he complained. "The people are demanding, critical, opinionated, fickle, hypocritical, and gossipy . . . you can't give me one good reason to go."

"Yes I can—you're the pastor!"

At times we can identify with Bob.

I was thirty-six years old when I candidated at the Highland Park Baptist Church in Southfield, Michigan. After having begun my pastoral ministry by helping to plant a church with a small body of believers and then having been led to minister in a stable, highly traditional congregation in Indiana, I felt pressed beyond my boundaries as I found myself in the candidating process in such a well-established and, in the best sense of the term, sophisticated church with a long history of effective shepherds and a demanding, multifaceted ministry.

The environment was replete with reasons for me to feel insecure and to fear failure. The previous pastor was an older man with a grandfatherly image who had been universally appreciated and accepted in the church. The church was large enough to have a staff that was assigned to the various functions of pastoral ministry, leaving the senior pastor to cast a vision, manage the staff, and be the primary teacher of the Word of God on Sundays and Wednesdays. And while this was appealing to my desire to develop my preaching and teaching ministry, I soon came to realize that while pastors in smaller churches had several "cards to play" in their ministry, i.e., calling in the hospital, marrying, burying, visiting in homes, etc., my ministry would rise and fall primarily on my capacity to measure up in the pulpit. This was an especially tense issue since the chairman of the pulpit committee, when talking to me about the priority of preaching in the church, had said, "We expect five great sermons out of four."

My insecurities were compounded by the fact that many of the leaders in this church were high-profile business leaders in the automotive community, and others were wealthy entrepreneurs and successful career persons. It didn't help that a colleague warned me, "Those high-powered executives will chew you up and spit you out." To cap it off, I was coming from a different denominational background to this church, and some perceived me to be a threat to the depth and breadth of the church since they thought me to be from a background that would be too restrictive for them.

In spite of all of this, God extruded me from the comfort of Kokomo and in essence said, "Back on the rack again." He put me in a context that was beyond myself, which is not a bad place to be if you know God has called you. It forced me to be God-reliant and humble in the process. I recall that as the time came near to go to Highland Park, the thought of it tightened my stomach. I wondered, "If this is God's will, why don't I have peace?" I finally came to realize that I had His peace in the decision, but the decision was still a frightening thought.

All of this personal history to say that all of my insecurities bubbled to the surface, and I found myself asking on more than one occasion if I was really the one to be able to carry out the task for that church.

We can talk about the fundamental functions of the church and their priority over the forms through which they flow, but at some point we have to address the reality that, while these functions are clearly delineated and carefully defined for us in Scripture, the functions really rise and fall on the person who is called to facilitate them, the shepherd of the flock. A realization of this causes a serious shepherd to deal with two haunting questions in regard to his task. "Can *I* pull this off?" and "How will I know when I've succeeded?" It is the issue of adequacy and success.

Functions are entrusted to facilitators, and therein lies our struggle. As Pogo once said, "We have seen the enemy and it is us." The true weight of ministry lies not in a textbook commitment to the task but in the successful management of the one mastering the task. When we understand that we are stewards of such significant endeavors, a sense of inadequacy and a fear of not succeeding are the legitimate responses.

Given the weight and strategic importance of the ministry of evangelism, identification, and discipleship in the face of the antithetical pressures of our society, it is little wonder that most of us live with a gnawing sense of being beyond ourselves. As more than gnawing. It is often debilitating and sometimes defeating. And while we understand God's call and the gracious capabilities that He gives us to exercise the call, we do struggle. As though the weight of the task weren't enough, our insecurity and fear of failure are complicated by three ever-present factors that are part and parcel of the shepherd's life.

The all-time worst of these is CRITICISM.

I'm reminded of the story of the pastor who after his first sermon at his new church was intercepted by a lady who said, "We've had a lot of pastors come and go but I've never heard one preach a sermon that poorly." Devastated, he determined to do a better job the next Sunday only to have the same woman stop him and say, "This series is quite irrelevant to the needs of our congregation." Determined again to improve, he worked harder than he'd ever worked on a sermon only to have her approach him again and mention that his suit and tie were in poor taste. Later the chairman of the board said to the pastor, "I see that Edna's been talking to you. Don't worry about Edna, she only repeats what everyone else is saying."

Although "Edna" was not a member at the Highland Park Church, going there was a challenging step for us. And while the six years there were happy and profitable years of ministry, I can still remember vividly the compounding influence that criticism had on my resident insecurities. I found the congregation at large to be accepting, affirming, and encouraging, but there were just a few whom God sovereignly assigned to keep my head and heart in perspective.

The chairman of the board of deacons, who was, interestingly enough, one of the proponents for my coming to the church, took it upon himself without the request of the board to take me out to lunch twice a year to evaluate my ministry. He did this for the first two and a half years of my time there. And while he remained friendly to me through all of those encounters, he would at each lunch take a list of things that he felt were not good about my ministry, go over them with me, usually couching them by saying, "People are saying . . ." The lists were long, and what was particularly painful was that at none of the lunches was there ever one word of positive affirmation about my ministry at the church.

I remember another time early on in my ministry when one of the high-level executives in the church came to my office and sat across the desk, kindly but clearly sharing with me that he felt that my messages weren't hitting home. We had a good talk, and I took it as from the Lord, as constructive input and impetus to work harder on my preaching.

Several months later, while at a social gathering, he walked up as I was socializing with a small group of people from our church, interrupted the flow of conversation and said, "Pastor, by the way, I've just returned from being out of town where I was with a group of people who attended a retreat that you spoke at." He went on to say how excited they had been about the material and how they had told him what an effective speaker I had been. For a fleeting moment I felt vindicated and was just about ready to thank the Lord for resolving his perspectives on my ministry when he concluded the brief intrusion by looking at me, smiling, and saying, "For a moment, I wondered if they were talking about the same guy I know." Needless to say, it went to the core, particularly given the fact that I was standing in front of a group of others from the church.

If we're not careful, criticism will distort our whole capacity to shepherd well. Why is it that, while the vast majority of the church may respect, honor, and encourage us, if there is just a small handful of critics, our hearts are enslaved to their attitudes? Why is it that we prepare sermons with them in mind? Why are we tempted to gossip to others about them? To discount their influence? Why is it that we feel our shepherding hearts disenfranchised from them and incapacitated to serve them regardless of their attitude toward us?

Our critics and our resultant insecurities make us defensive, divisive, and disenfranchised.

As the years of my life and ministry have worn on, I've come to value some aspects of criticism and believe some truths about criticism that help to liberate me from its defeating effect. First, there is most often a germ of truth in what is being said. And, if my critic is someone who is really on my team, who has already proved that he loves and cares for me, there is probably a lot more than a germ of truth. There may be a whole ton of truth riding on the words. And if indeed I'm committed to being the best servant possible for the Lord, I need to carefully weigh and evaluate what is true and how I should effect a change in my life to be a better shepherd.

If you're like me, the criticisms that really cuts to the core are those criticisms that malign our motives, that misunderstand our words, and that we know in our hearts are not really true. A friend once said to me, "Joe, time and truth walk hand in hand." What a profound blessing that has been to me. If what they're saying is true, then soon everyone will know that flaw in the ointment of my ministry. But if what they're saying is not true, in time—after people have observed my life and ministry, they will say, "That wasn't really true after all, was it?" Time and truth walk hand in hand!

I've also come to realize that there is a certain blessedness to the insecurities that criticism fans in my heart. When I feel insecure, I am most prone to be more dependent on God, to spend more time in prayer, and to not feel self-sufficient. There are fewer curses in the ministry worse than the curse of self-sufficiency. We desperately need to know how much we need Him. And isn't that why Christ wrapped up the Great Commission by assuring us that He would be with us all the time, even unto the end of the age? Because He knew we really couldn't do it by ourselves. So in moments of biblical sanity, I have learned to view even my critics as sovereignly placed messengers of God in my life, to keep me blessedly insecure that I might be more God-reliant and more genuinely humble in my work for Christ.

It has been helpful as well to realize that I am called to shepherd even those who, for some reason, don't like the shepherd. Some people don't like those of us who have position, power, or success. It really has nothing to do with us; it's just that they don't like people like us. Some people may feel free to criticize because we haven't lived up to the expectations they had for us. Maybe they wanted to be our best friend and possess our social life, and we weren't able to satisfy that. Perhaps they thought that we would excuse their behavior patterns, but instead we have called them to righteousness and they haven't liked that. There are a myriad of reasons why people don't like us and/or don't appreciate us. Some are reasons in our lives, and some are reasons in their lives. But the reality is that all in our flock are precious to God. He died for all of them. And if they are precious to Him and forgiven by Him, then they must be precious to us and forgiven by us. This liberates us to be total shepherds. Shepherds to all of the flock regardless. Good shepherds not because they always deserve our shepherding, but because we are the under-shepherd for Someone who deserves our very best on behalf of a people that He loved and gave Himself for. And that includes our critics.

Being liberated from the bondage of our critics liberates us from preaching sermons at them. Isn't it interesting that when we are in bondage to our critics, regardless of where we're studying—it can even be the "begat" passages—we see their problem. And so we prepare with focused applications and mount the pulpit, and as we open our Bibles we look across the faces of the congregation and notice that they're not there. A wasted sermon! And if they are there, it's interesting that no matter how much we veil the application, many people in the congregation will know that it is no longer a message but a billy club. And even if they don't agree with those who are being gouged by the message, they will often feel mercy toward the victim and for the most part lose confidence and respect for us. They know that if we would do that to someone else in the congregation, someday we might do that to them.

If criticism doesn't compound our sense of inadequacy, then COMPARISON will. Who knows why it is in life that we are always discontent with who we are and where we are . . . wishing we could be like someone else or be where they are? No matter who we are or where we get to, there will always be those who are bigger, better, more famous, or more wealthy. There will always be those who seem to have been given greater, more abundant gifts, who have had more opportunities than we have had, and who seem to suffer less than we suffer. There will always be those who have fewer problems and more fun.

A shepherd who compares himself with others becomes quickly discontent of not only where he is but who he is. He is driven into moods of introspection, wondering why it is he got stuck with that which is smaller, lesser, more troublesome, and less rewarding. He finds himself starved for affirmation and living on the edge of embitterment which only compounds his sense of inadequacy and insecurity.

And when we aren't comparing ourselves with others, we inevitably are victimized by those who compare us to others.

The problem with our propensity to compare is that at the core of it all, we have really ceased to be content with God's assignment for us in His vast vineyard, discontent with the gifts He has given us and the part that He has graciously given us to play within His body. It also reflects that our perspectives are really earthbound. That we measure life in terms of fame and fortune, position and power, acclaim and affirmation, comfort and convenience. And that we measure these commodities in terms of what we get on this side of heaven, not by what we have when we get home. Is it not our task to humbly accept as a privilege the place that God designs for us and the place for which we have been designed? And then to count ourselves as servants—servants first and foremost of Him who loved us, and second of those whom He loves and has called us to serve?

In Matthew 20 the disciples find themselves arguing again over who should be the greatest in the kingdom. James and John came with their mother to Christ and beat the other ten to the punch. As she filed the request, the text says that the rest of them were moved with indignation. Nobody was willing to play the lesser part. Everyone wanted to play the big part. Christ reproved them by telling them that this was the way the Gentiles functioned and that it should "not be so among them." He went on to say that he who would be great in His kingdom would be the servant, and he who would be administrative chief would be a slave. He capstoned the exhortation by saying, "the Son of Man did not come to be served, but to serve, and to give His life a ransom for many" (vv. 22-28).

Comparing ourselves one with another denies the reality that our affirmation ultimately comes from Him, in His time, in His way. And for some of us the affirmation may not come until we get to the other side and hear Him say, "Well done, thou good and faithful servant."

Comparing ourselves unfavorably to others also denies the realities of life in the long view. Our ministries may be small and unnoticed, but who's to say that in the context of those ministries there isn't one young man or one young woman who grows up watching our example, honors our ministry, and ends up being the next Billy Graham or Elisabeth Elliot to impact their generation for Christ? All because one faithful shepherd was not concerned about comparison, but about the consecration of his life and ministry right where God put him. I remember my mother-in-law sending me a birthday card when I turned 35. It lamented my advancing age and then culminated with the statement, "Bloom where you're planted." Great advice!

Which leads me to a third source of our sense of inadequacy, and that is CARNALITY. When we as shepherds live in unresolved patterns of sin we breed an insecurity within that plagues and disables us. Insecurities that focus on "What happens if I get caught?" and the sense of inadequacy that results when we wonder, "Can God continue to bless me?" and "Perhaps I'm just doing all of this in the flesh." Carnality engenders in our hearts an environment of fear, positions us in defensive postures, and makes our ministry a forced function of our calling rather than a spontaneous expression of our unhindered love and growing intimacy with Christ.

Needless to say, this may be the easiest source of inadequacy to resolve, through repentance, accountability, and growth. It's amazing what measures of security we sense in our hearts when we know that God is pleased and unhinderedly present with us. It's a special privilege to express our love for the flock "from a pure heart and a good conscience and a sincere faith" (1 Tim. 1:5).

Given the prevalence of these three sources of insecurity that are added to the weight of the tank, I think most of us will readily admit that our sense of inadequacy will live close to the surface of our lives. There is, thankfully, a biblical answer to our feelings of inadequacy that source themselves in the massive responsibility of managing the threefold task of the church. In fact, it is given in the very same text that deals with the second ramification of being a facilitator of the functions of the church. "How will I know when I've succeeded?"

Given the high profile of the Highland Park Baptist Church, its reputation, its size and scope, it may have been possible for me to go there and immediately feel that I had arrived. For us, success is so often measured in position and place, when in reality it should be measured in the outworking and outcomes of how well we have managed the fundamental functions that He has called us to.

In education we focus on "outcomes." The accrediting agencies demand that we structure basic expectations for the outworking of our mission statement and then measure our success by how well we conformed to our expectations in terms of the final product reflected in our students. Our success in ministry will be measured in how well we have ministered in relation to God's standards. What are the standards that God measures our ministries by?

Ephesians 4 and Acts 2 are passages that cast important light on our task. They speak to the issue of our insecurities and inadequacies as well as to the measurable outcomes of a church that is successfully functioning according to biblical patterns. They address the important questions, "Am I capable of leadership?" and "How will I know when the venture is succeeding?"

ADEQUATE SHEPHERD

In Ephesians 4, Paul declares that each one in the body of Christ has been given grace, i.e., special enablement, "according to the measure of Christ's gift" (Eph. 4:7). He follows this with an interesting statement regarding the ascension of Christ. In essence he says that when Christ left this planet to function as our Advocate and High Priest in heaven, He "gave gifts to men." The inference is that when He gave us the task of carrying out the work of His church, He also graciously supplied supernatural enablement for us to carry out the assignment. In the midst of all of our insecurities, we must remember that He empowers us with enabling gifts of ministry.

Paul went on to say that He specifically bestowed four types of leadership gifts which in essence drive the function of the church toward successful outcomes. The gifts are apostleship, prophecy, evangelism, and pastor/teacher.

The gift of APOSTLESHIP is the capacity that He gives to certain church leaders to advance the Gospel through church planting, authoritative leadership, and what we know today as missionary work. These were all ministries that were specifically given to the apostolic group that launched the New Testament church. There is no indication in Scripture that there is a continuation of the absolute apostolic authority that gives one a right to decree *ex cathedra* His will for the church as though it is of divine origin. The apostolic gift today is the gift that carries with it the authority of the already-revealed Word of God in terms of the functions of a New Testament ministry.

The gift of PROPHECY would be reflective of what was both the experience in the New Testament and also in the Old Testament, and that is that by and large prophecy did not deal with the telling of the future, but rather the forthtelling of a clear message of God calling people to repentance and requiring righteousness of the saints. Those with the gift of prophecy have a particular ability to see the reality of righteousness applied and have a sharp, discerning spirit regarding sin and error. This is the gift that keeps truth in tension and protects it from the insidious nature of error.

The gift of EVANGELISM is a unique endowment upon some within the church to provide leadership to the flock in terms of reaching the lost. These are individuals who have an uncanny capacity to passionately witness at every opportunity and, surprisingly, to be phenomenally successful in leading people to Christ. Whether it is in the public proclamation arena or an individual who can sit down on a plane and before the plane lands have led the stranger sitting next to him to the Lord, these individuals are especially equipped with an unusual advantage in witnessing.

The fourth gift that God has given to church leadership is the one who carries the gift of PASTOR/TEACHER. Of all of the four gifts, this is the most relevant to a resident shepherd of the flock. The other three gifts may find themselves being carried out in broader contexts than the local church, though it certainly is possible that they may reside as well among a group of elders and/or a staff within the context of a local church. In fact, it would be a rich church who had a covey of leaders who reflected the variety of these gifts. If, however, there had to be one gift in terms of local church leadership, certainly the most effective would be this one. The gift of pastor/teacher combines two key elements of local church leadership; one being the ministry of caring and concern, combined with the indispensable ingredient of instructing the flock in the truth of God and its ramifications for their lives. Those with the gift of pastor/teacher are individuals who are particularly inclined toward the needs of people and who as well are committed to meeting those needs not just through the ministries of personal resourcing, but public proclamation. Interestingly, the tension in this double-edged gift is that ofttimes those of us who are the pastoral types (i.e., high relational, high-touch people) find it difficult to be disciplined in sufficient measure to stay away from people and their needs long enough to adequately prepare the effective teaching ministry that is the vital, in fact, the most important part of our caring ministry. Most of us as pastors/teachers will fault toward pastoring more than teaching or teaching more than pastoring and must constantly strive to blend the gift into a balance that moves us toward the described goal of the function of our ministry.

It is important for us to know that these gifts are supernatural enablements for us to carry out the task. They enable us to adequately minister in the face of our feelings of inadequacy. Knowing that God has indeed gifted us to do what we are doing breeds a special sense of security. It is important as well to know that all four of these gifts describe functions that are the responsibility of the shepherd. And while we must faithfully exercise the essentials of each of the four, God will have given us one through which to funnel our responsibilities.

It is strategic for us as shepherds to discover what our specific leadership gift is and to find ourselves in places where the needs are compatible with our gifts. Discovering our gift may mean that we stop coveting or clinging to senior pastoral roles and happily opt for staff positions that enable us to focus all our energies on the enablement that God has given to us. Someone helped me greatly when they encouraged me early on in my ministry to discover my leadership gift by targeting what it was that brought joy to my heart when I exercised it, what I seemed to have energy for, what the Lord made fruitful through my life, and what others affirmed to be my strength. In time the convergence of these four measurements of our gifts will point to the exact type of equipment that God has sovereignly bestowed upon us to enable and empower us to carry out the task.

Knowing our gift and being in a place where it can be used will go far to minimize our sense of inadequacy. If He has called us to a task and equipped us for the task we can be assured that He will use us to be effective in the task in His *time* and His *way*.

Which poses the next vitally important question in regard to facilitating the function, and that is, "How will I know if I am succeeding in fulfilling God's intended purpose for my ministry?"

THE SUCCESSFUL MINISTRY

Ephesians 4:11-15 clearly delineates God's expectations for His church. These are the measurements of our ministerial success. The text has noted that the fulfillment of these expectations are through the gifts that we have been given (vv. 11-12). In an interesting twist of the text, the indication is that these are not only gifts that have been given to shepherds, but that the gifts in this text are indeed gifted individuals who are gifts of God to the church. It would be well for us to envision ourselves in the best sense of the word as God's gift to the church for an intended purpose. We've all gotten gifts in our lives that are outwardly attractive, but when it has come down to it, we have found them to not be very useful at all. It does little good for us to put on the cosmetics of ministry without finding ourselves to be indeed useful gifts to the body of Christ. Our usefulness is measured by the remainder of this text.

The text in essence creates targets at which we can aim. These targets are preestablished, unmovable goals for us and as such measure our success as marksmen. I'm reminded of the town fool whose barn was covered with targets painted on its side. In the middle of each bull's-eye there was a puncture mark from his arrow. A passerby remarked about what a great marksman he was. He replied, "It's easy. I shoot my arrow at the barn and then paint my target around it."

Some of us have manufactured our own targets of success—buildings, programs, notoriety, popularity, or even large crowds. Regardless of how many of our own targets we've painted, the only ones where bull's-eyes count are the targets that God painted long before we picked up our bow and arrow.

Target 1: We are to be busy about *preparing people for works of ministry.* This is a fascinating word in the original language which was used for mending the nets to enable them to be useful in terms of the fishing business. We start with people who need to be prepared for ministry. Some of that preparation may be transitioning them from the ways of darkness to the ways of light. Some of it may be exposing them to the reality of the gifts that God has given them and then give them training and opportunities to fulfill those gifts. Some of the mending may have to do with the brokenness of bitterness or past baggage that disables them and disenfranchises them for effective ministry. Whatever it is, bringing people to a place of usability in the hand of God is a measure of success.

Target 2: Usability is defined in the text as usefulness in *acts of service.* We might reflect here on Romans 12 where primary gifts of service are enumerated. They are the gifts of prophecy, serving, teaching, exhortation, giving, leading, and mercy. God has given all of the adherents in our church ministry gifts for service, and the goal of our ministry should be to see them prospering in and maximizing the gift in a get-busy pattern of ministry for Christ within the body of Christ. There are many great helps on the market today that enable people to start the process of discovering their spiritual gifts. We should be constantly encouraging our people to seek to know how God has built them to function within the body. But instead of sitting around wondering and waiting, the best way to help our people discover their gifts is to encourage them to get busy doing something that seems intriguing to them. If after a little while they've discovered that they really aren't equipped for that particular type of ministry, then we know that that's not their gift. Routine busyness for the Lord will soon separate that which is, from that which is not, in regard to our gift. As we have noted, parishioners will know that they are operating in their gifts when they have energy for the task, joy in doing the task, fruitfulness from the exercise of the task, and affirmation from others as they fulfill the task.

Interestingly, a megachurch that has often been the brunt of criticism for putting form before function has, at this writing, over 5,000 believers in its church who know what their spiritual gifts are and who are exercising them within the context of the ministries of that church. This is a ministry that, for all of its criticism, is functioning the way God intended a church to function in this area. To its credit, it obviously has a form that enhances the function, at least in regard to believers getting busy and being equipped to carry on the work of Christ as a means to the building up of His body.

Target 3 tells us how well we're doing by seeing our focused efforts on the functions of the church to bring people to a point where there is unity in the body based on a mutual faith and knowledge of God.

Target 4 relates to maturity in individuals in the flock whose lives reflect the likeness of the fullness of Christ.

Note that all of these targets relate to qualitative change in people's lives.

One of the things that makes pastoral leadership so much more difficult than almost any other task in the world is that most other tasks involve people working with people to build a material product or to provide a material service. In those material products and services there is a measure of predictability and reliability in the outcomes. Ministry, on the other hand, is people working with people to produce people whose lives are solidified and unified in their Christlikeness. That is a far more risky, unpredictable, and challenging endeavor. There aren't two people alike in terms of background, mind-set, perspective, and aspirations. And yet our challenge is to take this assortment of lives and bring them into a unified oneness in faith and knowledge of God, stretch them into biblical reflections of maturity, and develop their life attitudes and responses to reflect the pure and powerful character of Jesus Christ.

It's interesting to survey the temperaments and backgrounds of the disciples whom Christ called together. What an unusual and interesting variety of outspoken, timid, affluent, and common folks gathered in that first group of twelve! Most notable in terms of differences is the fact that Matthew was a tax collector. Tax collectors had sold themselves out to the occupying Roman Empire to collect the exorbitant taxes and attach personal assessments that they could keep for themselves. They were the despised traitors. And then there was Simon—the zealot. He was called a zealot because he was a member of the underground resistance force plotting and planning to overthrow the yoke of Roman rule. And yet the two of them were thrown into this cadre of colleagues who followed Christ. Christ gave them a commonality that eclipsed their preferences, politics, temperaments, and personalities, and drew them to Himself, that together through their diverse characteristics Christ alone would be reflected and glorified. The disciples paint a picture of what a successful ministry would look like.

Target 5. Paul goes on to say that the result of ministries that are managed in a way to prepare believers for acts of service, to be unified in faith and knowledge, growing in the likeness of Christ, is a body of believers that becomes firm in their faith, unshaken, and unseduced by false patterns of thoughts and values that erode not only life individually but the life of the church as well. And on the positive side, all of this is to produce a group of people who know how to speak the truth in love, unto the building up of one another, into a closer, more intimate fellowship in and with Jesus Christ.

This, needless to say, is a relevant point of success. There has never been a success in the history of the American church when there are so many seductive influences that threaten to toss believers "to and fro." From New Age philosophies to relativistic pluralism, to sensualism and a preeminent place for tolerance, our world offers a whole litany of seductive systems that with great subtlety seep into the hearts and minds of God's people.

A successful ministry has so effectively built up the saints in knowledge and faith that they are no longer vulnerable to the doctrines of secularism. And this success is reflected not only in believers who are equipped to stand firm against godless influences but, according to this text, are prepared without intimidation to speak the truth from a loving spirit.

In addition to these Pauline measures of ministry success, Luke notes that the ministry of the early church was characterized by a continuing devotion to "the apostles' teaching and to fellowship, to the breaking of bread and to prayer" (Acts 2:42). Authentic ministries then are measured by adherence to and celebration of truth in terms of conformity to the orthodox teachings of our forefathers; productive and positive involvement of the believers within the community of Christ so that an encouraging environment of fellowship is thriving; the bonding to Christ and the worshiping of His work through both attendance and attentiveness to the ordinance of the Lord's Table; as well as a church that is characterized by prayer. Volumes could be written about the tension that our society places on each one of these commodities that Luke mentions. The measure of a church's success is about enhancing truth in the midst of a nontruth culture; community involvement and fellowship in a culture that resists commitment to others and celebrates privatism and isolation; the celebration of history in terms of our rootedness in the cross, pictured at the Lord's Table in a world that has little time or interest in the implications of history on our present lives. And what of prayer in a society that celebrates self-sufficiency?

These measures of ministry success are the outcomes of a church empowered by adequately gifted shepherds who are non-negotiably committed to the best of things. Successful ministries measure up as a result of evangelizing persons into the body of Christ, leading them to identify with the legacy and life of the community of Christ, and patiently processing them into conforming their lives to the character of Christ.

Thankfully, both the functions and the measure of their success are transcultural, transdenominational, transliturgical, transemotional, trans-faddish-forms-of-ministry, transmethodology, trans-racial, trans-class, and attainable. These are the functions and measures of the church triumphant through all generations. These are the fundamentals. These are the best things in any time and certainly the best things in the worst times. Our forms must follow these functions, and the success of the forms must be measured not in their popularity or their compelling draw on people's interest, but on how well they have produced the kind of church that Paul speaks of in Ephesians 4 and that Luke observes in Acts 2.

Forms that enhance evangelism, identity, and discipleship; that are managed by a shepherd who is aware of and has confidence in his gift; that encourage the preparation of believers for acts of service as they grow toward unity in their faith and knowledge; that enable growth toward Christlikeness and grant protection from Satan's seductions so that the church can be rich in fellowship, founded in doctrine, focused on our Lord's death, and committed to prayer, are forms that God will see fit to prosper.

The ultimate test of it all will not be in our mental grasp of and allegiance to the functions and their ability to move us toward the measures of success. It will not be in our professional prowess or the praise of the crowd. The ultimate test of our management of functions and forms will be in our people. If we say we have a successful ministry then it is measured in the quality of our people.

THE SUCCESSFUL PASTOR

While we're speaking of success, we might as well focus on the primary issue of a successful ministry, and that is a shepherd who understands what *personal* success is all about. The whole issue of what makes a pastor a success needs a fresh look. In fact, there are few traps more deep and destructive for a shepherd than a distorted view of personal success.

I must admit that one of my least favorite pastimes as a pastor was attending ministerial meetings. Primarily because we all worked so hard to communicate how successful our ministries were—which, needless to say, was discouraging for the vast majority of us who had dropped out of the "Can You Top This" game long ago and wondered why it was that God wasn't letting us be very successful.

The wrong definition of success will divert us into thinking that power and significance are the true measures of success. This theory of success brings the downsides of self-sufficiency and pride, as well as a distorted perspective on self, life, and the community of believers that we serve. It will increase our level of insecurity and fan the flames of jealousy and covetousness, and will ultimately discourage us since external power and significance are not universally attainable—in fact, seemingly they are commodities that are granted to only a few.

It's interesting how Scripture challenges our assumption of what the standard of success is. Again we can learn from the disciples who were distraught over the fact that two of them had come with their mother to ask Christ for the successful places in the kingdom. Christ instructed them that true clout in kingdom work came through servanthood, not through the attainment of positions of power and profile (see Matt. 20:20-28).

Nor is our success to be measured in terms of prosperity. The rich young ruler was asked whether he would be willing to give it all away for Christ (see Luke 18:18-23). In Luke 12 the disciples who were anxious and distracted by earthly prosperity are refocused to seek first the kingdom of God and to be committed to laying up treasures through their lives on the other side (see vv. 22-34).

Success is always formed in terms of character and not cash in Scripture. Paul instructed Timothy to not serve for money but to remember that godliness with contentment is the formula for gain (1 Tim. 6:6).

And when we think about success being measured in terms of great productivity, we must remember the stories of the widow's mite and the little boy with the fish and the loaves. These didn't have much to give. Nor were they very productive in and of themselves. Yet when they gave the little that they had in faithful service to Christ, it was Christ who was able then to multiply their small and humanly insignificant means into ministries that were significant for Him and that glorified Him and His name. Hence Francis Schaeffer's sermon entitled, "No Little People, No Little Places."

If then position, prosperity, and high-profile productivity are not biblical standards for success, then what is?

Success in Scripture is a matter of living out our lives according to God's expectations and standards in undaunted routine faithfulness. There are at least three biblical elements to this standard of success. First of all, the reflection of His character and likeness through us. We are redeemed to glorify God (1 Cor. 6:19-20; 10:31). That really is the primary essential *what* of success for any believer. Second, the *how* of accomplishing His glory is through our commitment to goodness, faithfulness, and servanthood. If glorifying God is routinely reflecting Him through my life, then goodness, faithfulness, and servanthood are routinely submitting to His agenda. Third, the *where* of our success is measured not in the zip code of our ministry. It is not in terms of buildings, acreage, or location. Nor is it measured in the kind of house we live in or the prestige of the neighborhood in which we find ourselves. While none of these things are wrong in and of themselves, within the context of good stewardship, they are not the measures of our success. The place where success is measured is in eternity. It's what we do on this side that makes a difference on the other side that is the measure of our success. Both in Luke 12 and 1 Corinthians 3, it becomes readily evident that the only true significance and success in this life is what we do in terms of significance and success in the world to come. So while success is measured by our routine reflection of His character to His glory and our routine submission to His agenda, it is also measured by the routine investments that we make in His eternity. I use the word *routine* because it is rarely the spectacular that makes us successful, but simply the regular, ongoing faithful cadence of our lives in terms of our commitment to Him in the routines of our existence.

We need to keep in mind that some of the treachery of false notions of success is not reserved for those who are seeking to be successful, the "wannabees," but for those who have become what the world would view as successful. The position, profile, productivity, or prosperity that God may have seen fit to have given needs to be cast in the context of biblical perspectives on success as well. We should not assume that there is something inherently wrong with these kinds of achievements. What we must remember, however, is that they have been given to us and not gotten. If we feel for some reason that it has been of us, then we will slip into self-destructive forms of glorifying self and feeling that we are sufficient in and of ourselves. We must always remember how we got where we are and give Him the credit. We would never do anything of significance if it weren't for the fact that He had sovereignly opened the opportunity, sovereignly put us in the place, sovereignly equipped us with gifts that make us capable, and sovereignly energized the process to His designed ends.

In a moment He could take it all away.

And the purpose of our success? It is to glorify His name and to enrich eternity. It is not to glorify us and enlarge our kingdoms. This kind of biblical sanity guards and guides us from the seduction of false notions about success. It is not our drive for success that is wrong. God built us to succeed. The important reality is that He built us to succeed in the context of His definition of success and for His glory and gain. Success is not about the stellar moments in our lives. It's rather about the ongoing development of faithful adherence to the task and our continuing growth into the character of Christ. It's not our moments in the sun, it's our momentum toward the Son that is the measure of our personal success.

I was recently asked to speak to a gathering of over 60,000 men in the Hoosier Dome in Indianapolis. Needless to say I have rarely been with that many people at one time, let alone spoken to that kind of crowd. Thankfully, the message was well received. To be candid, it felt successful to be asked, to have it go well, and to be affirmed. Until the Lord reminded me that that moment was not my success but His. God wanted to reach into the hearts of those men. He could have done it without me or in spite of me. It's humbling for me to remember that He spoke through a donkey in the Old Testament. My success is measured by my life before my God. By my growth into His likeness. By character and not applause.

The wrong view of success will stymie us with satisfaction when we think we have finally arrived. The biblical view motivates us with gratitude to remember that the highest satisfaction in life is to know Him, to serve Him, and to continue to grow toward arriving at His likeness which in turn will glorify His name and not our own.

I recall as a college student committing my life to Christ in terms of two fundamental desires. I told the Lord that what I really wanted in life was to be *His kind of man in His place.* It wasn't important to me that I be famous, but I would feel that I had served Him successfully if He could look down with pleasure at my life. My desire was that someday He would stop all that was going on in heaven, call the angels to His throne, part the clouds, and point downward to me and say, "Look at Joe . . . that's My kind of man." Second, I never wanted to be anyplace but His place. It didn't have to be large or significant. It just had to be His place for me. It is still my desire to live in the context of that commitment. If Christ would take me through a reduction in terms of my position and place of service, I would continue to cling to the reality that my success in life would be measured by whether or not I was still being His kind of man and fulfilling that dream in His assigned place. Wherever He sent me I could still work toward that goal and grow toward success in His eyes. In the same vein, Paul wrote, "I eagerly expect and hope that I will in no way be ashamed, but will have sufficient courage so that now as always Christ will be exalted in my body, whether by life or by death. For to me, to live is Christ, and to die is gain" (Phil. 1:20-21). He wrote those lines after his ministry was dramatically reduced by imprisonment in Rome. As he noted, the goal of his life was not his own gain but Christ, enhanced through his life.

Having said all of this, it is true that what we do and accomplish for Christ is important. Within all of us we want to feel that our lives are maximized for Him. We wonder if God will ever give us the capacity to do great things for Him in terms of numbers and breadth of impact. These are not illegitimate desires. If you love Christ and His cause and want to see it prosper, then who wouldn't want to be a part of the breadth and depth of that prosperity? Our problem is that we often demand it on our terms, in our way, in our time, for our own glory. Successful impact in terms of breadth and scope is up to God in His way and in His time. And sometimes the impact will be known beyond ourselves and in generations to come.

It was Dwight Lyman Moody who led Wilbur Chapman to the Lord. Wilbur Chapman became a great national evangelist in the generation succeeding Moody's. During Wilbur Chapman's ministry in Chicago, a baseball player with the White Stockings had a Sunday off, as all professional ballplayers did in that day, and was standing in front of a bar on State Street in Chicago when a Gospel wagon from the Pacific Garden Mission came by playing hymns and inviting people to the 2:30 service down the street. This ballplayer, recognizing the hymns from the home he grew up in, attended that 2:30 service and received Christ as his personal Savior. That afternoon encounter with Christ dramatically changed the life of Billy Sunday. He played ball for two more years and then left professional sports to minister in the YMCA in Chicago which was then a fine and effective organization for Christ. Wilbur Chapman came through town and talked Billy Sunday into joining his crusade team as an advance man to help organize the pastors and set up Chapman's meetings. Billy Sunday enthusiastically agreed. Upon signing up with Chapman, Billy Sunday received word that Chapman was going to leave evangelism and take the pastorate of one of the leading churches in America. This left Billy Sunday stranded, but refocused on national crusade evangelism. He soon began scheduling his own meetings which launched his ministry across America for the cause of Christ. In one of Billy Sunday's meetings, a young man by the name of Mordecai Hamm accepted Christ. Mordecai Hamm became a great evangelist in the Southeastern United States, ministering to massive crowds south of the Mason-Dixon Line. One night in one of those large crowds, a young man and his friend came forward to accept Christ. One was Billy Graham.

And now you know the rest of the story.

What a phenomenal line of the succession of faithful, stellar, maximized servants of Christ. But that's not really the rest of the story. The rest of the story is told where it begins: with a Sunday School teacher in Boston who on one Saturday committed himself to visiting every one of the boys in his Sunday School class, to make sure that they knew Christ as their Savior. One of the boys worked as a shoe clerk in his uncle's shoe store in downtown Boston. Edward Kimball walked through the store, back to the stockroom where Dwight Lyman Moody was stocking the shelves, and confronted him with the importance of knowing Christ as Savior. It was in that stockroom that D.L. Moody accepted Christ as his Savior. Kimball had no idea that that routine faithfulness on his part would reap such unparalleled results in terms of populating heaven.

And what of the pastor who encouraged Kimball to be a faithful participant in ministry? The pastor whose modeling and mentoring had put the passion for eternity in the heart of one of his Sunday School teachers? Perhaps the most encouraging and significant part of the story is that none of us know the name of that pastor who created a church environment where a lay member would initiate such a powerful sequence of events. It's that kind of faithfulness in the trenches that, when placed in the hands of Christ, becomes multiplied in His time for His glory.

It's no wonder, then, that when Paul instructs Timothy on the essentials of ministry, he starts with the basic issue; that is, Timothy's commitment to live a life that is worthy of God's affirmation and hence worthy of people's respect.

Chapter Four

Platforming: Effective Leaders Start Here

The Foundation

St. Simone Stylites was a fifth-century ascetic monk who wanted to make a point. In the aftermath of the embracing of Christianity into the Roman Empire by Constantine, commitment was on the decline and laxity had set into the church. As Kenneth Scott Latourette observes, "The level of the morality of the average Christian appeared to be sinking, and the ardent, their consciences quickened by the high standards of the New Testament, were not content."[1] This early environment in the church gave rise to a host of individuals who wanted to demonstrate that the essence of Christianity was not the popular easy kind of Christianity that had become so prevalent. These ascetics chose the monastic life, depriving themselves of the prosperity and pleasures of life in an attempt to demonstrate that the true road to God was through the passage of difficulty and self-denial.

It was Simone's approach to asceticism that created an environment in which he could command peoples' attention and clearly communicate his commitment to what he felt was a more authentic kind of faith. He erected a sixty-foot tower east of Antioch with a platform on top of it and lived there for thirty-six years. His fame spread, and as Latourette states, multitudes, including some high state officials, came to see him.[2]

While other ascetics chose to seclude themselves out of public notice, Simone had a message to communicate and designed a way to draw the attention of the masses. He was so effective that the Roman Catholic Church ultimately made him a saint.

Though in many ways vastly different, the struggle for today's shepherd is not unlike what Simone faced. Recognizing that the church was endangered and adrift, he needed to establish a way in which he could not only capture the attention of people, but also establish a medium through which he could effectively communicate his message. People in our generation, by and large, have secluded their minds and their hearts behind encasements of individualism, privacy, and a healthy dose of cynicism regarding public figures. The key question for the shepherd, then, is, "How can I position my life and ministry to break down the encasements that surround hearts and minds, capture their attention, and effectively lead them to the personal growth and communal development that we studied in the previous chapter?" If there is not a significant *touchpoint* through which the power of God can flow from our lives to theirs, then our effectiveness will be minimal.

Since we live in a culture that is often cynical toward leaders, our position is not adequate in itself to create an avenue into their hearts. Given society's disdain for absolutes and authority, we probably won't create a touchpoint through the proclamation of truth alone. It's harder today to crack open the modern heart and mind to enable ministry to flow in transforming power. Yet the key to developing the capacity for effectiveness is as old as a piece of advice that Paul gave to Timothy regarding his effectiveness in a similarly pagan environment. This advice is without a doubt the foundational issue for a shepherd who wishes to do the best things in the worst times.

In the metaphor that Simone Stylites created for us, we might ask ourselves, "What is the platform from which we must minister, so that we can effectively capture the attention of those to whom we minister and transmit truth into receptive hearts over the long haul?" In 1 Timothy 4, the Apostle Paul isolates the key platform for the effective shepherd. It is a platform that is timeless, transgenerational, transcultural, and attainable by all of us. Before we deal with this foundationally strategic platform, it would be well to evaluate some of the more convenient platforms that we tend to opt for as shepherds, that, though compelling, ultimately discount and sometimes debilitate our success in ministry.

SHAKY PLATFORMS

There are some who are prone to lead from the platform of PERSONAL CHARM. These are shepherds who for some reason have been gifted by God with a wonderful personality and have found that they can draw people to follow them simply because they are so compelling. Leading from this platform can be quite successful until the first crisis hits, and then charm carries little clout. We might remind one another as well that there are some people who have very little charm and have taken it upon themselves to not like anybody who does have charm, and to carefully disengage the charm factor by being as negative as they can be about compelling people who are charming. There is always a group in every church which is uncharmable.

Others may fall to the seduction of using POPULARITY as a platform, feeling that if they can please people and simply be well liked by the vast majority, then they will be able to effectively lead. No one stays on this platform very long, especially if they're realistic about ministry. I don't know how you please the charter members, the baby boomers, and the busters. Or, how do you please those who love Bach and those who love rock, or those who love Bev Shea, and those who can't worship well unless it is to the strum of guitar and the pulsating sounds of a trap set? How do you please the teens and the old timers? And what of those Calvinists and those Arminians? Well, needless to say, if the platform of popularity is our hope for effective leadership, we're in trouble. Ministry leadership is not a popularity contest, and those who lead to please may soon find themselves looking for another flock to shepherd.

There's an ancient torture called being "drawn and quartered." In this particular torture each of the victim's arms and legs are tied to a horse, and then the four horses are slowly walked in opposite directions, slowly pulling muscles and ligaments and bones from the victim's sockets and joints. Trying to manage a ministry from the platform of popularity is ultimately a self-inflicted version of being drawn and quartered.

Some seek to lead from the platform of the latest PROGRAMS and ministry fads coming down the kingdom pike. While programs and new wave techniques certainly have their place, a leadership style that is built on programming and reprogramming and reprogramming will soon have people out of breath and leave them with a distinct impression that they are there to serve the results of our last trip to another seminar. I once had a friend who was pastoring across town tell me that the only way to keep your people excited about church was to keep them in a building program. It struck me at that time that there was something flawed about that perspective on leadership.

Some like to lead from the platform of rallying people to CAUSES. Whether it be political causes, or causes within the church or denomination, it is possible to keep people rallied if you can keep them stirred up about causes which readily raise our temperature. Leading people to vent their frustrations about abortion, homosexual rights, the demise of America, crime, drugs, or condoms in school will cultivate a climate where people can stay excited about the latest evil and feel wonderfully exempt from the challenge of personally growing in Jesus Christ. It's interesting that shepherds who lead based on the latest cause can fill the church for a protest rally, but rarely get a smattering of people out to prayer meetings.

Or, we may be tempted to lead from the platform of SELF-PROMOTION, subtly turning the focus of the ministry on the qualities and capabilities of "me," the beloved pastor. This is perhaps the most compelling yet most costly platform because it plays directly into the myth that our capacity to lead is based on our personal accomplishments and our ability to control the admiration of those who follow. The leader who leads from this platform is seduced into patterns of criticizing others to keep themselves on the top of the pile, taking credit for things that other people should rightly get the credit for, competing with staff and lay leaders for the limelight, and initiating efforts to remove or sideline those who are threatening and reward those who affirm him and happily yield to his control. This platform of leadership engenders an environment where the critical, self-promoting spirit of a leader soon begins to be reflected in the lives and attitudes of those who follow, which in turn creates an environment of competition, division, and dissension of which sometimes the shepherd himself is the ultimate victim. It is servanthood in reverse.

The platform of ASSUMED AUTHORITY is equally as dangerous. A shepherd who walks into the flock and immediately lets his adherents know that he is in charge, that he spells pastor with a capital P, and that the sooner people understand that the better off the church will be, creates an immediate tension and polarization that may in fact create a power struggle which the pastor finally will not be able to win. Given the cultural ethic of independence and the autonomy of thought and lifestyle that is grilled into us at nearly every level, very few people will have the fiber to gladly bow their wills to the demands of an authoritarian leader. While this may be more acceptable in some churches, particularly those with largely blue-collar flocks whose jobs are basically managed by an authoritarian structure in which they have little or no say and where in order to keep their jobs they must simply comply, an authoritarian ministry will certainly not create a long-lasting platform of effectiveness in churches where white-collar professionals worship. These are people who all week long have a piece of the action in the marketplace and who are involved in vision-setting, decision-making, and charting the course at the office. They come to church with a sense that their mind and perspectives will be valued as they are in the workplace, and that, while they may not always get their way or be right, that they should at least be respected and listened to for their input. And even in settings where there may be greater tolerance to the assumption of authoritarian rule, the attitude will soon sour as struggles over authority will be set up within empowered constituencies within the church (i.e., the board, charter members, staff members, large donors, etc.).

While it's important to recognize that an effective shepherd does lead from a position of authority, it must be kept in mind that authority cannot be assumed or demanded. Over a length of time people become willing to yield to leadership once they have learned to trust and feel genuinely loved and cared for by the shepherd. Authority is grounded not in the shepherd's authority, but in the clear authority of the Word of God in issues of life that relate to holiness and growth in Jesus Christ. The problem with a platform of assumed authority is that the shepherd moves beyond the authority of the Word and seeks to exercise unchallenged authority and control in preferential issues and matters of church policy.

Real authority is given, not gotten. Every time we grab for it, problems inevitably follow.

There is yet another platform that is a prescription for failure, that is the platform of managing the church through cultivating systems of internal POLITICS. Every organization has some politics involved. It's vitally important to take other people's views into consideration, to be diplomatic in implementation, and to delay for a better moment or a better situation in which to make advance. These kinds of "politics" are not only normal, but necessary. The problem comes when a shepherd seeks to maintain his power and position by playing one group against another, one deacon against another, or one staff member against another, and in so doing politicize the process and environment of the church into camps of distrust and deceit. Shepherds who give here to get there, who negotiate for personal advantage or promise one group something to placate or to get something in return, will create a tangled web of complex relationships that will finally ensnare the ministry. At best, the church will learn how to get and gain through political means rather than through the patient process of biblical principles in relationships and a trust in God to both resolve and supply. In fact, the pastor himself may very well be the victim of a politicized environment when enough groups get together and figure out how they can politic the pastor to another parish.

Some of us have sought to serve from the platform of our TRAINING. The fact that we have degrees from prestigious places may get us in the front door, but after that, they're only decorations on the office wall. Or, in reverse, we seek to capitalize and glory in the sense of false humility about the fact that our training has been so miniscule. And no appeal to undertrained stellar servants of the past like D.L. Moody and Billy Sunday will help you if that undertraining is being lived out in undereffectiveness and underachievement.

It's hard to say which of these platforms is more debilitating to the long-run process of ministry, but if I were forced to take a position, I'd want this platform near the top: the platform of BUILDING OURSELVES UP BY TEARING OTHERS DOWN. While this is not unlike the platform of self-promotion, it deserves to be a platform all on its own, because its characteristics and damage potential are so unique. When we have little to offer, or feel insecure about what we have to offer or how people are feeling about us, the easiest and most destructive response is to tear other people down so that we look better. This hopefully leads people to the conclusion that if everyone else is really that bad and unreliable then maybe the only one left to follow is this pastor, who has told me how bad everyone else is. Shepherds who are openly critical of other Christian leaders reveal a chink in their armor that defies the very truth they try to teach. I know it's hard for us to think that others are better preachers than we are, better administrators, or more highly gifted and more capable. It's doubly tough when our people become enamored with and awestruck by stellar leaders, either in the bigger picture of the body of Christ, or perhaps by an adult Sunday School teacher, an elder, or otherwise effective layman in the church. How we act toward and what we say about these who have attracted the respect of those in our flock will dictate how well our people are able to trust our leadership in their lives.

In a strange twist of reality, when we celebrate the strength of others, even in light of the lack of strength in that area in our own lives, people admire us for being big enough to affirm someone besides ourselves—even at our own expense. On the other hand, when we seek to destroy the reputations of others, we may feel better about ourselves for a while, but others will quickly see our smallness and our capacity to effectively lead will be effectively diminished. And even if we could get away with it and people would admire us in spite of it, are there any of us who really want to set that pattern in motion in the flock in which we serve? Once we begin tearing others down, forgetting that Scripture tells us that true love covers a multitude of sins and that we are to rejoice with those that rejoice, we will set in motion permission in the flock for the sheep to do the same. An environment of criticism, cynicism, and negativism will inevitably rebound as, given the right set of circumstances, the sheep will feel perfectly free to tear us down for their own gain.

I think it needs to be said that while God has given some shepherds a measure of charm, these should not feel guilty or seek to be as obnoxious as possible to balance out the equation. Nor should we try to offend as many people as possible so that we are not popular, or ignore programs and programmatic changes that will benefit the church, or even fail to recognize which causes are critical to feature in our ministry. And while there may even be a time to defend ourselves and in the right context to exercise our biblical authority, the point is that none of these can be the platforms from which we guarantee effectiveness. In fact, when we understand the biblical platform from which we minister, all of these lesser platforms become enfolded into a larger process in a guarded and balanced way, enabling us rather than disabling us.

THE FOUNDATIONAL PLATFORM

What then is the platform from which a shepherd can effectively break down the encasements of resistance, capture hearts and minds, and effectively infuse the biblical functions of ministry to affect lives and develop a community of belief that resounds to God's glory?

It is the platform of RESPECT. Granted, this foundation for ministry is not a spectacular, engaging, or compelling thought at first. In our fast-paced, fast growth, big-bang ministry environment, the platform of respect seems to be a rather mundane foundation. Yet, Paul's admonition to Timothy makes this platform his precise point when he exhorts Timothy to "let no man look down upon your youthfulness . . . show yourself an example of those who believe" (1 Tim. 4:12). Paul is requiring Timothy to do what is necessary to engender a sense of respect among those that he is called to serve. Hendricksen observes, "Timothy must not permit anyone to despise him because of his youth. He must see to it that he is respected. . . ."[3] In fact, it's interesting that even the difficulty that youthfulness brings to achieving effective leadership can be overridden by living the kind of life that people readily respect. While "respect" is not trendy, it is the element that can keep a shepherd leading over the long haul. Even when people disagree, they can still respect their leader. Leaders who engender respect draw people's attention to their character and stimulate a hunger in those who follow to replicate that character in their lives. When followers respect their leader, even though he calls them from their comfort zones and challenges them to deeper levels of commitment that require personal sacrifice, the fact that they respect him will keep their hearts open to the challenge. People feel safe with leaders they respect. They feel certain about their future with a leader they respect. For any number of reasons there may be some things they don't like about us, but if they respect us we can minister to them.

I don't need to tell you that ministry is a people-intensive business. We have no other commodity to work with and no other measurement of the ultimate success of our ministry investment. People are the meaning and the measure of ministry. It is clear that Paul wants Timothy to immediately focus on healthy, positive, and productive relationships with the people he ministers to. Respect is a relational issue.

Periodically, during a discussion of ministry, someone will ask me what I think the most important ingredient of ministry is. And while that's a tough question given the fact that you need more than one thing on your list, I always get around to talking about relationships. Ministries are really going nowhere unless relationships are stable and harmonious. Some of us are saying, "But you don't know the people I work with . . . it's impossible to build relationships with them." As we have mentioned, God places in all of our ministries a few people who make it impossible to have a growing, satisfying, productive relationship. In every church I've pastored God has placed a few key people who don't like me, misunderstand me, ascribe less than good things to my motives, and who often take it upon themselves to share my weaknesses with others. We cannot disregard the reality of how difficult it is to build meaningful relationships with some people. Romans 12:18 has instruction for us when it speaks of dealing with our enemies and says, "As much as lieth in you, live peaceably with all men" (KJV). It really does take two to fight. In fact, how you and I face opposition will model powerfully the biblical process in terms of loving our enemies, blessing those who curse us, and praying for those who despitefully use us (see Matt. 5:43-48), instead of lowering ourselves into the fray to meet them on the level of involvement that they've established.

There will indeed be challenges in terms of relationships, and we as shepherds must do everything in *our power* to create an environment in which we can have positive and lasting relationships so that our ministry is not impeded by roadblocks that are attributable to our mishandling of people's lives and of our mismanagement of ministry situations. And while we will periodically stumble, an honest response where we ask for forgiveness and communicate that we desire to be a better, more effective shepherd, will usually regain the lost ground.

It's interesting to note that Scripture does not require that we have positive growing relationships with everyone, but it does require that we minister in relationships marked by respect that will enable even those who do not like or appreciate us to follow our shepherding work.

Unfortunately, people rarely give respect as a gift to a new leader who comes into a ministry context. Older people who grew up in a generation where pastors were respected for their position may grant the gift of respect at the onset of ministry, and children will look at their shepherds with a sense of awe. I'll never forget walking into church one Sunday morning and hearing a little boy walking behind me say to his mother, "Mom, is that Jesus?" Obviously, he hadn't talked to my wife! But the fact that I was his pastor automatically elevated me to levels far beyond what I deserved. He had lots of respect to offer, but a relatively poor theology. There will be a few who graciously will say, "We believe God's called you here and are ready and willing to follow you," but most of the flock will have the arms of their hearts folded and will be waiting to see what kind of shepherds we will be.

As I mentioned, coming to the pastorate of Highland Park Baptist Church in Southfield, Michigan was a dramatic challenge for me. I was young and not only followed a godly, gifted expositor, George Slavin, but also a whole host of well-known names in preaching who had filled the pulpit during the interim. In one of the first staff meetings I sat with these new yet older colleagues whom I had not chosen and who had little voice in choosing me. I said that I thought that one thing which would be important in our ministry through the days and years ahead would be that we would share mutual respect for each other. A staff member sitting across the room who had been there the longest and who had led the church in the senior pastor's absence, stopped trimming his fingernails long enough to look up and say to me, "Respect is something that has to be earned." As brutal as that seemed, I knew that he was right. Some may give it as a gift at the outset for you to keep as a stewardship, but those gifts are few and far between. It's not unlike the ad for Smith Barney Securities, where a studied old gentleman, who cast an image worthy of respect, states, "We make money the old-fashioned way . . . we earn it!" In ministry, respect comes the old-fashioned way . . . we earn it.

After calling Timothy to the platform of respect, Paul goes on in the passage to delineate the process through which it is acquired.

The word that Paul uses for "look down on" is highly instructive. It comes from a Greek construction of two words put together, which literally means "to think against," or to have someone's mind set against you. J.I. Packer, in his article in *The Dictionary of New Testa-*

ment Theology, says that the word means a "lack of due respect," and goes on to indicate that those who do not respect you "act in such a way as to show contempt or disregard . . . on account of something."[4] Nothing can be more detrimental than to have those to whom we are hoping to minister disregard us or show contempt toward us. The "something" in this passage that might cause this alienation is Timothy's youthfulness. There really are two categories of things for which people might show disregard for us, one being things that we can't control, like our age, and then those things that are within the scope of our control. It would be well for us to think about things in our lives that erode people's capacities to respect us—those things over which we have a measure of control.

There probably is a short list of things that are in our control that create significant erosions of the platform of respect. Near the top of everybody's list needs to be the *lack of integrity.* People expect us to be honest in our words, relationships, and promises. And while few of us would be directly dishonest, honesty goes far deeper than being truthful in our words. An honest person has a life that lives up to the truths that he proclaims. Honest people deal squarely and in an aboveboard way with money. They do not use the truth in ways that manipulate and serve their own purposes, nor do they withhold information to advance their own agendas. People perceive us to be dishonest when we refuse to admit that we're wrong, promote ourselves without warrant, and take credit that is due to someone else. If a shepherd has obvious gaps in his integrity, then respect will soon be undermined. It's difficult to respect someone you cannot trust.

Slothfulness in ministry is also a lethal blow to people's capacity to respect us. Unfortunately, there are fewer positions in which you can so easily work beyond the limits of emotional and physical capacity, or at the same time, if you choose, do so little work. Most people we serve put in a good week's work for their boss, do chores around their home on Saturday, and then give most of their Sunday in service to Christ. Needless to say, they expect that their shepherd is hard at work in the ministry. I think we'd all be surprised at how symbolic it is when people drive by the church on a regular basis and don't see our car parked near the study. Or when they call and we are rarely there. Even if we are hoping that they will give us the benefit of the doubt that we are out and about the King's business, it may be their perception that preachers don't work all that hard. In some cases, the perception of "what does he do the rest of the week?" can be true. This is not to say that shepherds don't need space to come up for air and do a few things that they enjoy. We desperately do! But it is to say that it is important for our congregation to believe and know that we are hard at work for them, to help build their lives and to create the best church environment possible. There are a few ways that we can demonstrate, even if in a symbolic way, that we are on top of our game plan when it comes to our task. Having agendas done in advance and coming to meetings well prepared. Returning phone calls. Responding to emergencies. Keeping our promises. Taking the initiative when someone needs a word of encouragement by picking up the phone and letting them know we've been praying for them. Preaching sermons that demonstrate that we've done something besides sit around and shoot the breeze with the staff all week. These are important ways to show that the work is getting done. There are other impressions we can leave to show that we know what it means to work hard and to work well, such as dressing appropriately instead of slothfully, keeping our car relatively clean and our office as neat as possible. While I've always felt that a clean desk is a sign of a sick mind, most people equate some semblance of order with a well-organized work life. Perhaps the worst way for us to demonstrate a less than slothful spirit is to tell people how hard we work. Very few want to hear about it from us. They just want to see it in us. While many of us in the ministry consistently work half-days . . . twelve hours . . . it needs to be seen to be appreciated.

Among the controllable aspects in our lives is *manipulation* – managing the ministry in a self-serving, manipulative mode. When our flock feels that we have used them, their sense of respect for us is eroded. It doesn't go down well when we charm them, spend time with them, or court them for a task in the church, and once they say yes we never pay attention to them again.

Disloyalty to our flock also disengenders respect. We can be disloyal to them by not loving the things that they love. If most of them have grown up in the community and love the community, though it may not be a place that we particularly love, it's important to affirm their love for their locality. We need to be loyal to their past and to their history. A good shepherd is quick to celebrate the past and stand on its shoulders. Disloyalty in terms of sharing things from the pulpit that are other people's secrets, not keeping confidence in private conversation, talking about people behind their backs, flirting with other men's wives, or tearing down your own wife in public all serve to shake their confidence in us. If we appear to be a disloyal person, people will know that someday we might be disloyal to them. It's hard to respect someone who may turn on you. It's hard to respect someone who has little respect for others.

People will set their minds against us when we use our *power* and *position* to gain personal advantage. Using the sermon series and the power of the pulpit to berate individuals in the congregation for their offenses toward the pastor never . . . let me say that again . . . *never* comes to a productive end. No one can stand during the sermon and defend themselves or try to set the record straight. It is the process of being publicly shamed and embarrassed and at the mercy of the guy behind the microphone. Not only will the one who has been clobbered cease to respect you, but many within the congregation will identify not with the preacher but with the persecuted. You can count on it. The flock expects that our power and position will be used to empower their lives for glory and gain and to reposition them in places of healing and growth. When pastoral power is used against them, they will immediately feel abused, and respect will be in jeopardy.

Thankfully, these issues in our control can be remediated by repentance and a good dose of Spirit-led reformation in our lives. As you go down the checklist of the kinds of things that engender contempt, disregard, and distrust for the shepherd, it would be good to specifically isolate individuals, situations, and habit patterns that you have been involved with that have discounted the respect factor in your leadership. Sincere words and acts of repentance toward the Lord and toward those who have been involved will be in order, and an attempt to remediate them through a commitment to honesty, hard work, true love for the flock, loyalty, and fairness will begin the process of rebuilding the platform of respect upon which we all must stand.

Yet there are some things, as in Timothy's case, that are out of our control. Height, shape, ethnicity, age, background, gifts, and health are all things sovereignly assigned to us by the One who has called us to the task of shepherding. In these areas, respect is not gained through repentance, reformation, and remediation, but Paul says that respect can be gained in spite of these through the exercise of three essential ingredients. Not one of the uncontrollables in our lives needs to hold us back. It may go without saying that we need to be in a place where the needs of the ministry match our gifts. It is helpful as well to minister in a context that our own background enables us to understand and into which we can effectively integrate both ourselves and the truth that we proclaim. But given the fact that everything else is equal, the unchangeables in our lives are not the factors upon which respect rises and falls.

What fascinates me is that the first of the three ingredients in effective leadership that Paul isolates is not a matter of technique, style, or task performance. I might have expected that Paul would go into a lengthy dissertation on ministry from a management point of view with case studies on how ministry has been effectively done in other locations, citing the ministry leaders of his day as prime examples. Instead, Paul begins with character, the matter of exemplary *personhood.* He writes, "Let no one look down on your youthfulness, but rather in speech, conduct, love, faith and purity, show yourself an example of those who believe" (1 Tim. 4:12). Paul notes in this word to Timothy that the unchangeable factor of his youth *can be overcome* by exhibiting exemplary character. Guthrie, in his comments on this passage in the *Tyndale New Testament Commentary,* says, "In this way it would become evident that in Christianity, authority is contingent on character and not age."[5]

In my third pastorate, I learned something that I wished they would have told me in seminary. I had been pastoring the church for some time and felt that for the most part, things were going as well as could be expected. Most of the parishioners seemed responsive and supportive, but to my surprise I found myself pondering the fact that on this particular night, in this particular board meeting, things seemed different. The difference that I sensed was that the board members were interacting with me on a deeper level. They were listening carefully to what I had to say, interacting with my thoughts and ideas as though they carried weight and significance, and while I had always sensed that they had listened, this night *was* different. As I was driving home, I sensed that I had moved into a new phase of ministry. That now I had been received and perceived not only as a colleague by these to whom God had called me to minister but as a leader they were willing to take seriously. What I realized that night was that when you first lead a body of people, their verbal agenda will probably be something like, "We're so glad you're here. What are your ideas for this ministry and what can we do that will be significant for the kingdom?" While that is their verbal agenda, their heart agenda is far different and really more strategic. Their heart agenda simply is "Who are you? What will you do with us? Can we trust you?" It's not until those questions are adequately answered that people will look to us as their leader and be willing to follow. The answer to these questions is grounded in the kind of person we prove ourselves to be.

Personhood is ultimately the make or break issue in effective leadership.

So Paul gives Timothy a short list of issues to be concerned about in regard to his personhood. First on the list is his speech—what he says about people, what he says to people, what he is not willing to say, and what he is willing to courageously proclaim.

Paul goes on to say that *conduct* is also a critical element in personhood. Conduct toward our children and our wives. Conduct toward individuals of the opposite sex. Conduct toward those who oppose us and those who support us. Conduct in areas of personal deportment. Conduct is the art of how I do the business of life and how I relate to others around me. Conduct is what those who follow us constantly scrutinize.

Third on the list is the issue of *love.* Are people able to see that I genuinely care about them and others, or am I in the business of basically caring about me? Of protecting, enhancing, enlarging, defending, and advancing me? Or do I have a genuine heart concern for the needs of others who have been trusted to my care? It might be well here to remind ourselves of the old adage that says, "People will not care how much we know until they know how much we care." Effective leaders love others as Christ loves us (John 13:34), which raises to the surface issues like loving our enemies, loving unconditionally, loving with our time and our talents, and loving regardless of the temperaments or idiosyncrasies of those that we are called to love. Loving not just our kind, but all kinds at all times.

Faith is added next in this list of personhood issues. Faith is that capacity to visibly and undauntedly trust in God to keep His word and accomplish His will through our lives, regardless of the uncertainty, pain, or pleasure that we might experience in the process. It is the capacity to actualize in our responses to life the fact that He will deal with our enemies; that He will supply our needs; that He always prospers His dreams; that His Word will not return void; that the courageous proclamation of the truth will set men free; to have faith fundamentally in the Word, the will, and the character of God . . . to visibly, consciously, and without compromise demonstrate that kind of unshakable faith to a watching flock who seeks to follow.

Last on the list, but certainly not least, is the issue of *purity.* While we could spend hours discussing the issue of moral purity, it must quickly be said that purity is an issue that goes beyond sexual propriety. This relates to purity of motives, purity of heart, purity of conscience, purity in regard to money, and purity in managing our time and our relationships. Purity simply means that in all matters of life we are not perfect, but we keep ourselves clean.

Think about it. If we were around a person who exemplified these five qualities in his or her life, not perfectly but on a consistent growing basis, we would be compelled to respect that person. In fact, he or she would be the kind of person whom we would admire and be willing to listen to and to whom we'd readily go for advice. This is the kind of person people are ready to follow. *Personhood* is the beginning point for the grooming of a life worthy of respect.

As I think of those I know who have failed as leaders in ministry, I realize that so often it hasn't been a failure in management principles or leadership capacity, but rather a fatal flaw in their personhood that has given the adversary an opportunity to accomplish subterfuge and to either discount or debilitate their capacity to lead.

Paul sums up this first aspect of the three nonnegotiable elements of the infrastructure of respect by calling Timothy to be an "example believer"—which has a lot to say about the primary focus of a leader's life. As *believers* in Jesus Christ, we are followers of Him. It's only in that believing relationship, where we humbly submit to His leadership, that we can develop the kind of character from which we then can lead. Interesting thought, isn't it, that leaders are first and foremost followers. Followers of Christ. When we cease to be good followers, we erode respect and debilitate our capacity to be leaders of His flock.

With the personhood project well underway, Paul turns Timothy to the second issue undergirding respect. It is a dedication to the priority of *proclamation.* Paul tells Timothy, "Until I come, give attention to the public reading of the Scripture, to exhortation and to teaching" (1 Tim. 4:13). The fundamental need of every believer is to understand, know, and live in the context of the Word of God. People come to our ministries expecting that their innate spiritual hunger will be in some measure satisfied. When that spiritual hunger is satisfied the shepherd's stock is greatly enhanced in terms of respect and admiration. Again, we need to define what it means to be one who effectively proclaims the Word of God. While most of us in our early years of feeding the dream of being the world's next Billy Graham or Chuck Swindoll, very few, if any, of us will be sovereignly placed there by God. The goal then is not to be the greatest preacher, or even the greatest preacher in our people's lives. It is rather to be an effective proclaimer—one who effectively communicates the truth of God to the spiritual needs and hunger of His people.

It's interesting to be around people and hear them talk about their pastors. I frequently hear people say something like, "Well, he doesn't have much of a bedside manner, and we wish he could be more friendly, but he feeds us the Word of God." When fundamental spiritual needs are being dealt with and the flock's expectation to be well fed is being met, respect is a natural by-product.

Effective proclamation relates directly to several issues, one being accuracy in dealing with Scripture. Spending our words on our own ideas, philosophies, and perspectives makes us just another voice among many in our people's lives. Clearly, concisely communicating what God has said in and from a particular passage puts our communication in a different realm, gives it the authority of God's truth, and creates a compelling point of accountability for attitude and behavior.

Effective proclamation also relates directly to the needs of the flock. While the shepherd may find great pleasure in scholarly pursuits and minute nuances of language and context, most of the sheep have been struggling all week against the wolves in the wilderness of their lives and come perplexed about how to be victorious in places like the marketplace, family, friendships, and other contexts that doggedly pursue and confuse them. It's interesting to note that the public ministry of Christ was practically focused. It's not that we ignore accurate hermeneutics or the nuances of exegesis, but it is that shepherds go one step further in their meal preparation and bring well-researched, well-understood food to the sheep where they are in terms of their real needs. I had a deacon at my first church who was a successful businessman from the hills of Kentucky. He was full of great backwoods sayings, of which one was, "Pastor, don't hang the hay too high for the goats." Effective proclamation must be both anchored in ancient truths and at the same time clearly contemporary.

Effective proclamation must be based in good doctrine. Yet it must also recognize that every doctrine has direct implications on our lives. It is doctrine that guards and guarantees our thinking; it is the application of doctrine that transforms the value systems of our lives. Great application without doctrine is foundationless. Great doctrine without application is cognitive and tiresome. Effective preaching is not manipulative, controlling, self-serving, or bullying. It is quite simply the clear and concise communication of the changeless truth of God in a contemporary way to the needs of our people. We might say as well that the effects from effective proclamation are rarely seen in one sermon, but over the long haul. When a shepherd is faithfully feeding, in time the sheep will grow.

If our people sense that we have concocted Saturday night and early Sunday morning specials for their dining pleasure, they will remain hungry and disappointed. And that disappointment has a way of settling into a dissatisfaction that breeds less than a respectful perception of the leader.

Paul then establishes the third nonnegotiable element of the infrastructure of respect by exhorting Timothy to "not neglect the spiritual gift within you, which was bestowed upon you through prophetic utterance with the laying on of hands by the presbyters" (v. 14). While personhood and proclamation are essential, the matter of *proficiency* must be added to the list of the three fundamentals that engender respect. All of us who are called to lead have been given particular gifts through which God expects us to exercise our influence on others. Some of us are gifted to be teachers, others of us are mercy people or servants; others approach the ministry from an exhorter's perspective. Some of us are gifted in prophetically pointing out evil and calling people to the good, while other leaders have been gifted to lead from administrative strengths. One thing is certain. None of us has all the gifts and each of us has a lead gift through which we can carry on the work of our ministry.

Unfortunately, some of us spend most of our lives coveting the gifts of others instead of recognizing the sovereign decision of God to make us the way we are and the bestowment upon us of His wisely chosen gift for us. Exhorters may covet the studied, measured ministry of those who are gifted to be scholars and exercise their gift as a teacher. Those with the gift of mercy, who fundamentally work in hurting relationships, may very well wish they had stronger administrative skills and could master the details more effectively. Those with the gift of prophecy may admire those who are naturally built to exercise a servant's heart. In reality, Scripture requires that we practice all the ministries of the various gifts (i.e., serving, giving, mercy, etc.), but we have a lead strength through which these qualities are to be exercised. Our challenge is to maximize the gift and to avoid the distractions of people's expectations who thought we would be gifted otherwise; to avoid the distractions of demands that people may make on us that we are not gifted to fulfill, and thus try to do all that we do through our own strength.

Proficiency demands as well that we not spend all of our lives working on our weaknesses. A friend of mine wisely said that he had spent many years trying to shore up the weak sides of his gift and had neglected to maximize the gift itself. While we should be attentive to the potential casualties that could be mounted by a weakness out of control, we must concentrate on maximizing the strength of the equipment that God has so wonderfully bestowed upon us.

When our sheep see that we are proficient in what we do, it will engender a sense of admiration. Not that we are the best they have ever seen, but that we do what we do well because we're doing it through the equipment that we have been given. Proficiency engenders respect.

Admittedly, this is a pretty heavy assignment for leadership. In fact, the weight of building respect through personhood, proclamation, and proficiency may seem like an imposing task. Some of us may sense that Paul is calling us to perfection. If it takes perfection in the areas of personhood, proclamation, and proficiency, then none of us will ever be an effective shepherd. Before we walk away in despair, we need to note that Paul concludes by saying to Timothy, "Take pains with these things; be absorbed in them, so that your progress may be evident to all" (v. 15).

There is a postlude to this whole matter of leading from the platform of respect. Ministry is not a matter of perfection but rather of *progress.* Effective leaders are out in front. That's the very nature of leadership. But if our lives grow stagnant and static, distracted by the lesser things of this material world that stymie growth, then in time our sheep will pass us by.

Progress is a compelling trait in a leader's life. I try to be around people who are out in front of me. People who stimulate my heart to say, "I need to be like that." People who have strength in a quality or an attribute that lacks maturity in my life. These people are magnetic and stimulate me to growth. So a shepherd, if he is to be an effective leader, need not be perfect but must be making progress. People need to be saying, "You know, he's a better person . . . better proclaimer . . . more proficient today than he was two years ago." While we may be tempted to take that personally as a negative reflection on our past, we really ought to see it as an affirmation of the fact that people are noticing that we're making progress. Leaders who desire to see their people grow need to realize that it probably will not take place until we as leaders are growing ourselves.

Take heart. Effective leadership does not demand perfection, just progress.

Effective leadership demands that we examine the platforms from which we have chosen to do the best of things. If we find that we have left the platform of respect for more comfortable and convenient platforms, then our leadership will be discounted—for some of us fatally so. Others of us may have a series of platforms upon which we rely, conveniently skipping from one to the other as the context of the moment dictates. It may provide a little more longevity, but it doesn't position us for respected leadership.

There is only one platform, and it alone is God's platform for the kind of leadership that makes a difference. It is the platform of respect. Respect that is earned the biblical way through making obvious progress in our personhood, proclamation, and proficiency. As Paul concluded to Timothy, "Persevere in these things, for as you do this you will insure salvation both for yourself and for those who hear you" (v. 16).

In his book, *Power of the Presidency,* James Fisher refers to St. Simone Stylites, who after twenty years of being on the platform said,

"The most difficult part was getting on top of the platform."[6] If we were honest about this task called ministry, we probably would say the same thing. Getting to the platform, climbing the ladder of training and experience, and having the courage to step out and grab the staff and accept the job of shepherding are really not the tough part. Getting onto the platform of respect and staying there is the challenge of effective ministry. Particularly in the midst of a society that is so alienated from all we claim to be and all that we proclaim.

The remainder of this book is dedicated to helping us get on the platform and to making its foundations sure by strengthening the underpinnings of personhood, proclamation, and proficiency. It is about Paul's exhortation to "Take pains with these things; be absorbed in them, so that your progress may be evident to all" (v. 15).

Chapter Five

A Career in Modeling: Turning the Fishbowl to Christ's Advantage

The Follower

One of my all-time favorite *Leadership* magazine cartoons shows a carload of people driving down a street pointing to a giant house-sized fishbowl located between two homes, saying, "Our pastor lives there."

Like it or not, shepherding is a highly visible occupation. The fact that we are pastors automatically attracts the attention of both the adherents of the church and the citizens at large in our community. To the community, for the most part, we are an object of curiosity. To our parishioners we are the object of their attentive analysis. From the time we first come to the church, they wonder about us. Who are we, really? What are we like? What do we like? And what don't we like? They watch what we wear, what we drive, where we live, what excites us, and what disgusts us. They watch how we treat people. How we treat our wives and children, staff members, secretaries, musicians, young people, elderly, new people, and those who have been hanging around for a long time. They watch what we put on our plate at potluck suppers, hoping that we take what they have made, feeling slighted if we pass it by. The risk is that once they find out what we really like, we are served that dish constantly in their homes! The wise pastor never fibs about what he likes and doesn't like, lest he be banished to the fate of having to eat what he does not like when he is entertained in his people's homes.

It would be safe to say that there isn't a moment of our public lives that is not weighed and measured in the perceptions of the people we serve. And in their minds, what they see is what they get. For the most part, people form their perceptions about us based on their observations, and unfortunately those perceptions, whether right or wrong, are cast into the context of reality. What makes all of this so dangerous is that people feel free to share their observed perceptions with others. Pastors are a favorite topic of conversation. Not because we're pastors but because we're public figures. Public figures are fair game at dinner tables, in car pools, and on picnics. And all of the data—observed, perceived, and shared—weighs in to cast conclusions about who we are and what we are like.

What is so critical is that the outcomes of this inspection process create a sense either of *regret* or *respect* in our people's minds. Parishioners who form conclusions of regret are difficult to effectively shepherd. On the other hand, when the observation leads to respect, hearts are wide open to our shepherding impact on their lives.

VISIBILITY AND VIABILITY

While it's easy to resent the visibility factor of shepherding, it is important for us to remember that it is our *visibility* that gives us *viability* in the work. Were God to grant us our wish to be invisible, we might be happier, but there would be no ministry. But when our visibility casts positive and compelling images, it is to our advantage since it platforms our capacity for effectiveness. In fact, that is exactly what Paul says to Timothy when he requires that he be an exemplary leader. One has to be seen to be an example, and being a positive example is what respect is built upon.

One important benefit to exemplary visibility is that it becomes the shepherd's best defense against his detractors. Shepherds who isolate themselves from the flock are particularly prone to destructive rumors and false conclusions about their lives. If a negative word begins to move through the grapevine, and no one has ever been close enough to experience the reality of our lives, then no one will be able to say, "That's not true; I've seen him in action and know him well, and I can tell you that that would not be true about our pastor."

In seminary our professors constantly placed in us the fear of moral failure. I recall one professor saying that our behavior with women in the church should be so above question in how we look at them, talk to them, and relate to them, that if someone would ever accuse us of immoral behavior, others in the church would come to our defense on the basis of their observations regarding our relationship to women. Our best protection is our exemplary visibility.

Our presence among the flock is a priority commitment.

One of the key ingredients for effective leadership is to trim our list of responsibilities down to those few things that only we can do to make a real difference in our ministry. Once the list is established, the strategic leader pours his life into those few things and delegates everything else to others. I have come to realize that one of the things that only the pastor can do to bring effective impact on his ministry is to lend his visible *presence* to the flock. I'm still amazed at how important, how deeply appreciated it is, when we as leaders show up. Before we get bigheaded about the issue, we need to realize that it really has nothing to do with us. If it were simply us without the position we hold, people probably wouldn't care much whether we were there or not. However, due to the fact that we hold an esteemed position, our presence lends value and worth to the group. More importantly, our presence enables people to understand the real us. Being with our people enough for them to get to know us and understand us is better than a dozen sermons that defend the position of the pastor and demand respect for the office.

It's not just a matter of showing up at functions like Sunday School socials, dinner parties, and other official expectations. Sometimes we can cast positive shadows of our presence by walking through a Sunday School class and standing in the back for a few minutes, nodding approvingly to the teacher. Or showing up to greet and affirm volunteer workers or the missionary prayer group. It may be going to a high school basketball game where a bunch of the kids in your church are playing. Or intentionally going out to lunch with business people and showing an interest in their lives, their struggles, and their success. At times our presence need not be visible. It may be through phone calls promptly returned or strategically initiated. Through notes and responses to correspondence.

EXAMPLING

Of course, all of this presupposes that our presence brings something that people will respect. Which is exactly the point that Paul is making to Timothy (1 Tim. 4:12). Effective ministry rises and falls on whether or not our lives are exemplary. No doubt that's what some of us don't like about the ministry. Having to be an example can be perceived as a burden, a confining part of the job description, rather than an expression of the outworking of Christ through us. It's easy to see the ministry of *exampleship* as "faking it," as we try to appear sanctimonious, sacred, serious, stoic, overly dignified, and all the other expectations that seem to belong to the clergy.

Growing up as a "Pastor's Kid," I was often summoned to a quiet corner and told by a concerned adult, "Young man,"—and every time someone talked to me like that I knew I was in trouble—"you're the pastor's son. You need to be an example to your friends." They always said this in hopes that it would lead to some measure of behavioral modification of which I was in dire need. My problem was that I was a kid, with all the "let's have a good time" stuff that makes a kid's life exciting. To be an exemplary pastor's child in terms of what that meant to these demanding adults simply didn't suit me. I would have to be someone I wasn't—someone, quite frankly, I didn't even want to be. No doubt some of us look at an exemplary ministry life in those terms. And if we do, trying to be an example will become a tremendous burden. And the more we resent it, the worse our example will ultimately become.

Thankfully, that is not what this text requires. When we rightly understand what it means to be the kind of example that Paul is talking to Timothy about, we realize that it is not the *duty* of our life which is in focus, but rather the *direction* of our life. Our exampling is a natural expression of our continuing growth in Jesus Christ as we on our pilgrimage become more and more like Him in our attitudes, actions, and reactions regarding both life and ministry. It is the outgrowth of a relational dynamic that is stimulated by our belief in and commitment to Christ. It is not being perfect. It is simply being out in front of the pack in terms of growth patterns so that others will sense that they really do have someone to follow in their pilgrimage to become increasingly like Jesus Christ. Nor does it mean that we never slip or publicly fail. It does mean, however, that when we do, we have an exemplary response by admitting that we're wrong, asking people's forgiveness, and seeking to be accountable for the development of character in the arena where we failed.

Early in my pastoral experience, my Sunday School superintendent reminded me to order the Sunday School materials for the next quarter. "They need to be here in time for the teachers to prepare their new material." I assured him I would be delighted to do it, and immediately I forgot. I didn't procrastinate; I didn't deprioritize it in my mind; I simply straight-out forgot. It never crossed my mind again.

The following Sunday morning I walked through the foyer with briefcase in hand containing my prepared message for the day. As I walked by the Sunday School superintendent, he asked, "Pastor, did you order the material?"

I am embarrassed to tell you—in fact I trust you won't lose all confidence in the future of the Moody Bible Institute—but without giving the question a second thought I blurted out "Yes."

And as soon as that word came out of my mouth, my heart was struck with shame and guilt. Wanting to protect my sense of significance, I walked resolutely to my office, shut my door, and opened my briefcase to review my sermon. It was randomness in its rawest form. There I was preparing to communicate the Scriptures from a God who can be nothing but truth. This morning I would stand on His behalf and be a truth-teller to the congregation. Yet I had lied to protect my own sense of significance.

The randomness did not stop there. Though the Spirit was urging me to go speak to the superintendent and his wife, confess my fault, and ask them to forgive me, my flesh was frantically looking for a way out. *I can order it tomorrow and have it sent to the church by overnight mail. He'll never know.* But the nagging prompting of the Holy Spirit was urging me out of the office door to seek to repair the damage caused by my less than exemplary behavior. I asked myself, *How can I be a truth-teller when my life outside the pulpit contradicts what I purport to be? How can I teach the sacred text and ignore its word to me?*

I began to open the door to my office to go find this couple, and every internal energy tried to stay my hand. What I had defended so recklessly earlier—my significance—would now be left open and vulnerable to their perception of me as their pastor. But I had just lied to them; I had to meet with them.

At my invitation, they walked with me back into my office. I said to them, "I am committed to being the right kind of pastor to you, and you need to know that I just failed you. I not only have not ordered the material, but even worse, I have not told you the truth about it. I have wronged you, and I want you to forgive me."

Thankfully, the superintendent reached out his hand and said, "Pastor, we all make mistakes. Of course I forgive you." His wife with tears puddling in her eyes assured me that she forgave me as well. It was a random moment in my life that I will never forget. The amazing quickness with which it happened and the heavy weight of regret it placed upon my soul taught me a strategic lesson. Exampling required a commitment to recovery. I was not a perfect example but I was making progress.

Nor does exampling mean that this exemplary life cannot be interpreted through the reality of who we are. We're all built differently in terms of temperament, gifts, perspectives, humor, and the lack thereof. Being exemplary doesn't mean we become cloned to a predetermined personality through which the character of Christ uniformly flows. At times exampleship will be funneled through serious shepherds, through laughing shepherds, through scholarly shepherds, through highly relational shepherds. Exampleship will be reflected through visionary shepherds and maintenance shepherds; through tailored shepherds, and shepherds whose suits come from K Mart. An exemplary life will be exhibited in a variety of colorful reflections in the body of Christ, but it will always be grounded in the unchanging, nonnegotiable principles of righteousness that reflect the character of Christ.

When it comes to defining this modeling ministry of exampleship that engenders *respect,* Paul slates a list of five qualities for us to develop that we referred to earlier as being the arenas in which exemplary actions should be displayed. I've always been thankful that God is a God of short lists. If I think about what a holy God might have prescribed for me in terms of exemplary behavior, there could probably be volumes written to cover the topic. But God in His typical manner gave us a few strategic, fundamental areas in which to concentrate. The first two, *speech* and *conduct,* are publicly perceived. The remaining three are inward qualities that work themselves out in powerful actions on the surface of our lives. They are *love, faith,* and *purity.* In the chapters to come we will deal with each of these qualities in terms of their definition, scope, and application to pastoral life in our increasingly pagan culture. But for now imagine your shepherding reflecting a positive posture in these five areas. Not only would there be respect generated for you, but you would also generate a magnetism that would draw others to want to grow in these areas as well. That's the power that visible character lends to ministry.

Before we move into the specifics of these five areas, we need to be certain that we understand the precise sense of what Paul meant to be an *example* and what he meant when he qualified our modeling as being an example *believer.*

MODELING BELIEF

The word that Paul uses in this text for "example" is a rather graphic word in New Testament Greek that means "to model or reflect the form or likeness of a particular entity." According to H. Müller in the *New International Dictionary of New Testament Theology,* an example is "what an object leaves behind when pressed against another, such as a trace, a scar, the impress of a seal. . . ."[1] In effect, what this means is that the authentic example is one whose life reflects the likeness, the particular entities of belief. An *example believer,* as Paul has urged Timothy to be, is one whose belief has made an obvious impression on one's life, and has left a clearly discernible mark. We as shepherds are authentic examples when we have been so struck by our beliefs that our lives bear the resemblance of what we say we believe. H. Müller reflects on 1 Timothy 4:12 by noting, "These passages are not simply admonitions to a morally exemplary life; they call for obedience to the message

(2 Thes. 3:6). It stamps those who proclaim it and gives them authority. The shaping power of a life lived under the Word has in turn an effect on the community (1 Thes. 1:6), causing it to become a formative example." Müller points out that not only are we to be visibly impacted by our belief system, but its impression on and through our lives makes its marks on other people's lives as well within the broader context of the Christian community. It has been well said that the pastor will be his people's example or his people's excuse.

True belief does affect behavior. What I really believe about life will ultimately be reflected in how I conduct my life. In fact, the word that is used in this text for *believer* is a word that belongs to the word group that covers the broad sense of *faith* in Scripture. It is the concept that prompted James to remind us that true faith is a faith that behaves accordingly, and that if we say we have faith but there is no quantifiable difference in our lives, then we probably have no faith at all. The *New International Dictionary of New Testament Theology* states of this word *belief,* "the word group denoted conduct that honored an agreement or a bond."[2] We have a bond with Jesus Christ that subsequently impacts behavior.

All of this to say that being an example believer is not a burden or an inhibiting part of our job but rather an outgrowth of our faith in Christ, and our obedient heart submission to Him as Lord. This submission to what we claim to believe results in a radical altering of the direction of our hearts and minds in ministry life. Those of us who have not anchored our thoughts, motives, responses, and behavior in our relationship to Jesus Christ and the principles of His Word will find that our eroding character will jeopardize ministry. It is all too easy to respond carnally to situations, people, and a host of disappointments that come with the territory of shepherding. When people criticize us, don't follow through for us, don't reflect the admiration and affirmation that we think we deserve; if our minds are not focused on what we believe to be true about Christ, then speech, conduct, love, faith, and purity will all be at risk. On the other hand, if we are bonded to our belief in Christ and His truth, we will find ourselves looking instinctively to Him for signals of responsive behavior in times such as these.

I recall speaking at a Bible conference in the Midwest which, for many years, had always been held during the same week of the year. This annual conference was so old that I wouldn't be surprised if Methuselah had attended it at one point. It was a rather high-profile week of meetings, and this was my first time to be asked to be a part of it. I was honored. I was there with several friends of mine, including David Jeremiah and Richard Strauss. All of us were relatively young compared to the seasoned veterans who normally filled the pulpit at this conference. As far as I was concerned, all seemed to be going well until Wednesday after the evening service when a lady marched resolutely toward me, planted both feet in front of me, looked sternly at me and said, "I've been coming to this conference for years and have anticipated the deep teaching of the great men of God that normally come and speak at this conference. Why is it that only you younger men are here this year? Where are all the seasoned veterans of the Word that normally come?" I guess she'd thought I would know, but even if she did, she didn't give me a chance to reply. She went on intently, "It's already Wednesday night and, young man, quite frankly it has not been much." As she thrust the sword into my heart, I instinctively knew how I might respond. I felt like saying something gracious like, "In your face, sweetheart!" or something more spiritual like, "Well, if you would come looking for a blessing, I'm sure it would be possible to get something from the sermons."

I knew, however, that if I were to remain bonded to my belief in Him, I would have to, figuratively speaking, rock back on my heels, let my eyes glaze over, and check in with Him. I would need to inquire of Him, "What does Your kind of man do in a moment like this? What do I believe about You and about Your Word that could form my response in a way that would be consistent with what I say I believe?" It seemed that almost immediately the answer came as Matthew 5:43-48 came to mind.

> You have heard that it was said, "You shall love your neighbor, and hate your enemy." But I say unto you, love your enemies, and pray for those who persecute you in order that you may be sons of your Father who is in heaven; for He causes His sun to rise on the evil and the good, and sends rain on the righteous and the unrighteous. For if you love those who love you, what reward have you? Do not even the tax-gatherers do the same? And if you greet your brothers only, what do you do more than others? Do not even the Gentiles do the same? Therefore you are to be perfect, as your heavenly Father is perfect.

And so, I replied with something like, "Thank you for being concerned about my ministry this week" (bless those who curse you). "I really want my ministry to be meaningful in your life" (love your enemies). "Why don't you pray for me through the rest of this week that God will give me something for you, and I will pray that God in turn will meet the needs and expectations of your heart since it is so hungry to hear from Him this week?" (pray for those who despitefully use you) Hopefully this rendered me like my Father in heaven who is motivated out of the depth of His compassion, mercy, love, and grace, and not out of retaliatory responses of self-protective defense and the protection of significance.

As I reflect on that conversation, I realize that my belief in and submission to Christ that drove that moment of behavior enabled me to be an example in terms of speech, conduct, love, faith, and purity. And I must say I walked away not having gotten even, but having made progress in terms of the personal implication of what it means to be a believer and a visible reflection of such. And, believe it or not, that felt better than treating her like a sacred sparring partner.

One other item should be noticed about Paul's instruction that we are to be an *example believer.* Understanding that this is a matter of living lives that are driven by the impact of what we believe in Jesus Christ, we go beyond being an example *to* the believers—which is not what the text says; but rather we seek to be the prototype of what believing is all about. For those of us who seek to be simply an example *to* the believers, it will indeed be a burden, and there will be a propensity for us to only practice it when our lives are publicly noticeable. Hendricksen notes, "Paul does not really say that Timothy should become a model *for* the believers, that is, for them to follow, but that ever increasingly he should become a model *of* what believers are . . . in five respects."[3] To be an example believer means that we are indeed, from the very core of our beings, a prototype, a model of what it truly means to believe in Jesus Christ. It is a life not driven by duty to a project, but by devotion to a Person. It is driven by a dynamic, growing relationship with Christ.

Given the reality that exampleship is an expression of our belief in and relationship to Christ, we need to remind ourselves that this kind of respected leadership is rooted in a commitment to first and foremost being a *follower* of Jesus Christ.

FOLLOWERSHIP

Effective biblical leadership always begins with the nonnegotiated commitment to followership. Interesting, isn't it, that in all of our talk about leadership we rarely have any discussion of followership? No leader can be truly effective until he is first and foremost a follower of Jesus Christ. Think of leaders who have failed. Rarely do they fail because they have lacked management skills, a grasp of paradigms of programmatic growth, or an understanding of the mechanisms of leadership. Our failure as leaders is most often in the realm of ceasing to be a good follower of Christ. Of breaking ranks with Him in terms of our thought life, our private lives, our self-serving attitudes, and the resultant impact on our relationships with others.

It's interesting to note that the most trusted and perhaps most capable leader among the disciples was Judas. He was given the high-level privilege of keeping the money and none of his colleagues believed that he was the one who would betray Christ. Even after Christ gave him the sop and Judas left, the others assumed that he had gone to buy bread. We probably would have agreed with the consultant who studied the profiles of the disciples and concluded:

M E M O

TO: Jesus, Son of Joseph
FROM: Jordan Management Consultants

Thank you for submitting the résumés of the 12 men you have picked for management positions in your new organization. All of them have now taken our battery of tests, and we have not only run the results through our computer, but also arranged personal interviews for each of them with our psychologist and vocational aptitude consultant.

The profiles of all tests are included, and you will want to study them carefully. As part of our service we will make some general comments. These are given as a result of staff consultations and come without any additional fee.

It is the staff opinion that most of your nominees are lacking in background, education, and vocational aptitude for the type of enterprise you are undertaking. They do not have the team concept. We recommend that you continue your search.

Simon Peter is emotionally unstable and given to fits of temper. Andrew has absolutely no qualities of leadership. The brothers, James and John, place personal interest above company loyalty. Thomas has a skeptical attitude that would tend to undermine morale. It is our duty to tell you that Matthew has been blacklisted by the Greater Jerusalem Better Business Bureau. James, the son of Alphaeus, and Thaddeus have radical leanings and show a high score on the manic-depressive scale.

Only one shows great potential—ability, resourcefulness, a business mind, meets people well, ambitious, highly motivated. We recommend Judas Iscariot as your controller and right-hand man.

Yet he was the only one who ultimately failed! Precisely because, though he was working for Christ, he was not a follower of Christ. He was a follower of his own desires, passions, and plans. He was in it for all the wrong reasons. As John noted in retrospect, he was a thief and often stole from the treasury of the Twelve. Judas was committed to his own personal gain in the context of his work with Christ. All the leadership gifts and skills can't stop the inevitable failure of those who are not first and foremost followers of Christ. And, by contrast, those who are less capable can become immensely successful if they are first and foremost followers of Him.

There is a sense of liberation from laborious ministry when we realize that effectiveness as a shepherd flows out of a relationship with Jesus Christ, whom we have committed to follow in such an intense and intimate way that His character, perspectives, actions, and reactions become replicated through our lives. This truth is liberating because there are a lot of us, even in ministry capacities, who feel down deep inside that we're really not built to be leaders. In this particular sense, leaders lead not by merit of temperament or gifts, but by living a life that is so compellingly like Christ that others naturally want to follow them. To follow them to Christ. We may not have a lot of programmatic vision or affirmation for managerial accomplishments, but our lives as a result of the management of our relationship to Him will be a vision of the distinctiveness of Christ. We will see the affirmation of changed lives, of those who, because they came under our shepherding, followed an exemplary model of what it means to believe.

In fact, leaders who lead from instinctive leadership gifts and capabilities need to recognize the down side of their gifts, that people tend to be attracted to, bond with, and glorify them. Transitioning them to Christ is a major challenge to the gifted leader. Those of us who may not be as significantly endowed, but whose lives as followers of Christ create a desire for the flock to follow us, will find it easier to bond people to our Savior.

It should not go unnoticed that the primal call to the leaders who ultimately turned their world upside down for Christ was, "Follow Me, and I will make you fishers of men" (Matt. 4:18-22). Note the order in which that comes. We are to follow Him, and then in the process of our followership, He will develop our effectiveness in ministry. He will *make* us fishers of men.

The challenge to their commitment to follow was, however, that they had some things going on in their lives that they would have to abandon if indeed they would be complete followers of Christ. They would have to leave their careers. In James' and John's case, it was the family business, *Fish by Zebedee and Sons.* When you think of what their career as fishermen meant to them, you begin to understand the weight of what they had to abandon. Their career provided security, significance, position, worth, value, income, and in some regard, meaning to life. This was a high-risk, high-sacrifice step. But what is amazing is that all of them immediately left that which hindered them from being followers and stepped out to follow Him.

NETLESSNESS

When we think of the joy of shepherding from the posture of an exemplary life that flows from our growing relationship to Christ, we too must realize that in order to be an authentic follower we must be willing to yield those things that inhibit or prohibit our capacity to be nonnegotiated followers. The metaphor is dramatic in the case of Peter and Andrew. The text says that they *left their nets.* As long as they clung to their nets of security, which symbolized the known and comfortable routine of their lives, they were going nowhere in terms of following Christ.

Christ comes to us and says, "Follow Me," and in order to do that we may have to drop the nets to which we have clung for so long. We must be constantly looking to our hands to see if there are nets that we're clinging to, that in some way inhibit our capacity to be a follower and hence a respected leader. Nets like material treasures or living for material gain. The nets of relationships—some legitimate, some not. Personal plans and dreams. Moral compromises. Security-producing patterns of self-serving, self-advancing actions and reactions to life. Nets of comparison to others, and covetousness in regard to our colleagues' gifts, recognition, position, influence, and affluence. Nets that relate to family and friends. Nets that create for us a sense of security and comfort. Nets that are familiar and functional. Yet nets that rob us of the capacity to be the shepherd that Christ wants to make us to be.

An example believer is a netless follower—one whose life can be shaped, formed, and made from scratch by the influence of a yielded commitment to Jesus Christ, the Leader and Shepherd of our souls. What's interesting, however, is that even those of us who drop our nets, who leave behind all which inhibits our capacity to be fully followers of Him, find that along the way the adversary offers us new nets to distract us, delay us, and ultimately debilitate us.

SERVING

Though these twelve disciples had left everything to follow Christ with a clean slate, they kept reaching back for the one net that is undoubtedly the most destructive net in terms of limiting leadership potential, and that was their constant interest in "who would be the greatest" when they came into the kingdom. It seems that whenever there was a break in the hectic pace of ministry, the disciples' discussions would inevitably turn to this *obsession with their own significance.* The most dramatic case of this obsessive tendency in all of us is, as we noted earlier, reflected in Matthew 20, where James and John came with their mother who on their behalf asked Christ to make them the greatest in the kingdom. The text indicates that the other disciples were "indignant," no doubt because they wanted this position themselves. At this point, Christ gathered the disciples together and reminded them that their attitude was like the world since Gentile rulers seek to lord it over those around them. He then transitioned them to what it meant to be a follower of Christ by saying that the greatest in His kingdom would be those who serve, and those who would be administratively powerful would carry the attitude of a slave. He claimed to be the example that we should follow by saying, "Just as the Son of Man did not come to be served, but to serve and to give His life a ransom for many" (v. 28).

This moment was not unlike the moment in John 13 when the disciples were gathered for that Last Supper with Christ in the Upper Room. One thing was missing, according to the common practice in that day, and that was that a servant had not met them at the door to wash their feet. One thing was for sure—none of them were going to humble themselves to wash the feet of their brethren. They were too interested in posturing themselves for places of position and power when the kingdom would finally come. In fact, Luke indicates that this is exactly what they were discussing (Luke 22:24). And in that context it is the Lord of the universe, in a beautiful metaphor of the voluntary yielding of His glory (Phil. 2:5-8), who stands and drops His robe, puts a towel around His waist, draws a basin of water, and washes the disciples' feet. He then instructed them, "Do you know what I have done to you? You call Me Teacher and Lord; and you are right, for so I am. If I then, the Lord and the Teacher, washed your feet, you also ought to wash one another's feet. For I gave you an example that you also should do as I did to you" (John 13:12-15).

Dropping the net of our own significance to follow Christ down the road to servanthood is complicated by the fact that some of us are so struck with our position as shepherd that we are short-sighted to the issue of serving. Yet it is critical for us to be serious about this issue. Shepherds who view their leadership mode in terms of flocks who will serve their dreams, desires, visions, and plans will soon have fewer and fewer who will want to buy into his agenda. Shepherds are first and foremost servants of the flock. They guard, guide, feed, and at times sacrificially give themselves to the needs of the flock. Undershepherds were particularly serious about this since they knew their flock was a large part of their master's wealth. We should be reminded that the flock of God over which we have oversight is a highly valued possession of our Lord. In fact, so highly valued that He Himself served them all the way to the giving of His own life on a cruel instrument of ancient torture.

What is instructive about Christ's example and call for us to follow Him in servanthood is that though He had a high position, in fact the highest position of the universe, He was willing to use that position as a platform from which He could serve. Pastoring is not a pedestal. Pastoring is a platform from which we minister to the flock on His behalf.

Getting our position in line with this practice of following Christ will not always be easy. This obsessive addiction that we have to our own significance will often get in the way. Our administration building at the Moody Bible Institute, Crowell Hall, is an eleven-story structure and since my office is on the ninth floor, I spend some of my time in the elevator. The inside of the elevator doors are stainless steel and show fingerprints easily. Our housekeeping staff regularly rides the elevators to keep the doors clean. Getting on the elevator one day I noticed that the housekeeper was probably not more than 5′ 1″ and was struggling to clean the doors all the way to the top. There was about an 18-inch shortfall that was impossible for her to reach. As the door closed I thought to myself, *Pity that someone else didn't get on here. If they had they could help her. Certainly the President of the Institute is not here to clean doors.* Well . . . not really. Having recently been impacted by the reality that Christ used His position to serve, I asked her if I could take the rag and spray bottle and get that part that she couldn't reach. With a somewhat surprised look she handed them to me and as I started to clean the upper parts of the doors the elevator stopped, the doors opened, and some of our students and staff got on the elevator. I kept cleaning the doors. I asked the housekeeper a few weeks later how the doors were coming. She glowingly said, "Just fine; in fact, lots of people are helping me now." It is that step of laying down the net of our own significance, being a follower of Christ, which then creates an exemplary magnetism that draws others to follow Him as well.

On the other hand, think of the destructive outcomes that we inflict on ministry when we do not see ourselves as servants and configure our ministry from the context of our obsession to our own significance, expressed through self-serving, self-promoting, self-enhancing, self-defending, self-maintaining attitudes. Think of what it means in staff relationships and in the relationships we have with the volunteers that come to help us in the shepherding cause. Think of what it means in terms of our actions and reactions toward those who criticize, misunderstand, or simply don't appreciate who we are or what we've done. When we are unappreciated or maligned it is a major blow to our sense of significance. And if we are not following we will lash out in subtle or not-so-subtle ways and compound our problems.

Being a netless follower of Christ in this struggle with our desire for significance not only relates to serving but to suffering as well.

SUFFERING

Peter focuses our attention on the pattern that Christ set for us when we suffer. If we follow Him we should suffer patiently without self-defense or acts of retribution, but rather commit ourselves to God who judges all men righteously. The point is that as we continue to do what is right, God will manage the outcomes. We don't have to jump in to defend ourselves or destroy those who are perpetuating the suffering. What is instructive and highly significant is that this is exactly how Jesus Christ responded. Peter notes that a person finds favor with God "if for the sake of conscience toward God a man bears up under sorrows when suffering unjustly. For what credit is there if, when you sin and are harshly treated, you endure it with patience? But if when you do what is right and suffer for it you patiently endure it, this finds favor with God" (1 Peter 2:19-20). He then points us to what it means in this context to be a follower of Christ by saying, "For you have been called for this purpose, since Christ also suffered for you, leaving you an example for you to follow in His steps, who committed no sin, nor was any deceit found in His mouth; and while being reviled, He did not revile in return; while suffering, He uttered no threats, but kept entrusting Himself to Him who judges righteously" (vv. 21-23). The context goes on to say that because He did not lash back at those who were imposing lashes on Him, that He then had the capacity to have a ministry of healing, remediation, and restoration. "And He Himself bore our sins in His body on the cross, that we might die to sin and live to righteousness; for by His wounds you were healed. For you were continually straying like sheep, but now you have returned to the Shepherd and Guardian of your souls" (vv. 24-25).

The critical point here is that Christ was willing to commit His enemies to God and continue to be concerned about their needs. This probably is the ultimate test of shepherding. Our trust in God is based on Paul's exhortation to the Romans, where he taught us not to pay back evil for evil but rather to put wrath in its legitimate place—i.e., the hand of God who judges all men righteously. And once we have committed our enemies to Him and His care, we are then liberated not to live in modes of vengeance but in modes of love and concern. As Romans 12 says,

> Never pay back evil for evil to anyone. Respect what is right in the sight of all men. If possible, so far as it depends on you, be at peace with all men. Never take your own revenge, beloved, but leave room for the wrath of God, for it is written, "Vengeance is Mine, I will repay," says the Lord. "But if your enemy is hungry, feed him, and if he is thirsty, give him a drink; for in so doing you will heap burning coals upon his head." Do not be overcome by evil, but overcome evil with good (Rom. 12:17-21).

It is the privilege of the shepherd to model to a watching flock what it means to not be overcome by evil but to overcome evil with good.

In my first pastorate, one of the parishioners in the flock who had been a long-time friend of mine since before I became pastor of the church began to take it upon himself to share his list of secret prayer requests with other people in the church concerning the weaknesses that he observed in my life. Needless to say, this was unsettling for me in that it threatened my sense of security. First of all, I had no idea what was on the list, so I felt unable to defend myself, and second, I didn't like the thought of my perceived weaknesses being spread throughout the congregation, particularly to those who had not noticed the now-advertised weaknesses. As more and more people came to me, some mentioning that they were joining my brother in a prayer ministry on my behalf, I decided that I needed to follow Paul's exhortation and Peter's articulation of the pattern of Christ and not retaliate but rather trust God to resolve the problem in His way and in His time. And while this was not easy for me, I found my heart bolstered by Psalm 37 which exhorts us not to fret because of wrongdoers, but rather to trust in the Lord and do good. The flow of exhortation concludes with the encouraging words to my heart, "Rest in the Lord and wait patiently for Him; fret not yourself because of him who prospers in his way, because of the man who carries out wicked schemes. Cease from anger, and forsake wrath; fret not yourself, it leads only to evildoing" (vv. 7-8).

It was all I could do to resist the self-defending promptings of my heart, particularly when I had the opportunity to share with people what I perceived some of his weaknesses to be. I had to resist dragging him into my messages and being in bondage to his behavior. The only way that became possible for me was to really trust that God would deal with him in His time and in His way, and to ask God to use this time in my life to develop and shape me into what He wanted me to be.

Since Scripture gave me permission to go to one who had wronged me, I asked him if we could go out for coffee one night after prayer meeting. As I unfolded my heart to him, I asked him if there was something that I had done to offend him, because I had sensed a real distancing in our spirits and a negative feeling toward me. He said that there was nothing he could think about that I had done to offend him, but that he had been praying for me and that one of the things on his prayer list was that I would become more sensitive. And it was obvious now that God was answering his prayer, since, at least in this regard, for me to approach him like this was a reflection of a new sensitivity in my heart.

I walked away from that moment feeling that I had been stepped on once more and that I had moved farther, not closer, from resolution.

Several months later during prayer meeting, he stood up and announced that he would like to say something to the congregation. To my shock, he shared that he had been unfair to me as his pastor and that he had shared things with people that he had no right to, and that he wanted to ask my forgiveness in front of the flock and also forgiveness from the congregation for his attitude. I could have hugged him for an hour. I thanked him for his gracious spirit and forgave him, as did the congregation, and the problem was settled.

I thanked God that, indeed, in His time and in His way He does deal with those who oppose us. I have often looked back on that situation thanking the Lord as well that His way was best—because if I had gotten in and put on my biblical boxing gloves and tried to hammer my opponent into submission, it would have been worse, not better. In fact, it's hard to tell what may have ultimately happened if I had started that kind of sequence of events.

I wish I could say that I've always been so anchored in my followership responses to Christ in times of difficulty. Sometimes it's hard to learn our lessons. At times I have tried to use the pulpit to settle scores with enemies. I have fallen to the temptation of protecting myself by subtly, sanctimoniously sharing negative things about those who oppose me. And there have been times that I have permitted my spirit to become angered and to flirt with bitterness for what someone has said or not said, or done or not done. In each case I stopped trusting Him to do what He promised to do on my behalf, and in the process shut down my capacity to be a total shepherd toward all who were in the flock—those who liked, loved, and cared for me and those who for one reason or another did not. It's tough—perhaps the toughest job in ministry—to deal with those who dent our sense of significance and threaten our comfortable place on the pedestal. Yet followers of Christ have a Leader who has cut a path before us in regard to our response to suffering.

Dropping the net of enhancing our significance through a self-serving, self-defending approach to ministry is strategic. Shepherds who will engender the respect whereby effective ministry can proceed need to maintain a commitment to dropping the net of the promotion of our own significance and follow the leadership of Christ by being non-negotiably committed to a spirit of servanthood and a willingness to suffer patiently if necessary to please God and heal our enemies. Christ served intentionally and suffered graciously, that He might continue to have open and unhindered relationships through which God could use Him to transform lives as He would draw people to Himself, the Shepherd of their souls.

It seems strange that we, of all people, should be consumed with our own significance. Paul wrote to the church at Philippi that they were to stop living in self-serving, self-elevating patterns of life, but rather to in humility focus on the importance of others rather than on the importance of self. And the way that we would change this ever-present propensity would be to follow Christ by taking His mind as our own in matters like these. The text then goes on to say that regardless of His high position as God, He "did not regard equality with God a thing to be grasped, but emptied Himself, taking the form of a bond-servant, and being made in the likeness of men. And being found in appearance as a man, He humbled Himself by becoming obedient to the point of death, even death on a cross" (Phil. 2:6-8).

Herein lies the fourfold pattern of the Christ whom we follow: *surrendering* to an agenda beyond ourselves; *sacrificing* whatever is necessary to accomplish the agenda; considering ourselves to be *servants* to our Father and to those He came to save; and *suffering* if necessary to get the job done.

For all of us who wonder if, in the process, there is anything in it for us, we must remember that the text goes on to say, "Therefore also God highly exalted Him, and bestowed on Him the name which is above every name, that at the name of Jesus every knee should bow, of those who are in heaven, and on earth, and under the earth, and that every tongue should confess that Jesus Christ is Lord, to the glory of God the Father" (vv. 9-11). And while it would be right to think, *Yes, but that was what God did for Christ,* we must recall the words of

1 Peter 5:6-7, "Humble yourselves, therefore, under the mighty hand of God, that He may exalt you at the proper time, casting all your anxiety upon Him, because He cares for you." Exaltation is not *grabbed.* It is *given* by the Father, in His time and in His way. For some of us, it may be on the other side when we hear from Him, "Well done, thou good and faithful servant." Fascinating, isn't it, how so many of us in spiritual leadership program our lives around ways in which exaltation can be gotten in our time and our way? And when it never comes, we are discouraged and defeated. A proper view of authentic Christianity is that it is not about the exaltation of ourselves, but about the exaltation of Him. It is not about building and gaining our kingdom, but about the advance of His kingdom.

Yet our significance obsession drives us to enhance ourselves and advance our own kingdoms. How then can we be liberated from this major barrier to exemplary leadership?

SIGNIFICANCE SECURED

It is not the desire for significance that is at fault. We are built for significance. It's rather that we spend our lives searching for it in all the wrong places, assuming that it is something that we can manufacture in and of ourselves and our own efforts.

Early on in human history, when God created Adam and Eve, they were beyond a doubt sufficiently significant—not in and of themselves but in the fact that they were without hindrance, fully related to the significant One of the universe. He was their God, and they were His pinnacle of creation. He had given to them the most significant task on earth: to be stewards of His created order and to, through that stewardship, bring glory to Him. They were fully significant in the fact that they related to and were responsible to the only significant One in the universe.

A satisfying significance can never be gained in and of ourselves. It is only realized in our relationship to the One who is fully and supremely significant, that is our Father in heaven. Our sense of significance is not a search, but something that is secured in our relationship to Him. And while the Fall severed us from the Source of significance, sending our fallen souls in search of significance lost, redemption has restored us to God and in the process restored a secured significance for us. As such, significance is not a search, but something that has already been fully secured.

In Colossians 2:10 Paul writes that we have been made *complete* in Him. When we think of that completeness in terms of significance, we note that redemption has made us significant in every aspect of our longings for significance. We are significant in terms of *identity,* in that we are children of His; in terms of *position,* in that we are a chosen race, a royal priesthood, a holy nation, a people for God's own possession (1 Peter 2:9); in terms of *prosperity,* in that we are heirs and joint heirs with Jesus Christ; in terms of *power,* in that we are empowered by the indwelling Spirit; in terms of *worth,* in that we have been not born into His family but purposefully chosen through adoption to be a part of His family; in terms of *possessions,* in that regardless of temporal, material wealth, we possess the treasures and the reality of all that is on the other side. And all of this need not be sought after, but is already secured through the finished work of Jesus Christ. In fact, since most of us feel that significance will be ours through performance, it is liberating to remember that all of this significance is not based on my performance but on the completed performance of Jesus Christ on the cross. I am not called to perform in order to gain significance, but rather, since my significance has been secured, I am called to gratefully serve the One who has made me fully significant in Him.

Given this redemption-wrought liberation from the shepherd's fatal obsession, those of us who have applied these redemptive realities to our minds and hearts are finally free to be committed to glorifying and magnifying His character through us instead of our own and to sacrificing anything that is an impediment to our commitment to serving the advance of His kingdom, even if it means a measure of suffering in the process.

Can you imagine what ministry would be like without feeling the need to be competitive with gifted lay leaders, colleagues on the staff, or others in the ministry around you? Can you imagine what it would be like to go to a ministerial meeting, not needing to manufacture some kind of bragging rights so that your ministry can look significant in the light of others? Can you imagine not having to covet another person's success or to complain about not being affirmed or recognized? Can you imagine a ministry where you delight in serving others by passing along the credit and affirming them? A ministry where you are free to serve, love, and care for even those who undermine your significance through harmful reactions to you? A ministry that trusts God to take you through the tough times and to guarantee you affirmation in the proper time? Can you imagine the release of your spirit when you no longer have to serve self but can know the joy of serving Him and others on His behalf?

This is the fundamental issue of followership, that the mind of Christ is ours, who was not obsessed with His own significance but rather ministered as the Suffering Servant Shepherd of our souls. And it's just this kind of followership that postures us to do well in the arenas of speech, conduct, love, faith, and purity. For if we have not dealt with the issue of our own significance, then our speech will be self-serving, our conduct self-promoting, our love will be for ourselves, and our faith will be in ourselves, leaving us evidently and shamefully impure before a watching flock and a curious community.

We will not be truly viable as shepherds until we are noticeably followers of Christ. Visible examples of what it means to believe in Christ. Followers who turn the fishbowl of ministry to Christ's advantage by so effectively exampling that when we lead, others will both respect and follow us.

Recently while talking with a wealthy executive our conversation turned to his pastor who is a friend of mine. He spoke of his admiration for his pastor and then said, "I often find myself asking, 'What would Don do if he were in this situation?' " Don's life has caught the respect of this macro mover in the marketplace and created a compelling exemplary life worthy to be followed.

Recently I found myself complaining to Martie about how the press takes such delight in magnifying the failures of people in ministry. I was ranting about the hypocrisy of the press who never seem to take delight in the fact that people in other professions fail morally all the time. Doctors, lawyers, butchers, bakers, candlestick makers—all have massive failure rates in these areas. But somehow their failures never command space in public attention. Martie insightfully responded, as she normally does, that there is a difference. She observed that as ministers we portray by the very posture of our calling that we live by a different standard. As a result, people expect us to be exemplary. They expect that because our names begin with "Rev.," we will reflect what the representatives of Christ should reflect. That we will live out what we believe and what we proclaim to be true. Not only does our world expect that of us, but so does the flock. When we do, they will respect us for it.

Amidst all the rubble of public failures, Billy Graham has lived an exemplary life that is above reproach. As such, he stands as a man respected in a world that is anxious to debunk and defraud what we believe and what we highly value. In a smaller context, the same thing is true in the communities where we live and among the congregations that we serve. They simply expect us to live out what we believe. When we do it with a good measure of consistency, respect will be engendered. And that respect will be the platform from which effective ministry is launched regardless of how decadent the society becomes.

Paul sets up five targets of exemplary living at which the effective leader takes aim.

Section Two

Personhood: *Character Still Counts*

"An institution is the lengthened shadow of one person."
—Ralph Waldo Emerson

Chapter Six

Leading from Living

Speech and Conduct

Reflecting on the leadership qualities that made Harry Truman one of our great presidents, journalist Eric Sevareid who covered him extensively observed, "I am not sure he was right about the atomic bomb or even Korea. But remembering him reminds people what a man in that office ought to be like. It's character. Just character. He stands like a rock in memory now."[1]

Somehow we've missed that point in our generation.

Fewer things are more challenged and more neglected in our modern society than the importance of character. Performing, succeeding, and doing all hold higher postures than being and becoming.

The prevailing conviction in American society today regarding leadership is that character doesn't count. This is particularly true in the political arena, as public opinion polls consistently underscore our societal bent that lifestyle and leadership are unrelated. Nothing, however, could be further from the truth. Who I really am and what I do in private will ultimately affect what I do in public. All that I am and do as a leader ultimately is sourced in the authentic me. Character is about what and who I am at the very core of my being.

Character still counts. In fact, in a society that minimizes values, the value of character escalates in terms of ministry. It is the shepherd who proves the point regarding the value and worth of character who becomes a trusted and readily followed leader. It is character that will be transferred to others and be used of God to transform lives.

In the despairing darkness of the encroaching century the light of character-centered leadership will blaze like a torch that will lead many to Christ and the joy of a Christlike life.

Character is the critical mass of ministry.

Given the shift of our society on this issue we are finding that more and more, our world and our people are expecting less and less of us as leaders in regard to *personhood.* However, we who are called to spiritual leadership need to expect more of ourselves and hold ourselves accountable to scriptural standards rather than societal opinions. The biblical perspective on effectiveness in leadership consistently postures character as the essential prerequisite (1 Tim. 3; Titus 1). In fact, as we have noted, Paul postures character as the leading issue in a pastor's life if he is to engender the *respect* from his flock that is necessary for him to maximize his effectiveness over the long term (1 Tim. 4:12). It's interesting to note that when *Webster's New Collegiate Dictionary* defines respect as a descriptive term it states: "respectable: adj.: decent or correct in character or behavior."

Since character is increasingly irrelevant in regard to leadership, our culture finds itself looking to credentials as the leading requisite for leadership. Ours is a credentials more than character, a performance over personhood, world.

Before Martie and I moved to the city, I used to periodically commute to Moody by train. I was joined by masses of other businesspersons on their way into the city. It was fascinating to watch us symbolically try to out-credential each other. Lower management used Bic pens, middle management Cross pens, upper management Mont Blancs. It was obvious that the upper management guys rarely wore button-downs, but always stiff, straight, white collars. We would try to out-pinstripe each other and out-wingtip each other. Then there were the guys with the alligator briefcases and the ones with laptop computers. The ultimate stroke of credentialed significance was the commuter with the cellular phone who did business all the way into the train station.

This is a world where it's not what you are as a person that counts, but it's what title you hold, what floor your office is on, and what your business card looks like. If you and I were involved in a panel discussion with some of the eminently successful leaders of our day, no one would ever think of asking, "Now, I know that you are successful as a leader in your own right, but what I'm more concerned about is how you got there. Tell me about your integrity, commitment, compassion, justice . . . and while you're at it, tell me a little bit about your home life—

what kind of a husband and father you are." No one would dream of asking questions about character, because performance and subsequent credentials are more highly regarded than the process by which they were gained.

In a sense, ours is a "Little Jack Horner" world where the quest for performance-based credentials ignores the deeper issues of character. It's that obsession with the establishment of our own significance that becomes more compelling than the issues of right and wrong. In a moment of what for him was a smashing performance, Jack stuck his thumb into a Christmas pie, pulled out a plum, raised it high in the air, and proclaimed, "What a good boy am I!" Pleased with his accomplishment, he went public with his performance, seeking the applause and affirmation of those around him.

But before our applause raises to a fever pitch we need to examine the scene more closely. If I remember correctly, "Little Jack Horner sat in a corner." As far as I know, the only reason little boys sit in corners is because they haven't been good. In addition, the pictures that I saw of Little Jack Horner in the nursery rhyme book depicted him sitting there with a whole pie on his lap. I know of few mothers who give their boys whole pies. Could it be that he had stolen it from the kitchen?

However Jack got the pie, and whether or not you buy my exegesis of the story to this point, we do have to question why he's taking the credit for pulling a plum out of a pie that his mother baked. She selected the plums, cleaned them, and put them in the pie. Even a naive level of decency would consider at least sharing the glory with her. And we would all have to agree that Jack is in clear violation of acceptable table manners by having his fingers in the food.

If we're not careful, it's this Little Jack Horner syndrome that will make us willing to do whatever is necessary to establish a credential-centered ministry. But focusing on credentials and ignoring the process will ultimately, though perhaps unwittingly, erode the platform of respect by leading us to compromise our character. Needless to say, shepherds are not exempt from this credentials-over-character response to life and ministry. Think of the times we exaggerate the successes of our ministries at ministerial meetings with our colleagues to establish our posture and place, rather than expressing the character of the mind of Christ in the context of Paul's exhortation to "do nothing from selfishness or empty conceit, but with humility of mind let each of you regard one another as more important than himself" (Phil. 2:3). As leaders it's easy to compromise the effectiveness of our ministry by making choices in ministry based on whether or not our own standing in regard to praise, profile, or prosperity will be elevated. Shepherds, however, who resist the temptation to violate the process of character for the gain of credentials, strengthen the platform from which they minister.

A friend of mine recently accepted a call to a large, affluent church in one of our nation's major cities. Soon after going there, a member of his church who was a car dealer took him to lunch and offered to supply him and his wife with two luxury model cars which would be recycled every six months. He said that he had done it for previous pastors and was looking forward to extending the privilege to him as well. My friend turned down the request. Not because it was not offered with good intent or from a sincere heart, but rather because he knew that, as he and his wife began their ministry, double-dipping in luxury car appearances might very well erode the platform from which he would minister. Although my friend didn't share this with me, there might be a sense as well that as spiritual leaders we need to be sensitive to whom we are beholden. If decisions in the church needed to be made that went contrary to the donors' desires, would we as shepherds ever be tempted to rethink what we would've otherwise thought best for the church, given this material bonding that had developed through the gift? All of this to say that there is no credential that could be gained in ministry that would ever be worth compromising the platform of respect that character supports.

It's interesting to watch pastoral search committees evaluate their candidates. Most of the profiles that I have seen are primarily related to performance and credentials. Can he preach? What is his educational background? What is the size of the churches he has pastored? Can he administer? Has he written anything? Does he speak at conferences? And while most of these searches don't center only on credentials, the credential issue tends to hold the upper hand. What we must remember is that even if credentials get you in the front door, character is what will keep you there. People quickly forget credentials, because the ongoing impact on their lives is at the level of their experience of our character. Credentials impress the mind and appeal to a congregation's ego. Character—either good or bad—impacts the life and legacy of the church. We need to remind each other, as we mentioned earlier, that the fundamental questions in the hearts of the people in our flock are not *What have you done? What can you do? What vision do you have for this ministry?* Their heart questions are *Who are you? Will I be able to trust you?*

Is it any wonder then that God's Word, when it speaks to the qualification of spiritual leadership, speaks always to the issue of the way we live our lives? Character is infinitely more strategic to effectiveness than credentials. For instance, character is universally obtainable. Credentials are attainable by only a gifted few. Character develops a legacy that will cast its shadow over generations to come. Credentials are quickly forgotten. Character is transferable from the leader to those whom he's leading. Credentials are not transferable. Character is a means to glorify Christ through our lives, since it is His character, the expression of our belief in Him, that is reflected through our lives. Character makes a point about Him. Credentials make a point about us. Character is both magnetic and motivating. As others see a growing, deepening sense of goodness in our lives, they will be drawn to us and feel stimulated to follow suit in their lives. Credentials set a distance between us and others and may discourage others who can't attain, or incite jealousy and covetousness. Character is what we will be held accountable for. Credentials won't count on the day that we stand before Him. Character is only forged through a growing, sincere relationship to Christ. Credentials can be gotten quite apart from Christ. Character is deepened and developed in crises. Character has value in a crisis. Credentials are of little avail when the chips are down. Credentials set us on a pedestal while character erects a platform from which we can minister.

Even some in the secular arena are starting to recognize the bankrupt environment that leadership without character creates. Speaking of the importance of character to respect, Kouzes and Posner observe,

> In the late 1970s and into the 1980s, self-help and management books boomed. But in large measure, this was a triumph of image over character, style over substance. In the 1990s, there is a growing recognition that gaining credibility is far more important than being dressed for success. Credibility is the foundation on which leaders and constituents will build the grand dreams of the future. Without credibility, visions will fade and relationships will wither.[2]

In Scripture the issue of character is more than a generic philosophical concept. God's Word clearly intends for us to understand the issue of character in terms of specific areas that need to be targeted for development and reflection in our lives. As we have noted, Paul calls Timothy to commit himself to progress in five areas.

SPEECH

The first target area of our life, according to Paul's list in 1 Timothy 4:12, is our *talk.* While we cannot be certain that Paul prioritized the list, it is interesting to note that the list begins with speech. This may be reflective of the fact that James states that we who are teachers will stand in greater judgment, and that the primary struggle of our lives—that which threatens to put us in the most jeopardy—is this dragon in our dentures known as our tongue.

Fewer things are more powerful in the arsenal of our ministry than our words. They can not only empower and enhance our leadership, but they can also discount our profile and devastate those in our charge. Some time ago I read the testimony of an individual who shared a life experience that illustrated both the power of constructive words to encourage as well as the power of destructive words to demoralize and defeat. He wrote,

> My junior high school had scheduled its annual operatic production. Talented students were quick to try out for the various parts. I was not so certain of my abilities and had decided that singing in an operetta wasn't really for me.
>
> Then Mrs. Wilson, my music teacher, asked me to try out for the role of the black servant. It was not a coveted role, but it *did* have three solos.
>
> I am certain that my audition was only mediocre. But Mrs. Wilson reacted as if she had just heard a choir of heavenly angels. "Oh, that was just beautiful. That was perfect. You are just right for the role. You will do it, won't you?" I accepted.
>
> When the time came for the next year's operetta, most of the students who had played the leads the year before had graduated. And Mrs. Wilson had transferred to another school. In her place was a rather imposing figure who had an excellent singing voice and a sound knowledge of music theory.
>
> As the tryouts began, I was ready. I felt confident that my talent was just what the operetta needed. With approximately 150 of my peers assembled, I knew everything would go well.
>
> But if I live for an eternity I will never forget the words spoken on that day. When my audition was completed, the teacher asked, "Who told you you could sing?"
>
> The timid youth of a year earlier was suddenly reborn. I was totally destroyed. Harsh words are bad enough under any circumstances. To a young idealistic boy, they can be devastating. From the time those six words were stated, it took eight years and the coaxing of my fiancée before my voice was raised in song again.

It is critical as well for us as spiritual leaders to understand that these powerful entities known as words are the essence of our trade. In our toolbox of talents and tactics, nearly everything we do flows through the words that we speak. This is particularly true of those of us who are proclaimers. Our words are the medium through which the Spirit of God transfers His truth from the pages of Scripture to the hearts of listeners. When we reflect godly, positive speech patterns in our lives out of the pulpit and away from other speaking forums, those who sit under the instruction of the Word when we are in the pulpit will have hearts that are open to the words through which the Spirit can move their lives to His glory and gain. On the other hand, when our words are less than honorable—perhaps punitive, manipulative, flirtatious, sensuous, or self-serving, then our proclamation ministries become discounted in the hearts of hearers. One of the most strategic aspects of our calling is to be truth tellers on behalf of God. If we violate integrity through our words in more casual and informal moments, then we will undermine the capacity of our words to carry appropriate weight when we speak on God's behalf.

Before we detail specific areas of speech that we as spiritual leaders need to both be on guard against and also the kind of speech that we must engender in our lives, it is important to note that there are two key aspects about the words that we use and the things that we say. First, words make *impressions.* When I say something or share information about someone, the words that leave my mouth move through the ear gate of those who are around me and lodge themselves rather permanently in the minds and hearts of those who hear. In a very real sense, when I speak I am stockpiling data in other people's memory banks. Data that will be used to draw impressions regarding the kind of person that I am and regarding the situations about which I have spoken. Once our words have logged the data and made the impression, it is very difficult to erase the impact. And one impact is the discounting of their respect for us. People have a way of measuring their memory bank against what they expect from spiritual leaders. And what makes all of this more sobering is that with some people we will only get one or at best very few opportunities to cast an impression through our words. One misspent word, response, or statement can cast a permanent shadow in regard to our character.

I was teaching a section of a course at a nearby seminary when one of the graduate students said during a time of discussion that he had been with a friend with whom I had played golf on the East Coast several years ago. He said that that person had shared with him a negative impression that he had concluded about me. He admitted that he had come to the class with his conclusions already drawn and was surprised to note that what he thought he would see in me he didn't see and wondered why it would be that his friend could have felt that way. Granted, golf is a test of anyone's sanctification, but for the life of me, I have no recollection of what I might have said to cause that impression to be made. In fact, I've always felt that as a Christian, the only trouble with my golf is that I don't have enough words to use on the course. The third time the ball goes in the water, "phooey" doesn't quite do it!

Something I said, some attitude, something that was misunderstood was logged and passed on to who knows how many people and, in turn, logged in their minds as a conclusive impression. Fewer things erode respect, trust, and admiration more than a consistent pattern of misplaced, misspoken, inappropriate words.

A friend of mine who serves on a staff of a rather large, influential church told me in brokenness about an experience that he had with the senior pastor. According to my friend, his pastor walked in his office and noticed that he was processing some of his work with a computer program that, for some reason, the pastor had asked him not to use. And since I didn't inquire further about that part of the story, it could be that this staff member was in the wrong, or perhaps there was a misunderstanding regarding the instructions of the pastor. When the pastor inquired about it, the staff member sought to explain only to be interrupted with a burst of angry words as the pastor said, "Listen, if you don't do what I tell you to do, I'm going to kick _____ all the way to California!"

Think of what the words in that encounter did in terms of impression and erosion of trust and respect. Think of the undermining of a key relationship that needs to be whole and productive for the sake of the health of the church. Granted, I do not know the whole story or all of the things that happened before and after. But it is a rather startling case in point. And while the vast majority of shepherds would not speak in those kinds of words, we are just as prone to use inappropriate, harmful, self-serving words when the heat's turned up. To use this as a teaching moment we might want to ask ourselves, if we had been in the senior pastor's shoes at that point, would there have been some other options that would have more productively dealt with the situation? If the staff member had been consistently insubordinate and this was the final straw that opened the door to a flood of anger, perhaps we should have simply walked back to our office until we had ourselves in control. If the anger level wasn't high, we could sit down and ask why he felt compelled to do it his own way. It's possible that a lot of understanding could have been gained on both sides with an encounter like that. Or perhaps it would have been good to simply ask the staff member to clarify whether or not he had understood the request, and if so, to reiterate that you expected him to comply.

As those words were logged in the staff member's mind and heart, they were devastating enough at the moment. But as trouble began to brew in the church at large, it was a memory that made it difficult to be loyal and supportive to the pastor as others began to express similar reflections on their experiences as well.

On one occasion I was privileged to go out for coffee and dessert with a high-profile communicator whose preaching has been a model for me. I was young to the ministry and perhaps idealistic about my heroes, but I was surprised at how free he was to talk negatively about others, their problems, and his perception of them. On that particular night his tongue of clay had tarnished his image.

Second, words not only make an impression, but they also grant *permission.* Permission for others to adopt the same speech patterns that the shepherd has. We all have a propensity toward problematic patterns of speech. It's a result of the intrinsic residuals of our fallenness that have not yet been fully eradicated by final redemption. People need little encouragement to speak out of the wrong side of their mouth. But when we as shepherds do it, there's a tendency for them to feel free to follow suit. Shepherds who exhibit godly Spirit-controlled patterns of speech that are lovingly yet firmly truthful, healing, helpful, and encouraging, will find that before long that will begin to rub off in the flock. On the other hand, if we want a flock of gossiping, complaining, slanderous, boasting, beguiling, critical, murmuring, and lying sheep, then the best way to foster that is to sprinkle our talk with that kind of speech.

It would be easy, perhaps, for us to see speech as an activity and not a measure of character—easy, that is, if it weren't for the fact that our Lord taught that *all talk is heart talk.* It was His point of view that our speech is a clear revelation of what's going on on the inside. The *New American Standard Bible* that I often use puts this title over the passage to which I'm about to refer: "Words Reveal Character." Speaking of the kinds of things that we say, Christ taught,

> Either make the tree good, and its fruit good; or make the tree rotten, and its fruit rotten; for the tree is known by its fruit. You brood of vipers, how can you, being evil, speak what is good? For the mouth speaks out of that which fills the heart. The good man out of his good treasure brings forth what is good; and the evil man out of his evil treasure brings forth what is evil. And I say to you, that every careless word that men shall speak, they shall

> render account for it in the day of judgment. For by your words you shall be justified, and by your words you shall be condemned (Matt. 12:33-37).

I like the fact that Christ speaks in terms of the kinds of treasures we store up in our hearts. Either good treasures or evil treasures. And that our words are spent out of that treasure. He likens us to a tree. Good trees bring good fruit; bad trees bring bad fruit. And this is the key to understanding why we will be judged based on our words. Quite frankly, for years I thought that that was a rather harsh reality. But even a casual review of this text indicates why our words will provide a point of accountability on Judgment Day. Because they reveal what our hearts are really like. And should any of us want to argue with the Lord about the true condition of our hearts, our words will simply stand as clear evidence of the condition of our inner self. In a sense, words tattle on our hearts. Words betray a confidence regarding the real me. And wouldn't this mean as well that words are a reflection of our relationship to Him? If He indeed is the treasure of our hearts, if our hearts are rooted in walking in ways to please Him, then our words will reflect that. If, however, all we have is a religion that is simply a habitual, professional, well-practiced ritual, then ultimately it's our words that will unmask the fact that our hearts are far from Him.

There's a relatively long list of speech patterns that erode the respect platform of a shepherd. They could be grouped into categories of words that express anger, penalize, manipulate, control, intimidate, belittle, or self-enhancing words that serve to advance the shepherd rather than the sheep. But regardless of the categories, there are specific types of words that, like termites, gnaw at the strength of the platform of respect.

Let's look at a list of types of talk that erode character. Though incomplete, the list is certainly long enough to get us started on some remedial heart repair that will produce speech patterns that establish a quality of talk worthy of respect.

Gossip

Gossip is sharing damaging information about someone or something with another person who is not a part of the solution. It may be true or untrue (at which point it becomes a lethal combination of gossip and lying), but the fact that it may be true does not provide sufficient rationale for sharing it. We don't need to tell everyone everything we know, even if it is true, and especially if it casts a dark shadow across another. When we look past our tongues to examine our hearts in regard to gossip, it may demonstrate that we are more concerned about ourselves than about others. When we share negative information, we somehow feel better about ourselves—"At least we're not like that . . ." which deters us, then, from taking personal responsibility for what we are like. And given the fact that it's self-serving at another's expense, it's clearly a violation of love. If we cared about the people we were gossiping about, we wouldn't want to tell what we know about them. But we would be thinking and praying about ways that we could help them. As God's Word says, "True love covers a multitude of sins."

I remember hearing some devastating news about a very dear friend of mine. Had I heard it about someone else, I may have been prone to hit the phone and share the news with someone who should know especially so they could "pray more intelligently" about the matter. I would have felt significant to be the one to have the scoop. But in this case my first impulse was to not tell a soul, but to call him, pray with him, and seek to help him. The reason that impulse was there was not because I'm not prone to gossip about others, but because I cared so much about him that I wanted to protect him and not expose him.

In addition to the fact that gossip reflects an unloving heart, it may also unmask an insecure heart that has not yet cultivated security and significance in our relationship to Christ but rather seeks to establish our significance by posturing ourselves against or above others.

Gossip and slander plant impressions that are often unjust. While the individual who is the brunt of the verbal abuse may have repented, reconciled, and redirected his life, those who have logged the data assume that they remain as reported and will probably continue to spread the outdated news with no awareness of what is gloriously new about the individual.

Unfortunately, when we realize the damage we have done it is often too late to undo it. One small informational leak quickly floods masses of hearts and minds. Everyone loves to tell a good story.

Realizing his error of spreading damaging information, a young man went to the village monk and asked him how to undo his careless talk. The monk said to take a basket of feathers and place a feather on the doorstep of each house in the village and when he was finished to go back and retrieve them. Obviously impossible. Once the feather of negative information is laid at the doorstep of another's life there is no hope of knowing to how many others it has blown.

Slander

While gossip and slander are very close, the definitive difference is that slander is sharing negative information with the *intent* to hurt. Slander is usually born out of some wrong that has been done either to ourselves or to another that we know. It is a means of revenge, a way to settle the score. Slander reflects that our hearts have not yet learned to give our enemies to God and permit Him to care for them (Rom. 12:17-21; 1 Peter 2:19-25). Slanderous speech as well may reflect a heart that refuses to recognize its own part of the wrong. In every conflict there is at least an implication that I may have played a part in stimulating the offense. Slander enables us to avoid personal responsibility by focusing on another's fault. Slander reflects an inability to place conflict into the kind of response patterns that Scripture teaches ultimately bring resolution (Matt. 5:43-48). It reflects as well an unwillingness in our hearts to suffer when necessary with a patient spirit, trusting God to protect us, deal with our enemies, and work all things together for good . . . the good of His glory and gain.

Lying

If I were to prioritize the most damaging erosions of the tongue, lying would have to be near the top. Primarily because it is our occupation to be truth tellers. To represent a God who is always, consistently, faithfully true. To represent a God whose words are always true.

It is sobering to note that one of the characteristics of those who endure an eternal punishment in hell fire is that they are liars. And we might note as well that when Christ reproved the Pharisees for being untruthful about Him, He associated it directly with the work of their father, the devil, who was, as Christ said, "a liar from the beginning." A case in point is the original invasion of God's perfect world by our adversary when it was through the well-crafted mediums of beguilement, deceit, and lying that the universe fell through two hearts that believed the lie. Which says something, doesn't it, about the victimization of those who believe us when through our false words we deny them the privilege of perceiving and responding to life based on reality.

A lying tongue betrays some very fundamental heart issues that need to be remediated. It reflects that at the core of our being, we are more concerned about the advancement, protection, and maintenance of ourselves than we are about the primacy of reality and truth. People whose primary agenda is centered on self will quickly prevaricate when something threatens that self-centered agenda. Lying may reflect that there are sins in our lives that we are trying to mask. Lying may reflect as well that we have been slothful and failed to live up to our responsibilities; hence we resort to dishonesty to cover the shortfall. Or perhaps lying simply reflects that we have become overcommitted and are unable to fulfill our commitments which tempts us to manufacture excuses to cover the residue of our overcommitment. Whatever the heart reason for lying might be, fewer things erode respect and undermine trust like lying.

Deceit

A close relative to lying, deceit seeks to gain some advantage by masking part of the truth, twisting the details, or manipulating the communication to effect a less-than-true communication of the set of facts. Deceit reveals the same core realities that lying does, except that it is not as blatant in its presentation. It's more elusive than a blatant lie, but equally as devastating. As the poet said, "Oh, what a tangled web we weave when first we practice to deceive."

Beguilement

We are beguiled when we draw a wrong conclusion from a set of facts, and our tongues beguile others when we share those false conclusions even though we believe that our conclusions are correct. This propensity has devastating impact on a community of believers. It probably tracks false information more quickly because it is so perceptually innocent.

When Satan sabotaged the universe he posed a set of facts in a way that would lead Eve to draw the wrong conclusion and act accordingly. God had said that they could eat of every tree in the Garden except for one. At that point one could conclude that God had been expansively generous in granting them access to all but one. When Satan came to Eve he staged the facts like this: "Indeed, has God said, 'You shall not eat from every tree of the garden'?" (Gen. 3:1) The conclusion would be that God was less than generous, restrictive, and limiting—a conclusion that quickly eroded gratitude, appreciation, and loyalty, and set the stage for her heart to be vulnerable to his devastating intent for her life . . . and ours.

While pastoring in Kokomo, Indiana I took our garbage can out to the curb and noticed a few empty beer cans that had been scattered on our lawn by someone who had no doubt thrown them out of the window of a car as they passed by. Innocently, I picked them up, threw them in the garbage can, put the lid on it, and went off to the office. Later that day it struck me that if the people who service our garbage noted the beer cans tumbling out of my trash can and knew that I pastored the local church down the road, it would be easy for them to come to the conclusion that the parson imbibes—worse yet, for them to share it with others in the town. And while nothing could be further from the truth, the facts did seem to point in that direction.

I have been amazed throughout the brief history of my life at how often I have drawn an initial conclusion from a set of facts only to find out later that when a few additional facts were added to the picture, my conclusions needed to be changed. And needless to say there was a warranted sense of shame when I thought of who I had shared it with and the damage that beguilement had done to the perceptions of others toward the situation. We've all been around ministry long enough, haven't we, to know that there are two sides to every story and that a wise person refrains from judgment until both sides have their say?

Hearts that are committed to patiently wait for all the facts; to love enough to believe the best until proven otherwise, are hearts that guard a shepherd's tongue from beguiling others.

Murmuring

One of the characteristics of the Children of Israel as they went through the wilderness was that they had a murmuring and complaining spirit. This brought tremendous displeasure to God, because, as the Old Testament notes, it was a direct reflection of a lack of gratitude in what God had provided and a lack of appreciation for His sovereign management of their lives. There probably are fewer groups of people more prone to murmuring and complaining than shepherds. We are so often unheeded, unheralded, underloved, and underpaid. If you stop and think about it, there are a lot of reasons for us to grouch our way through the ministry. A heart that has learned to trust God to provide for every need; to trust God to withhold provision or praise when it's in His best plan to do so; to realize that we all deserve nothing and that even redemption is more than we deserve, and to be grateful for it is a heart that reflects an attitude free of grumbling and complaining.

Paul stressed the importance of this area of character when he wrote to the church at Philippi, "Do all things without grumbling or disputing; that you may prove yourselves to be blameless and innocent, children of God above reproach in the midst of a crooked and perverse generation, among whom you appear as lights in the world" (Phil. 2:14-15).

Criticism

This devastating item on the list emanates from the all-too-prevalent pressure from our obsession with significance to tear others down. It often reflects a self-righteous heart that has ceased to be internally honest with its own failures. It's not that we shouldn't be discerning and careful to observe what is right and wrong. But it does mean that we process that observation in a way that is pleasing to God, by going first to the person and to that person alone, seeking to clarify misunderstandings and draw appropriate conclusions. As Matthew 18:15 teaches, if the brother responds, then you have won a brother. If he doesn't, then you should process it with another and ultimately, if necessary, to the church. Galatians 6:1-2 counsels, "Brethren, even if a man is caught in any trespass, you who are spiritual, restore such a one in a spirit of gentleness; looking to yourselves, lest you too be tempted. Bear one another's burdens, and thus fulfill the law of Christ."

A critical shepherd will foster a critical flock. And that critical attitude may very well someday rise up against the shepherd and derail his ministry.

Boasting

As shepherds we are prone to exhibit boasting tendencies. Perhaps because so few others seem ready to recognize and affirm our greatness. Yet, when Paul wrote to the Philippians in chapter 2, verse 3, and said, "Do nothing from selfishness or empty conceit," he phrased the term "empty conceit" in a rather graphic literary expression. The *King James* calls it "vain glory." The word for vain means vapor, nothing. The word "glory" means to enhance, enlarge, and advance. Paul reflects that self-centered talk is like puffing up our nothingness. Any great or glorious reality about our lives is always directly, completely attributable to God. He is the One who has given us our background, our temperament, our talents, and our gifts. He is the One who has provided opportunities and exposure to a hundred dozen influences that have shaped us and made us what we are. Nothing is more distasteful to our Lord than the glorification of ourselves when the glory belongs to Him. In fact, it might be well for us to remind each other that when Nebuchadnezzar in the Old Testament boasted of himself and his kingdom after knowing full well that it was God who had provided all this for him, that God, unwilling to have anyone compete with His glory, assigned him to the field like a beast to eat the grass until he repented.

At the base of a boasting tongue is a heart that has forgotten that God is the gracious reason for all we are and all we do and that the chief end of man is to enjoy God and to glorify Him forever. We cannot glorify Him and glorify ourselves. The two are mutually exclusive. A boasting tongue, no matter how subtle, sets up an environment where the glory is focused on us. Boasting tempts others to compete with our "can you top this?" attitude and will often create resentment toward our self-adulation. Is it any wonder that the writer of the Proverbs said, "Let another praise you and not your own mouth; a stranger and not your own lips"? (Prov. 27:2)

Exaggeration

Do we dare mention this, given that it is probably the most universal flaw of shepherd talk? Like one parishioner said, "My pastor doesn't exaggerate. He just blows up the truth so that everyone can see." It's so easy, isn't it, to stretch a detail, to expand a set of numbers, to give a story a spin that makes it more compelling? But at our heart level, it reflects a lack of trust that God can use just the average realities of existence to catch the attention of hearts, and that it is truth that wins in the long haul. If our people come to believe that we exaggerate, even if they joke about it as being "Evangelistically speaking," there is something that happens to our trustworthiness and ultimately to respect. How will they know when we are exaggerating or communicating reality? If numbers, statistics, or stories can't stand on their own, then they're probably not worth sharing.

How do we deal with our propensity to these kinds of lethal speech problems? Remediation begins within. Good and godly words are sourced in our relationship with Christ. When it comes to our words, it's not their recitation but rather this relationship that is paramount. Regardless of what happens outside of, around, and what is directed toward my life, Christ becomes the compelling, controlling influence in my heart and as such engenders speech that is consistent with Him. Christ's love inhibits gossip and slander. Our trust in Him and His truthfulness in us make lying, deceit, and beguilement unwelcome and unnecessary. Our gratitude toward Him muzzles murmuring. Criticism is cured in Christ's call to help and heal. And it is our commitment to His glory through us that puts boasting and exaggerating pastors back into the context of reality. As our relationship to Him blossoms, our words will be words that reflect warmth, healing, helping, careful inquiry, wise perspectives, discernment, righteousness, and justice. Our words will reflect His truth, spoken at times courageously but always compassionately. Words that are resourced out of the treasure house of all that Christ is within me are words that enable us to obey Paul's words in Colossians 4:6, "Let your speech always be with grace, seasoned, as it were, with salt, so that you may know how you should respond to each person."

When I took the pastorate at the Highland Park Baptist Church, I became quickly aware that the first pastor had been a giant of a man.

While he had long before gone on to heaven, his memory and the aura of his ministry remained. He served the church for forty-one distinguished years. He left a legacy that was fondly recalled.

I often wonder what it takes to do so well in the same place over the long haul. I got a glimpse of it one day when talking with the person who served for years as his secretary. She related to me that he was a wonderful and godly man. But what she unfolded next seemed to help me understand why he had been so effective. She recalled how his wife had become a serious problem in the church at one time in his ministry, he was falsely accused of a compromising relationship. Though it was clearly proven to be untrue, it was a long and arduous season of trouble for him. What was surprising to me was that his secretary was now telling me that, in light of these kinds of struggles, she never recalled hearing Dr. Coltman say a negative thing about anybody. Interesting, isn't it, that his heart-controlled tongue was a distinct and impressive memory? A reason for respect and admiration through all the years had stuck with her and had impressed her. It's interesting as well that this may have been the reason that his platform remained strong and his respect uneroded. He had been a shepherd whose speech directly reflected his belief in Jesus Christ, and that belief had created an exemplary life worthy of respect.

A good rule of thumb when it comes to talking is, *when in doubt . . . don't.* It's better to slow down, engage the brain, check with the indwelling Christ, the Manager of our souls, and carefully ponder the moment before a response leaks out. In fact, silence is not a bad option on occasion. Proverbs 17:28 tells us, "Even a fool, when he keeps silent, is considered wise; when he closes his lips, he is counted prudent."

Our prayer should continually be that of the psalmist when he closed the 19th Psalm: "Let the words of my mouth and the meditation of my heart be acceptable in Thy sight, O Lord, my rock and my Redeemer" (Ps. 19:14).

CONDUCT

Equally as important in terms of our visible exampleship, as Paul notes in his list, is the issue of our *conduct.* The word "conduct" in the New Testament is a general word for our behavior. And it's important to note that in both the Old Testament and the New Testament, this concept always demands a modifier. Everyone has conduct. The issue is what *kind* of conduct? Is it bad or good? Righteous or unrighteous? Admirable or reprehensible? Appropriate or inappropriate? Average or excellent? Paul instructs us to guarantee that our conduct accurately reflects our belief in Christ, who makes such an imprint on our lives that our conduct is above question and reproach. And while our public conduct can sometimes be disciplined to conform to people's expectations, it's probably well said that the true measure of character is what our conduct is like at home and in comfortable confines where we do not need to impress anyone, and more specifically what we are like when no one is watching and when we believe that no one will ever find out.

When targeting conduct, we could probably generate a hefty list of items that need to be conformed to our belief walk with Christ; conduct that expresses the kind of life that is not only above reproach but compellingly magnetic in terms of winning the hearts of others to follow us in similar ways. If we were to itemize a lengthy list we'd run out of room and might miss something that needs to be targeted. So let me suggest that each of us measure our own private and public conduct and cast it in the revealing light of the character of Christ.

Beyond the specifics, however, there are three conduct arenas which are critical for leaders in terms of maintaining the kind of respect that will keep the platform of ministry strong. They relate to our conduct in the arenas of *work, women,* and *wealth.* If not managed well, these create deep black holes in ministry.

Work

We dealt earlier with the important concept of not being slothful in our work but diligent in our assignments and our follow-through. Ministry is a marvelous place for people who like to let the work slide and increase leisure time. Let me say that we need to learn not only to work hard but to play hard, to parent hard, and to partner hard. These are four critical arenas of the application of our work in terms of time and energy.

Let's advance the discussion into *how* we work, to be shepherds who work with integrity, not short-cutting, cheating, or neglecting the way we handle the fundamental duties of our task. To work without grumbling, out of a genuine spirit of love toward those around us in gratitude for the privilege of serving Christ. The work will not always be easy, inviting, or fulfilling, but the work of Christ is always worthwhile. He is always worthy of our best—even if those we are serving don't present themselves as worthy objects of our service.

I am in the ministry today, from a human perspective, because of the attitude of my parents toward the work of ministry. As I grew up I watched them struggle through many problems that related to parish work. From my perspective there were times that they were unappreciated, unfairly and unjustly treated, and mostly underpaid—at least that seemed to be true since my dad's constant refrain when we asked for something we wanted was, "We can't afford it." Yet in all of the struggles of shepherding, I never recall my dad once complaining about the work of ministry. In fact, he consistently communicated to me that to be called to serve the flock of God was the highest privilege one could have. He worked throughout his ministry life with a good and gracious spirit, and it was that attitude toward the work of the ministry that made me willing to hear the call of Christ when it was my turn to pick up the torch. Given the value that my dad placed on the big picture of ministry, he was able to work *willingly* and *gladly*. There are other aspects to the way in which we conduct the work of ministry that will advance our capacity to be examples and enable a watching flock to respect us.

We need to work *efficiently*, making the best use of our time by prioritizing, delegating, and completing assigned tasks in the proper frame of expectations. We need to work *appropriately* in terms of appropriate timing, appropriate responses, appropriate promises, appropriate planning, appropriate performance, and appropriate dress. If we serve in an arena where people are up at 6 and off to work early, whether it be in the fields, or commuting, or whatever, then it may be appropriate for us to start our day early as well. It's a difficult issue for those who work hard during the week when they call the pastor only to find that he's still not up or still isn't in the office after they've been up and involved in their life tasks for three to four hours. We need to learn to work *smartly* by knowing our limits, our stress points, marking the boundaries clearly, and managing what happens between those boundary points with wisdom. We'll deal with this in greater detail later, but suffice it to say that if we're not smart about our work, we might very well be consumed by our work.

Women

Not only will our flock watch how we conduct our work, but they will watch intently how we conduct ourselves with women. There is probably no greater residual fear in the life of a flock than the sense that their shepherd might either be susceptible to or prey upon the women in his life and in his flock. Four years of exposure at Dallas Theological Seminary grounded in my consciousness the reality that a leader's conduct with women was one of the key areas to guard. The tragedy of failure in this arena, particularly if it's a failure with someone in the church, is that it violates the shepherd's primary duty to keep the flock safe and to provide an environment where his sheep can feel unthreatened, safe, and able to advance their lives in spiritual growth in the imitation of

Christ. A shepherd who preys upon anyone in the flock denies the very essence of what God has called him to do. It's betrayal.

It's probably not necessary to rehearse the downsides of moral failure, since it seems to me that we are all well aware of its pitfalls. But before we talk about guarding against it, we need to probably remind each other that fewer things are more immediately damaging and disqualifying in ministry than how our relationship to the women around us is perceived. Even if we don't morally fail, if our conduct is perceived as flirtatious or encouraging a relationship beyond the boundaries of propriety, our capacity to shepherd will quickly be discounted.

And it's not just that perceptual trust is eroded. Think of the statement we make to Christ when we value the ego massage of a flirtatious affirmation or enjoy a relationship with someone outside the boundaries of what is right. Succumbing to temptation sends loud signals toward heaven. It basically says that we love this—whatever it is—more than we love Him. Keeping our walk fresh with Him and our primary focus of expressing our gratitude and love to Him by pleasing Him will go a long way to protect our propensity toward using women to gratify our need for affirmation and gratification.

We can also guard our relationship with women by keeping focused on what it truly means to love another person. It means to seek their best. For spiritual leaders it means to create an environment that will stimulate them to growth, to the glory of Christ through their lives and the gain of His kingdom through their service. Shepherds need to know early on the difference between love and lust and avoid the lustful impulses that will in some measure be ever present, and continue to track their lives toward an expression of the love of Christ by keeping women safe and encouraging their sanctification.

The most helpful pattern to cultivate in our lives from a human standpoint, is to pour ourselves into our relationship with our own wife. Learning to love her and to know the joy of a developing relationship with her will build important fences around our hearts. And in case there are some of us who think our wives are rather unlovable, it may very well be that the way we have treated them is the reason that they seem to be somewhat less than desirable. Before we camp on any excuse to bail out of our responsibilities to God's chosen partner for us, we need to carefully examine whether or not we have loved them with the unconditional love of Christ, willingly sacrificing our time, energy, and attention for their best interests regardless of how they treat us or reward us (Eph. 5:25-33). When people get the distinct impression that we are deeply in love with our wife, that we adore her and still hold her in awe, it defends us against women who, for one reason or another, are drawn to us. And they will be drawn to us. By our very position we represent so much that their hearts long for. We are leaders—strong, compassionate, pastoral, sensitive, and portray an image of spiritual vitality. In reality, few of us measure high on any of those scales, but that is the image that our office communicates. Given that these qualities are so much of what a woman longs for in her man, we immediately have a measure of magnetism that we can never take advantage of for our own gratification but must always use for the advance of His cause and the glory of His name.

We protect ourselves against the dynamics of our office by cultivating a growing relationship to our spouse and communicating our love by the way we look at her in public and the way we don't look at other women. By a compassionate touch, loyal words, a wink across a crowded room that sends messages that no one can decode, and other verbal and nonverbal expressions of our love to her.

Martie and I would often walk out of the service together, and periodically I would hold her hand as we would walk the aisle during the postlude. I did it for no other reason than the fact that I like to hold her hand. I found it interesting, however, to see the kind of response that engendered. I got a note from a parishioner who said that every time she saw me leaving the service with Martie hand-in-hand, she would weep for the happiness that it brought to her heart. Obviously we don't stage these events for effect, but when we genuinely love our wife in a growing relationship that is fostered in the private confines of our home and is observed in our public life, we create a conduct that is exemplary and compelling. A conduct that not only sets a stimulating example, but shuts down suspicion, discourages false hopes in women's hearts, and erects a retaining wall against the ever-increasing overflow of our passions that threaten to wash the platform of respect down the river of our desires.

While we are managing our conduct as an expression of our authentic belief in Christ in terms of both our work and our relationship to women, a third area of concern in relationship to our conduct needs to be considered, and that is our attitude toward *wealth.*

Wealth

Wealth has a phenomenal power to manipulate both attitude and action. And while it is true that no one can live without it, no shepherd can afford to live for it. Apart from the profit of the kingdom and the glory of His name, ministry is a not-for-profit business. As soon as we begin to do what we do for financial gain, everything distorts.

God taught me a major money lesson early on. I was in my very first pastorate, in a small church planting situation, and was asked to speak at a youth banquet in Indiana. Since I was pastoring in Ohio, it was my first invitation to speak out of the state. I was enamored by the thought that someone from way over in Indiana would want me to come and speak. We were living on a subsistence-level income that the small faithful band of believers generously gave us out of their own sacrifice. Yet on many occasions, as Howard Hendricks says, there was too much month left at the end of the money. Through that time, we had watched God marvelously supply for our needs. In fact, those were years of the strengthening of our faith, and the anchoring of the reality of God's caring nature in the lives of our children as they, with us, observed His provision for our needs. But given the financial pressure that we were living in, part of the intrigue of this invitation was the ever-alluring honorarium. I drove to the banquet, gave my talk, said my prayer, and when it was all done waited for the coordinator of the evening to hand me the envelope. He didn't seem to be real quick on the draw, so I stayed and helped them take down a few chairs and chatted and lingered. Finally, after everyone was gone, I got in my car and drove home late that night. I went to bed wondering why it was that I had not gotten any pay. Not even a check for expenses.

Through the days ahead, I felt my heart sour toward those who had invited me, and wondered why they had taken advantage of me like that. It wasn't long into that process that the Holy Spirit began to work me over. *Why had I gone there? Had I gone there for money or for ministry? Was it for cash or for Christ that I had given my time that night? And hadn't I already learned that God would supply my needs in His way and His time? When it came to provision, was that the business of people around me, or was my prosperity managed through His hands?* I felt a growing sense of shame at my crude cash-oriented response. Martie and I confessed our attitude and committed ourselves that from that time on, we would never serve for money. It was a liberating moment that has charted the course of our lives through the waters of ministry ever since.

The next day, a check for expenses and an honorarium came in the mail. An interesting sequence of events in terms of timing. We're convinced that God delayed the reward until we had gotten such a primal issue of ministry straight.

And while I had the honorarium phase of it figured out, the salary issue became a haunting hindrance to my spirit as that planted church began to grow and flourish. In the early days, Martie and I found that the sacrificial generosity of the flock to pay us a salary that was clearly an expression of their love for us built gratitude in our hearts toward them. As the ministry went on, however, the growth of the flock permitted that the salary could be expanded, which was done on an annual basis. Our family grew, expectations for ministry that cost us money increased, and our housing needs changed. And while God saw fit to make sure that we could pay our bills, we sometimes struggled with the way in which we were paid. We had in our church several professional educators in leadership positions, and the prevailing attitude in salary formation became pegged to paying their pastor what an average salary for a teacher in the community would be. For them, that was a way to benchmark the salary to a community standard. But as we often struggled with our own finances, we viewed the perspective a little cynically. After all, teachers got all summer off, a couple of weeks at Christmas, and a spring break. My three weeks of vacation hardly seemed like a match for that, and many of my nights were taken up with ministry responsibility, as well as most of my weekends.

It's interesting that the same congregation that brought us joy early on from their sacrificial giving became a source of frustration later, even though they were giving us more than they had in those early days. The problem was not theirs. The problem was mine. My focus was all wrong. Instead of focusing on the Lord as the One who is the Provider for my needs, I had wrongly viewed the congregation as my provider and ended up struggling with my feelings toward some of them. A distortion of a shepherd's perspective! Particularly given the fact that God had worked overtime to prove to our family that He could and would, in His time and way, provide for all of our needs.

I repented. Again. And again.

The material seduction of the shepherd's heart is also played out in the arena of comparison and resultant covetousness. Some of those in that first church who were humanly responsible for our salary were teachers who in the summertime were able to have second jobs and through the year had alternative sources of income. Most of them drove better cars, lived in far better homes, and had greater financial capacities to satisfy some of their wants and desires. As we compared ourselves to them, it was easy to fall into the ditch of discouragement and disappointment—which, by the way, provided a field day for growing negativism.

Comparison not only to others in the church but even to others in ministry can be a defeating force in our hearts. Other shepherds and spiritual leaders who seemingly have flocks who care and provide for them, friends who pamper them with increased levels of prosperity, and high-level speaking engagements with honorariums more lucrative than ours. What we lose in the process is the valuable shepherding context of *contentment.* The contentment that sources its confidence in Christ's capacity to supply for our needs and delivers us from the seductive force of the wealth trap in ministry. Paul told Timothy to be sure to communicate the formula that godliness plus contentment is what gain consists of. Unfortunately, some shepherds switch the formula as though it reads "godliness plus gain equals contentment."

When we as spiritual leaders keep complaining that we "don't get what we deserve," we need to remind one another that if we got what we really deserved, there would be no heaven, only hell, for us. Christ has given us a full and eternal redemption. And none of us deserved it. Anything, whether less or plenty, that He gives in addition to our salvation is already beyond what we deserve. We need to have the attitude of the Puritan imprisoned for his faith who, when brought bread and water from the prison guard, would often lift his eyes to heaven in grateful prayer and exclaim, "All of this and heaven too?"

My dad gave me a piece of advice early on that has served me well. He told me that whenever he candidated for a new ministry, he never talked about money. He knew that if it was God's place, God would provide, and he never wanted the issue clouded with currency. I adopted his practice and found that God has always been faithful to provide. Needless to say, if someone offers a ministry position where the cash is far less than sufficient to provide minimal support for your family, it may be God's way of shutting the door. But it would be hard for me to believe that money should ever be an upfront issue when we are negotiating.

It's not only the attitude toward *gaining* wealth that becomes a conduct issue, but it is also the *distribution* of wealth. I'm appalled at how many of us as shepherds do not share our resources in faithful stewardship back to the ministries that we serve. I've often wondered what the financial secretary or treasurer—or whoever it is that counts the cash at church—thinks about the fact that there's rarely support expressed from their own pastor. Needless to say, an issue like this quickly erodes our respect and credibility and grants permission and excuse to others to not be financially involved. Shepherds should express in their conduct that it has been the joy of their lives to give sacrificially back to the Lord's work and to watch God provide, sometimes miraculously, for their needs.

Conduct is a reflection of character, and character is nurtured and matured in a growing, submitted, and committed relationship to Christ. When our character is developed by the application of our belief to our conduct, we strengthen the platform of respect to be effective.

All three arenas of conduct that we have dealt with are becoming increasingly out of vogue in our culture. We live in a culture that is obsessed with *leisure* rather than work, driven by *lust* rather than love, and dedicated to *loot* instead of spiritual gain.

A counterculture shepherd models that life in Christ is clearly and wonderfully different than life in this fallen culture in speech and conduct.

Chapter Seven

Leading through Loving

Substance, Sensitivity, Style

In their book *Credibility: How Leaders Gain and Lose It, Why People Demand It,* management gurus Kouzes and Posner cite their research on what people expect from and are drawn to in terms of relating to a leader. Three of the most frequently selected items in their research were honesty, competence, and inspiration.

In reflecting on Paul's list in 1 Timothy 4:12, it should be noted that *honesty* is largely communicated through the integrity of our talk and that *competence* is directly related to people's expectation for appropriate conduct in leadership. And if *inspiration* is what followers are looking for, as their research indicates, then the last three character qualities on Paul's list—love, faith, and purity—would certainly provide a basis for inspirational leadership. What could be more inspiring to a flock than to see their shepherd exhibit the dynamic love of Christ and project unswerving and nonnegotiated faith in all that He is and does, and who at the very core of his being is unquestionably pure?

Their research supports Paul's thesis that character is foundational to respect as they underscore the importance of leading from a platform of credibility that is bolstered by the qualities mentioned in our text.

> What we have found quite unexpectedly in our initial research and have affirmed ever since is that, above all else, people want leaders who are credible. We want to believe in our leaders. We want to

> have faith and confidence in them as people. We want to believe that their word can be trusted, that they have the knowledge and skill to lead, and that they are personally excited and enthusiastic about the direction in which we are headed.[1]

And while the direction for our lives as shepherds is not ultimately sourced in management material, it should not go without notice that, in a world that discounts character and encourages people to live lives that reflect style over substance, ultimately the truth of the way God has built us to lead does not escape even secular research. And if it is true for them, it must be more true for us. We manage an eternal cause and are dealing with not only the immediate needs of people, but ultimately their eternal destinies.

If the character qualities that are so essential to us as shepherds, our talk and our walk, are to be consistently reflected in our lives, then the three remaining qualities of which Paul speaks will provide both impetus and support. Our capacity to reflect exemplary speech and conduct will be supported and enhanced by our commitment to what follows on this list: love, faith, and purity.

The secularization of our society makes us increasingly aware of the fact that everything around us will work against our development of these three remaining nonnegotiable character commodities. Our world encourages us to be committed to a narcissistic sense of self-service and not to be lovingly concerned about others. This is not a world in which it's easy to believe or to have faith, but rather a world in which the departure from truth has made us skeptical and cynical about most everything. And yet God calls us as shepherds to exhibit a life that is motivated and managed by faith. And what shall we say about purity in such a hedonistic, pleasure-at-all-costs, impure context—both in relationship to our motives and to our morals?

If we have loving hearts and lives that are grounded in faith, lives that are clean to the core, then both our speech and our conduct will make it clear that love, faith, and purity indeed are imbedded in our being. Think of how solid a platform of leadership this creates in a world that sinks lower and lower in regard to these characteristics. A leader who demonstrates a growing dynamic in all five areas will shine as a compelling beacon to both his flock and his community. As such, there will be a magnetism about him that will be a touch point for the kind of relationships that are necessary for a shepherd to cultivate to effectively lead his flock. There is no leading if it is first and foremost not leading through living. Leadership is a matter not of pushing, demanding, or cajoling others to go somewhere they ought to go. Leading leaders go there first and by their lives compel others to follow.

Let's look in some detail at what it would take to develop love, faith, and purity not only as a support for our speech and our conduct, not only as an indispensable part of the infrastructure of our platform for effective shepherding, but also as a compelling counterstatement in a culture whose narcissism, cynicism, and hedonism have made them strategic values that are compellingly rare.

LOVE, THE RELATIONAL KEY

When Paul pinpoints love as the next personhood issue on his list, he anchors it directly in the heart of the list, preceded by speech and conduct and followed by faith and purity. Whether or not that was intentional would be hard to affirm, but when we understand love in its biblical dimension, it would be understandable if he had done it intentionally. A heart dedicated to the love of God will produce both speech and conduct that is useful in our Lord's hand. Loving shepherds speak like it and act like it and thus create a strengthened platform from which to be effective for Christ. It should not go unnoticed either that faith and purity follow. In order to unconditionally love, our love must be grounded in an unshakable faith in God, not in those we are loving, and must be exercised from both motives and morals that are unquestionably pure.

Love is at the heart of what it means to be a shepherd. Shepherds are caring, flock-focused individuals whose primary motivation is not the interest of self but the interest of the safety, security, and satisfaction of the flock. Given this, a discussion of love in terms of the shepherd's ministry is of great importance. And it must be more than a discussion. It must lead to a commitment that transcends the circumstances of the shepherd's life or the configuration of the shepherd's congregation. True love does not depend on its environment; it dramatically affects its environment. And speaking of environment, we need to recognize up front that love in the biblical sense is a counterculture commodity, given the fact that the only thing our culture seems to know about love is a distortion of it, which would be more properly called lust, and a reverse focus of it which is known as self-centeredness. If we are to be truly effective in this dramatically different society, we must demonstrate the difference that love can make in an unloving culture.

Love is the key to good relationships, and good relationships are indispensable to effective leadership. According to Kouzes and Posner, "Leadership is a reciprocal relationship between those who choose to lead and those who decide to follow. Any discussion of leadership must attend to the dynamics of this relationship. Strategies, tactics, skills, and practices are empty unless we understand the fundamental aspirations that connect leaders and their constituents."[2]

Love expressed from the shepherd and experienced by the flock is a link that "connects leaders and their constituents."

Perhaps we need to begin in terms of defining what Paul means here by love. True love is others-directed. And it's the *others* that make ministry such a struggle. The philosopher Rousseau is supposed to have said, "The more I get to know people the more I love my dog." You've probably felt like that at times.

In a *Peanuts* cartoon, Lucy challenged Linus about his dreams for the future. She said to him, "Linus, you can't be a doctor. You hate mankind!" Linus responded, "Lucy, you don't understand. I love mankind. It's people that I can't stand."

The trouble with people is that they can be our greatest joy and source of satisfaction, and at the same time our worst nightmare. I've often thought that ministry would be a cakewalk if it weren't for people. But then if it weren't for people, there would be no ministry. It is the inevitable commodity of our calling. Everything else is dispensable. Programs, buildings, budgets, and the like could all be peeled away, and as long as there were people, there would be a need for shepherding—the need for a shepherd who is committed to loving the sheep.

Given the importance of the love factor in our personhood, let's bring the quality into clear focus. There are at least four aspects to love. First, we must understand its specific *substance* so that it is not distorted into a warm, spineless, ethereal, mystical malaise of emotion that ultimately ends up working against the solid, substantive power of love. Enabling love to be what it needs to be in every situation demands that we not only understand its substance but also note that intrinsic to love is a *sequence* through which it flows. Additionally, there is an important *sensitivity* in the exercise of our love, without which the expenditure of love will drain our strength and leave us defeated and discouraged. And when all of this is done well, love develops a *style* of ministry in which not only the flock can prosper, but also from which the testimony of Jesus Christ can be enhanced.

SUBSTANCE

The ability of the Greek language to bring greater definition to words than English is a great benefit to our discussion of what the real substance of a shepherd's love is all about. As you probably know, there are several words in the Greek language for love, but the one that is used in particular here is a unique kind of love that stands in contrast to the normal cultural and instinctive kinds of love that often characterize our behavior. It is the love that is used of God for man and Christ for the lost as well as for His sheep. It is a love that transcends emotion, feeling, and fact, yet at the same time, when practiced properly, creates an environment in which a depth of emotion and feeling can flow based on the fact of a solid, unwavering love commitment from the shepherd. This *agape* love is the kind of love that *chooses to understand the needs of another and then responds to those needs by expending available resources to meet those needs.* It is the kind of love spoken of in John 3:16 when God so *loved* the world that He *gave* . . . He gave from the resources of His own capacities and abilities to meet us at the point of our need when we were hopelessly, helplessly lost in sin, so that we could be transitioned from the domain of darkness into the kingdom of His dear Son. Paul describes agape love in terms of Christ when he says, "But God demonstrates His own love toward us, in that while we were yet sinners, Christ died for us" (Rom. 5:8).

There are at least four elements to the substance of love that are relevant to leadership. These elements stand in sharp contrast to our society's spin on this quality. Substantive love is a *choice* that has a particular *direction* that creates a *feltness* and defines a particular *function* for the shepherd.

First, we should note that a shepherd's love is a *choice,* not a feeling. Count on it. There will always be a group of sheep that you'd rather send to the butcher. But shepherds who love only those whom they like fail the love test of shepherding. I doubt if God felt good about me as a sinner, about the fallen world, and the offense of sinners against Him. Love, however, drove Him to make a commitment to meeting my needs and to offering the option of rescue through the gift of His grace and goodness. If we wait until we feel like loving some people, we will wait a long time and deny ourselves a ministry characterized by the love of Christ. Seeing love as a choice enables us to minister to *all people,* even those we may not like. Even those who may not like us. I doubt if Christ always liked the skepticism of Thomas or the impetuousness of Peter. Temperament flaws have a tendency to rub us the wrong way and segment our love focus toward those who are likable and away from those who, for one reason or another, we don't like all that well. I find it important to remember as an undershepherd that God does not like my sinfulness, yet He loves me with all of His divine grace and power.

People come in lots of different configurations. They're not all cut out likably, conformed to predictable molds suited perfectly to my expectations and personality. But then God does not require that I like everyone. It's liberating to discover that true love enables me to choose to love even those I don't like. It releases me to be sensitively concerned about the needs of all in my care. True love seeks to look beyond the fault to search for the need that we can meet. In fact, love applied correctly would no doubt make some in our care more likable.

Biblical love also has a *direction* to it . . . a distinct outward focus. In fact, when we understand the true definition of agape love, we realize that the opposite of this kind of biblical love is not hate but self-centeredness. Which puts us as shepherds in particular tension since we so quickly see ministry in terms of self-centered agendas. Seeing ministry in terms of our own programs, prosperity, advancement, and affirmation will tempt us to use, manipulate, control, and even abuse people in the process of ministry. What a tragic contradiction of true love. Shepherds who cease to love their flocks but rather use their flocks for their own benefit, even when their self-advance is wrapped in the advance of God's work, end up destroying the flock. The Prophet Jeremiah spoke God's words to spiritual leaders in the Old Testament who led for their own gain and purposes when he wrote,

> "Woe to the shepherds who are destroying and scattering the sheep of My pasture!" declares the Lord. Therefore says the Lord God of Israel concerning the shepherds who are attending My people: "You have scattered My flock and driven them away, and have not attended to them; behold, I am about to attend to you for the evil of your deeds," declares the Lord. "Then I Myself shall gather the remnant of My flock out of all the countries where I have driven them and shall bring them back to their pasture; and they will be fruitful and multiply. I shall also raise up shepherds over them and they will tend them; and they will not be afraid any longer, nor be terrified, nor will any be missing," declares the Lord (Jer. 23:1-4).

The history of the church in America is full of tragic stories regarding shepherds whose focus was dedicated to using the church for the benefit of their own needs and desires, and in the process have battered the spirit of the flock, scattered the sheep, and damaged the testimony of Christ in their community.

It's interesting to note that God assures us that He will raise shepherds who have a tender and skillful touch to fill the void. Sometimes He will send them to replace the selfish shepherd and at other times He will send the sheep to follow another shepherd at an alternate church in the community. Sheep seek to follow a shepherd who lovingly cares for them and not for himself. It's the nature of sheep. It should be the nature of the shepherd.

One of the texts that has always been an anchor for my soul in terms of shepherding is the prayer of Solomon at the beginning of his reign. When God appeared to him in a dream and said, "Ask what you wish Me to give you," he could have asked for personal rewards as a result of the position to which he had just ascended. Instead he prayed for wisdom and discernment to lead the flock of God effectively: "And now, O Lord my God, Thou hast made Thy servant king in place of my father David, yet I am but a little child: I do not know how to go out or come in. And Thy servant is in the midst of Thy people which Thou hast chosen; a great people who cannot be numbered or counted for multitude. So give Thy servant an understanding heart to judge Thy people to discern between good and evil. For who is able to judge this great people of Thine?" (1 Kings 3:5, 7-9)

Mark this: "It was pleasing in the sight of the Lord that Solomon had asked this thing." Those of us who shepherd to please Him need to realize that God desires that we first and foremost care about what He cares about, and that is the welfare of His people. God's response to Solomon is highly instructive in regard to our own attitudes. He said, "Because you have asked this thing and have not asked for yourself long life, nor have asked riches for yourself, nor have you asked for the life of your enemies, but have asked for yourself discernment to understand justice, behold, I have done according to your words" (vv. 11-12). Then He went on to say that since Solomon had not asked for riches and honor, He would bestow those upon him as an act of His rewarding grace for Solomon's focus on the people of God.

A key principle: Shepherds need to be passionate in their loving care for the flock, and then trust God to bestow upon us in His time and in His way those things that we desire. When they are given as gifts from the hand of the Father who cares for His shepherds, they are never destructive or distorted in terms of our shepherding ministry. When they are grabbed at the expense of both the sheep and the shepherd's exemplary life, then a sure demise waits to claim its loss.

An effective shepherd understands that the substance of shepherding love goes beyond liking and chooses to focus on the needs of the flock. He understands that it is a matter of loving through a commitment that relates positively and constructively to the needs of those in his flock regardless of his own perspectives or pleasure. The shepherd checks his bag of resources to substantively meet real needs. He checks his time, talents, treasures, programs, alliances, and networks with other people and their resources. He checks the stockpile of the gifts of those in the extended flock and then seeks to marshal appropriate resources, whether his own or those of others, to focus like a laser beam of love on particular and personal needs within the assembly. Sometimes a shepherd's love response is personal, confidential, and pastorally intimate. Other times it is public and programmatic. At times it is carefully processed through a resensitizing of the congregation to needs within the flock through proclamation or education. Whatever the application, the shepherd must *choose* to *direct* his ministry toward a nonnegotiated focus on the real needs to which he is called to minister.

There is also a *feltness* to substantive love. When a shepherd is truly expressing love, his flock *feels* cared for; they will prosper in a context their felt needs are addressed; they will thrive in an environment where they are the objects of real compassion. The shepherd's reward is that he will feel a reciprocal sense of love and enjoy ministering to hearts that are open to his leadership. It has been well said that they "won't care how much you know until they know how much you care." And when they do know how much you care, an environment will be created where effective leadership can flourish. A felt environment that will resound with appeal in a world that cares less and less about one another, creating a culture where the increasing silence of isolation, loneliness, and despair is almost deafening.

Churches that build a caring, nurturing community in this increasingly lonely and despairing world lay out one of the clearest and most compelling welcome mats to those outside their walls. A church here in Chicago offers car repairs by mechanics in their church to widows and single parents. The Armitage Church, as we noted, opened school to the neighborhood when the Chicago school system failed to reach a budget agreement. Help for those in serious trouble with alcohol, abuse, pornography, and other deteriorations in our fractured society are finding hope and help in churches who are reaching out in the love of Christ with the bigger picture of ministry clearly in view.

As loving shepherds we will spend a lot of time rescuing lambs from thickets, extracting thorns, and cleaning wounds. But that is not the end. It needs to be done toward a larger purpose. Enabling sheep to come to wellness and safety is all done that they might grow and prosper on behalf of and for the benefit of the One to whom they belong. A shepherd lovingly heals, guides, guards, and feeds the flock ultimately to enable them to grow into the likeness of Christ, to enable them to glorify Him, and ultimately through their lives bring gain to the kingdom. The real need of the believer is to fulfill the role for which they have been created and redeemed. In fact, attending to the more immediate, pressing needs of the sheep takes on new meaning and energy when we realize that the purpose is to take them beyond their needs to the glory and gain of the kingdom of Christ. This goal realized will create a spiritual feltness that will radiate with vitality and energy on behalf of Christ in the life of the community of believers.

Loving as an expression of our choice directed to meet the felt needs of all the flock requires that we *function* as a servant to the sheep. Given the high position we hold as shepherds, servanthood is often put in tension with the perception that since we are leaders others should serve. Yet, lest any of us think that we are exempt from servanthood because of our position, we need to remember that Philippians 2 has taught us that Christ, holding the highest position in the universe, used that position as a platform from which to dedicate Himself as a servant to the eternal needs of mankind, that He might redeem a flock for the glory and gain of His Father. Unfortunately, we often perceive ministry through management paradigms that configure organizational charts that place the pastor, if not at the top, second only to the board of elders, and those in the church fall below them in a scattered array of functions. And while it is accurate that the shepherd does hold a particular sense of biblical authority in the flock, when it comes to function, the biblical organizational chart would have the mission of the church at the top; then under that, like a reverse pyramid, are the people in the flock, with the pastor at the point of the upside-down pyramid, to serve all of those in the flock with enabling resources to help them become all that they need to be in order to advance the mission of His church. This captures the mind-set of a servant shepherd. His heart lives in the what-can-I-do-to-help mode.

Love for the shepherd is a choice, not a feeling, to extend the resources of his life and ministry capacities to all of the flock, even those who for some reason are unlikable, focusing not on what is best for himself, but rather on what is best for them in a way that the love becomes a felt commodity among the congregation, the recipients of the generous and gracious acts of their shepherd who is functioning as their servant.

Love calls us to place our lives in sync with Paul's word to the church at Philippi when he said,

> Do nothing from selfishness or empty conceit, but with humility of mind let each of you regard one another as more important than himself; do not merely look out for your own personal interests, but also for the interests of others. Have this attitude in yourselves which was also in Christ Jesus, who, although He existed in the form of God, did not regard equality with God a thing to

> be grasped, but emptied Himself, taking the form of a bond-servant, and being made in the likeness of men. And being found in appearance as a man, He humbled Himself by becoming obedient to the point of death, even death on a cross (Phil. 2:3-8).

It was out of a heart of love that Christ became incarnate and functioned as the redeeming Servant of our needs. It was the key to a productive relationship with us and for us. We in turn need to become the incarnate likeness of Christ by replicating the same spirit of love. And it should not go unnoticed that in the work of the incarnate Christ on our behalf, He surrendered to an agenda beyond Himself; was willing to sacrifice the perks, pleasures, and comforts of heaven; counted Himself to be a servant, and suffered when necessary, that the redemptive work of the cross might be effected (vv. 6-8). This process of love acts as the pattern for our love as well. As such, our substantive shepherding love becomes a powerful tool in our portfolio of ministry assets when it is processed through a dedication to be a shepherd to others like Christ was to us. And it is that surrendered, sacrificing, serving, suffering-when-necessary process that produces the most pure and powerful form of love for our congregations.

A commitment to this substantive kind of love calls for deliberateness in our love. True biblical love is intentional and takes the initiative. While at times it is a response, it does not wait until it is forced to comply to the needs around it. Christ's love for us all the way to the cross was an intentional step on His part, in which He took the initiative to meet our needs. Good shepherds initiate acts of love in the congregation from a willing heart, and as Christ's love for us was intentional toward all mankind, so the deliberateness of our love must be all-encompassing, crossing lines that normally divide people and stymie love. A shepherd's love embraces old and young, strong and weak, traditional and contemporary, rich and poor, lovely and unlovely. It dismantles, no matter how hard the task or how high the cost, the barriers that divide races and classes, and seeks to convince a watching world that the love of Christ has arms that are big enough to embrace all those who come to Him.

But perhaps the shepherd's most difficult task when it comes to love is to love those who oppose him, to serve the needs of those who strive against him, and to seek to care compassionately for those who bring him anxiety and consternation. Can a shepherd's love be so encompassing and deliberate that it would include *all* the flock? If it's Christ's love, then it must. But how is that done? Bringing the substance of a shepherd's love to the flock demands that we understand that biblical love has a sequence. And it's the understanding and application of this sequence that enables us to initiate a deliberate love consistently without condition.

SEQUENCE

Love has a starting point. And interestingly, biblical love does not *start* with our initiative toward others.

The Pharisees came to Christ and posed a question of fundamental significance. In Matthew 22:36, one of the Pharisees, a lawyer, asked Him a question, testing Him: "Teacher, which is the great commandment in the Law?" Christ responded, "You shall love the Lord your God with all your heart, and with all your soul, and with all your mind" (v. 37). The most important relational expectation that God has for our lives, the primal expression of ourselves to Him, is that we love Him. What does it mean to love God? Answering this question is pivotal in learning how to love others.

Loving God, as you probably know, means more than feeling good about Him—thankfully, since there are times in our lives when we don't feel good about much of anything. The act of New Testament love, of agape love, is yielding to another. We express our love when we yield ourselves to Him—the totality of our being, as this text has just said. Notice that self is important in the process. God never intended that we would think badly about self or relegate self to lie in the bilge water of the ship of our existence. We are a treasure, not to be enhanced in self-alluring acts of self-advancement, but to be given to the One who fully deserves all of us. Love means giving the gift of me and doing it willingly and gratefully. Loving God means surrendering gladly to all He calls and/or asks us to do. It is total surrender.

And, love for God begins not in ourselves but is motivated as a grateful response to Him. Scripture teaches us that our love expressed toward Him is a response to His love for us. Love begets love. When someone does a loving act on my behalf, my first instinct is to repay that with an act of love from my life to theirs. When I understand the theology of God, I understand that, at the very core of it all, it's not that He acts in love or thinks loving thoughts toward me; rather it is that He *is* love, and that that love is intrinsic to His being. And because He is love, He does loving acts of kindness toward me and thinks loving thoughts toward me. None of us would have the capacity to express a consistent unqualified love to others if it weren't for the fact that this kind of love is stimulated by a response to a God who is love and who has graciously and wonderfully loved me far beyond what I have deserved. The Apostle John underscores this fact when, in speaking of our love responses in life, he writes, "We love, because He first loved us" (1 John 4:19). Shepherds who seek to manufacture reservoirs of love on their own from which they can draw refreshing and need-meeting water for the flock will soon find that their reservoirs run dry. Or they will construct exclusive clubs to which certain members can come and drink, and from which others are excluded. Our love for the flock begins with our love for God. And our love for God is only possible when we understand His love for us. That is the sequence through which shepherding love must flow. If you struggle to love, it may be that your loving is out of sequence.

It is in this sequence that love is resourced in my soul. He goes on to tell us that the first demonstration of our grateful, submitted response to Him is our willingness to love our neighbor. In Matthew 22:39, Christ says that the second greatest commandment is like the first, "You shall love your neighbor as yourself." This is a direct quote from the Old Testament, and the concept of "neighbor," both in the Old Testament and in the New Testament, is anyone—whether friend, enemy, or alien—who happens to walk through the turf of our life. So this love is to be extended to anyone within reach. And it's important to note that it means both friend and foe alike. When the Pharisee queried Christ concerning who his neighbor really was, He told a story about a man who was left in the ditch by thieves, ignored by those who should have naturally been good to him, yet ministered to by one who was his "enemy." The story of the Good Samaritan stands in the annals of time as one of the greatest short stories ever told. And yet it seems that in the practical outworking of our lives, we have forgotten its message. Our neighbors are not just our friends, but our enemies as well. Why, then, would we love our enemies? Because they deserve it? No. Because they're good to us? No. Because it's an enjoyable experience for us to meet their needs? No. Then why? What would ever compel us to initiate such all-encompassing love that it would include those whose lives are marshaled against us?

Quite simply, we love them because we love Him. That's how the sequence works. God has loved us and has asked that in return we love Him by fully yielding to Him. When we do that, He says to us, "Your first assignment, then—the outworking of your yieldedness and your love to Me—is to love those around you unconditionally, as an expression of your love toward Me."

Loving in this sequence is liberating. In this progressive flow of love I am free to love those who oppose me, misunderstand me, use me, talk about me, and expect more of me than I am capable of giving. I can love them regardless of their treatment of me not because they deserve it, but rather because Christ deserves it. Loving my critics is a way in which I can express the depth of my gratitude and love toward my Father who has done so much for me. As shepherds, one of the most powerful healing influences we can bring to the body of Christ is to love those who don't love us, bless those who curse us, and pray for those who despitefully use us. As Christ said in the Sermon on the Mount, "You have heard that it was said, 'You shall love your neighbor, and hate your enemy.'" That was street talk. That was the "I don't get mad; I get even" talk of Jesus' time. But note that He transitioned us to a kingdom response that would set us apart from the normal sword-to-sword ethic of our culture. After exhorting them to this powerful kingdom response, He said that when we love our enemies we are like "sons of your Father who is in heaven; for He causes His sun to rise on the evil and the good, and sends rain on the righteous and the unrighteous. For if you love those who love you, what reward have you? Do not even the tax-gatherers do the same? And if you greet your brothers only, what do you do more than others? Do not even the Gentiles do the same? Therefore you are to be perfect, as your Heavenly Father is perfect" (Matt. 5:43-48). Loving others because we love our Father enables us to act and react just as the Father does and to become a clear statement of what it means to be an undershepherd of the true Shepherd of men's souls.

One tension that love-active shepherds live with is that there are several categories of neighbors that he is to love. These categories are often in tension as we try to serve well. So it's important to recognize that loving our neighbor has a particular sequence of its own. There is a certain priority in the dispersing of love from a shepherd to his *neighbors.*

Our closest neighbor is our wife. Shepherds need to prioritize their love for their wives. It brings no greater joy to the church than to see a pastor who clearly is sensitive to, understands, and dedicates his life and resources to meeting the needs of his wife. When our attitude toward the needs of our wives is too busy, too bullish, too brutish, then we tarnish our ministry of modeling love. Ephesians 5 reminds us that as husbands we are to first and foremost love our wives. Which means in essence that if our lives are indeed Spirit-filled (vv. 18-21), then that Spirit-filled life will be reflected in a willingness to love, i.e., to submit to the needs of, our wives. And with the arsenal of our resources—our time, attention, energy, power, and prosperity—the opening of the treasure house of ourselves to satisfy our wives is a high-ranking priority for shepherds. It will prove the depth and reality of his love and will stand as a motivating symbol for other men in the church.

Second, shepherds must be sure that we demonstrate Christ's love as a gift to our children. For reasons best known to God I've had some unusual opportunities in my life to minister at conferences, to write, to pastor, and to serve at a place like Moody Bible Institute. I have to tell you, however, that by and large, my children have not been impressed by what I do in ministry, where I get invited to speak, or how many books I write. In fact, the discouraging reality is that I've written several books and, until recently, my children hadn't read any of them. I learned long ago that the basic need of my children in regard to their dad was for my *time* and *attention.* That was the only thing they were really impressed with. And that meant that early on I had to meet them with my time and attention at their level. When they were little, it meant playing Chutes 'N Ladders on the living room rug. Quite frankly, board games have never been my favorite pastime. They finally grew out of that, and then it was skateboarding and elementary band concerts. Then it was important for me to show up at basketball games and track meets and cheerleading, and everything else that went with their busy lives and schedules.

But then, isn't that exactly the way God loved us? He didn't stand on the edge of heaven and shout to us, "Come on up and be with Me!" He knew that was impossible. We couldn't get there on our own. So He left His world and came into our world and met us right where we are. And He takes us by the hand at the cross, and slowly but surely leads us into His world. It's that kind of Father's love that needs to be reflected by shepherds to their own children, that we might not permit anger to come up alongside of them, but rear them in the "discipline and instruction of the Lord" (Eph. 6:4).

There can be no greater love statements by the shepherd than the evident love that he expresses to his wife and his children. Family is the proving ground of a shepherd's love. Fewer things engender confidence and respect faster than an observable love from the shepherd to his family.

The love of the shepherd then flows beyond his wife and children to the flock at large. Wasn't it Christ who kept questioning Peter until he finally got the point, "Peter, do you love Me?" When Christ finally resolved the question of Peter's love for Him, He said, "then feed My sheep." The sustenance and nurturing of God's flock is vitally important. Particularly when we remember how precious they are to Him. They have been bought with His blood. That's helped me love a lot of people who were otherwise unlovable in churches I've pastored. A lot of them didn't seem real precious to me. But I knew that they were precious to Him. And since they were precious to Him, then they had to be precious to me. The needs of the flock are most readily met when they are nurtured with the life-changing, rearranging, remediating Word of God. And shepherds need to do that effectively through attentively listening to them. By tenderly guiding and directing them. By warning, disciplining, discipling, and growing them into the likeness of Christ. All under the authority of the Word.

Love is sequenced as well beyond the immediate flock to the larger flock of God. Do other churches in the community sense that we have a spirit of concern about them and their welfare and the advance of the cause of Christ through them? Or do we convey a spirit of competitiveness? Loving the larger flock can be a great example of the unconditional embrace of all of God's people within the context of the shepherd's love. The people in our churches will be prone to want to have the best church and to gossip and complain about the faults that they see in other people's churches. A shepherd can prove the breadth and depth of love by consistently expressing a sense of godly care, concern, and compassion for brothers and sisters outside of the local group to which he is assigned.

When I pastored in Detroit there was a church about twelve miles away that for years had postured itself competitively with ours. We had been portrayed by many of them as the loose liberals, and many of our people looked at them as the unloving legalists down the road. In reality, we were all a part of the body of Christ. Slightly different perspectives. Different approach to ministry. Different philosophy about church. But brothers and sisters in Christ, mutually committed to the cause of the kingdom.

While attending a conference I met a layman who, in the course of our conversation, began remarking how wonderful it was that every Sunday his pastor prayed for other churches and pastors by name. He prayed that the cause of Christ would be powerful through their ministries. I was struck by the fact that I had never thought of doing that and particularly convicted that I had looked at some of my colleagues in ministry as competitors. I resolved at that point to have the impact in my ministry like the love impact that that other pastor's ministry had had on this layman in his church. This layman was obviously encouraged and motivated by the loving response of his pastor to other churches and other pastors.

The next Sunday during my pastoral prayer I included this church down the road and mentioned the pastor by name, asking God to be with them as they met and worshiped and proclaimed the Good News of Jesus Christ on that Sunday. That afternoon at a nearby restaurant, the pastor of that other church and a couple of his people walked by the table of our church business manager. They had been longtime friends, and in the course of greeting one another our business manager said to him, "By the way, you'll never guess what our pastor did in church this morning." He went on to say that I had prayed for both him and the church, that God would prosper their work. The pastor was so struck that that night, in the middle of the evening service, he told his people what had happened at our church that morning and said, "We're going to take a moment now to pray specifically for Pastor Stowell and the church he pastors, that God would strengthen and use them for His glory." And they prayed. They prayed for us. Loving the larger flock in that way began to melt the barriers between believers in a way that we had never been able to do before.

There is one more aspect to the sequence of our love for God toward others, and that is the expression of His love through us to the lost. Interestingly, when Christ came He spent time with some of the worst elements of His society. In Luke 15, as Christ talked with the tax gatherers and sinners, the religionists of His day expressed great concern over the fact that He was spending time with people like that. To explain why, He told three stories: the stories about the lost sheep, the lost coin, and the lost son. In each one of the stories, He was making a profound point about why He would express care and compassion toward these kinds of people. In each story something of significance had been lost and the natural response of the one who had suffered the loss was to seek to reclaim that which was lost. That is why Christ loved lost people. His Father suffered a significant loss when the pinnacle of His creation was torn from Him in the Garden, left dead and unalterably separated. Having suffered that loss, He focused all the rest of human history on reclaiming that which He had lost. The pinnacle of the flow of history was when He came Himself in the form of His Son Jesus Christ to ultimately accomplish a redemptive transaction whereby life could replace death and alienation could be supplanted by restoration. Those of us who love God will feel with Him the significant loss that He has suffered. His loss will in a real sense be our loss as well. Which will drive us, then, to love the lost—even the most unlovable among them. And when the flock senses that we love the lost because of our love for God, the power of God's love to the lost will spread through hearts that are under our care.

As we have mentioned, all of this expression of the substance of God's love is rooted in our grateful love to God and exercised as an expression of our love for Him. Apart from that, our own attempts to manufacture love will be erratic, weak, and selective at best. Shepherds resource their love for their neighbors out of the limitless reservoir of their desire to love God because of God's great love for them.

SENSITIVITY

Not only must a shepherd's love have substance and sequence, but it also must be managed with *sensitivity.* And here again, Christ serves as our example. Christ knew the limits to His capacity to love. After busy seasons of pouring out Himself to the needs of others, Scripture records that He often went aside to rest awhile. There are limits to our resources and limits to our emotional, physical, mental, psychological, and spiritual capacities to give. Shepherds who do not learn to take a break and walk away will become depleted and defeated. A change of pace and a change of place, whether it be through time spent alone, playing golf, tennis, fishing, running with a friend, reading, or walking with your spouse—whatever it is, it is vitally important that we know when we are running on weary and be willing to walk away. There will always be plenty of needs to meet throughout the rest of our ministry life. If we don't pace ourselves, there won't be much of us left to meet the ever-present needs. A wise shepherd learns that he can't meet all the needs all the time all by himself.

Which leads to a second sensitivity that a shepherd who loves must have, and that is to the limits of his gifts. As shepherds we have all been equipped to do different things well. Some of us may express our love by spending an evening fixing a widow's car while others of us do well at the bedside, and still others are equipped to give in-depth wisdom in counseling situations to repair the brokenness of lives. But it is possible that a shepherd who is handy with the wrench may be frightfully disabling to a counselee. It's not that we don't address these needs; it's that we try not to address the needs that we are not built to address. A wise shepherd finds others who are equipped to help when the kind of help that is needed is outside the scope of his capacities. A wise shepherd knows how to say no compassionately and then tenderly directs them to someone who ought to say yes.

Some of us are holders; some of us are helpers; and some of us are healers. Those of us who are holders need to simply hold the lamb in need until a helper or a healer can be found. Helpers need to act in between to help sort out the initial needs until a healer can be found to finally fix what's broken. Helpers shouldn't try to be healers, and healers should not be content to be holders. But as shepherds we need to know who we are and what the limits of our capabilities are, and love in that context.

As shepherds we need as well to be sensitive to the limits of our love in terms of priorities. I remember well the temptation in pastoral ministry to spend hours and hours with just a handful of people, trying to meet their needs in depth. If that's all I was being graded for, then I did a fairly good job. The problem was that because of the time consumed with a few, I often neglected the time that I needed to take to prepare for my feeding ministry when there would be hundreds of the flock gathered under the holding, helping, and healing ministry of the Word of God in their lives. Sunday morning should be one of the most need-meeting times in the life of the church, when the entire flock feels the remedial nurturing impact of the shepherd's compassionate feeding of the sheep. The shepherd must guard his schedule to guarantee sufficient time to feed the flock at large, and pace the individual care to not intrude. Granted, there are weeks when emergencies arise that distract us from the proper time we need to prepare to feed the flock. People who die rarely call us in advance to see if it's convenient for us to conduct a funeral this week. Domestic and physical crises never check with our Daytimer. I've always found that on the Lord's Day after weeks of unexpected interruptions, God unusually blesses and enables my public feeding of the Word of God. I believe that He compensates when He calls us to unusual time commitments spent in love and care. My concern is, rather, for the weeks that are simply filled with the routine care and counseling of a few that puts the needs of many in jeopardy.

Part of this relates to not only figuring out who we can help, who we can't, and how many we should help, but also to our capacity to sensitively discern the people who really want help. Unfortunately, some of our parishioners are like bottomless buckets. We pour ourselves into them, feeling like that ought to fill them up, and the next time we look into their bucket it's empty again. I finally came to the realization that there are some people who have problems because they learned a long time ago that when they had a problem, someone would pay attention to them and they would feel loved and cared for. Their problem, then, is only a means to an end that has nothing to do with the problem. Suffice it to say that these individuals can never be helped. They will consume our time, possess our energies, and at times be frightfully manipulative. When you tell them that you've finally decided that you can no longer help them and try to send them to another counselor whom you think can help, they will usually resist, saying they've been to that counselor before or they've tried people like that before and you're the only one who can help them and that if you don't help them, no one will ever be able to help them. I've even had people tell me that if I cannot help them, they're going to commit suicide—the ultimate manipulative stroke to keep their thirst for attention satisfied at the well of our schedule. Regardless of the threats, however, it's important to understand when this dynamic is in play and try to transfer them to someone who can break through the barrier of the deeper need, freeing yourself to help those who can be helped in a short-term relationship.

It is not that we want to be insensitive or unloving, but rather that we learn to be wise in the sharing of that love. It's not unlike Christ who, after feeding the 5,000, got in the boat and went across the sea to minister in a city on the other side only to note that those He had fed the day before had followed Him to be fed again. But He did not feed them. In fact, He reproved them, saying that the only reason they were following Him was to get satisfied by earthly bread and to see another miracle. He told them not to expect Him to do another miracle or to feed them again, because what they really needed was the bread of His Word which was the bread of life. There are times when we need to be that compassionately confrontational with those who are sapping our love strength in an inordinate measure.

We must be sensitive as well in dispensing our love when it comes to the tension between expressing our priority love for our family and our love for the flock. Early in my ministry I assumed that every need that arose demanded my presence. On those special evenings when our family had planned to finally be at home together, invariably someone would call during dinner, describe their struggle, and ask if I might not come over that evening to help solve the problem. Before I knew better, I'd grab my coat, kiss my wife, say good-bye to my kids, and be out the door to be the loving shepherd that God had called me to be. Martie and the kids rarely seemed to be impressed with my pastoral instincts. It's as though they had a sixth sense about what was a true emergency and what wasn't. They had, as well, a rightful sense of the need in their own lives to have me around once in a while to relate to them as father and husband. Often to my disappointment I would discover that as I spent a portion of that family night in the midst of someone else's problem, that the problem hadn't been nearly as troublesome as it had sounded, nor had the solution demanded my immediate attention.

Subsequently, when people would call during one of those special evenings, I would ask them to summarize the problem and then ask as well how long they had been struggling with the matter. They would usually explain the problem and then say that it had been developing over quite a period of time. That gave me the opportunity to tell them that I had a commitment that evening that I could not break, and that while I wished I could come and help them, I wanted to see them first thing in the morning. I would mention that since the problem had been there for a while we could deal with it further in the morning. Then I'd share a couple passages of Scripture that related to the problem and ask them to spend time reading the Word and praying that portion of God's Word back to Him claiming the truth and the promises. We would pray together over the phone asking God to help them, guide them, and keep them stable and safe. I'd remind them to be sure to call me when I got to the office and we'd set up a time when we could get together. It's not quite like "take two Psalm 37s and call me in the morning" . . . but almost.

This temporarily ministered to the problem, preserved the time with my family, and interestingly enough, many of them didn't call me back the next morning, simply because the intensity of the moment had passed, God had met them in their own time in the Word, and in reality, they hadn't needed me to spend my entire evening with them. And the best part of it was that I was able to prove the priority of my love for my family by saying no to another need in order to meet their needs.

I should note that when a compelling emergency arose, my family was more than willing to let me go and be by the side of those who were hurting. In fact, my family gladly shared in the shepherding responsibility when the cause was of sufficient scope for them to sacrifice. It was those not-so-compelling needs that robbed them of their husband and father that troubled their hearts regarding my ministry.

When we're out of control in the helping mode it would be well to check our pulse regarding why we are so prone and ready to sacrifice other priorities to be a helper. If it's because we get more ego strokes in that mode, then we have let our own needs eclipse the priority needs we are called to meet. At that point we are into ministry for our own gain under the guise of gain for others.

Effective shepherd love reflects a substantive love that is sequenced in the context of our love for God and dispensed with balanced sensitivity. When this is done well it creates a style in our ministry that even a pagan world will not be able to ignore.

STYLE

It's tough to get churches in balance. It seems as though churches are either high-truth, cognitive congregations with little compassion and care, or high on touch and low on truth. Both are less than what they should be. In fact, both lead to dangerous outcomes. One shows a cold, cognitive sense of consecration that lacks a sense of the spirit of Christ, and the other tends toward compassion without consecration. When Paul wrote to the Philippians about his prayer focus on their behalf, he said, "And this I pray, that your love may abound still more and more in real knowledge and all discernment" (Phil. 1:9). Note the wonderful blend between a love that increases within the context of our commitment to knowledge and its application to life. The hunger in our society is looking for churches that are high truth and high touch.

One of my favorite churches was started by a ministry to prisoners. Individuals who left prison were encouraged to join themselves to a local body of believers where they could continue to nurture and grow within a community of the called. Unfortunately, they were often unwelcomed and marginalized in the churches they attempted to attend. Someone encouraged this prison ministry to start their own church where former inmates could worship. As a result, that church now has an effective ministry not only to former prisoners but to executives, homemakers, career persons, and street people. Its breadth of ministry is a credit to the love and compassion of Christ and His people. The pastors of the church are dedicated to the authoritative proclamation of the Word of God, and they do it well and powerfully. It's definitely a high-truth church. But it is also a church that understands the importance of expressing the love of Christ through acts of compassion and concern for genuine needs.

As a part of their morning worship service, while the congregation sings, they invite those who have needs in their hearts, whether it be for repentance, restoration, intercession, or some personal problem, to come to the front of the church if they would like to kneel and pray. The first time I was in their service, I was surprised came to the front and knelt, many of them with tears marking their cheeks as they met with their Lord. What I found to be particularly compelling about this liturgy of repentance, restoration, and intercession, was that as these knelt before the Lord, individuals from the congregation and staff came and knelt next to them, put an arm around them, and prayed for their needs with them. It is a touching moment in the service. I have been reared in high-truth contexts that rarely expressed the reality of brokenness and the healing power of the love of fellow believers in intercessory prayer. But this blend of both in the context of a public service made a statement about the heart of that ministry.

The church is obviously led by shepherds who value the place of love within a congregation. Shepherds who aren't afraid to manifest public compassion. It was in this same church that I noticed in the front row of the choir a lady who was visually challenged. Next to her was a lady whose crippling had gnarled her limbs to the point that she was disfigured. When it came time for the choir to sing, the choir stood, and as the choir director led in that anthem of worship, these two ladies raised their faces and voices in obvious liberated praise to God. It could only happen in a church that truly cared for the needs of people. In some churches these types of people might bring a sense of shame and embarrassment. But a church where love reigns would welcome these as equally valuable members of the community. And I have to say that their presence on the front row of the choir made a statement about the worthiness of Christ to be praised and worshiped regardless of our personal distress. It was a message that preached itself. But it only happens in a church where love is a theme that resounds from the depth of the shepherd's heart.

The impact of the obvious love in a church shepherded by loving leaders was spoken of by Christ when in John 13:34-35 He said, "A new commandment I give to you, that you love one another. . . . By this all men will know that you are My disciples, if you have love for one another." It is a style that has impact. In a disengaged, self-centered, isolated, and increasingly lonely world, the fact that God's people have learned to love, care, and compassionately reach out to meet one another's needs will be not only a compelling testimony to the reality of our relationship to a loving Christ, but will provide a magnetic draw to lonely lives that need His touch as well.

The early church was maligned and misrepresented. Its love feast, the Lord's Table, was reported widely to be a cannibalistic orgy. They were pictured as political subversives and accused of breaking up families. But one dynamic that could not be ignored by their pluralistic heathen culture was their love for each other. Early secular literature notes that what had really caught the attention of a watching world was the mutual love they shared for each other.

If the new paganism of our day has done nothing else, it has given rise to the narcissistic encouragement to live for ourselves, and to clamor for rights, privileges, and pleasure regardless of the ultimate expense. And the expense is high. As self-centeredness is celebrated, people become disenfranchised and victimized, leaving a culture of hurting, lonely, uncared-for persons looking for a place to be loved. Society welcomes its love-starved adherents to the temples of sex, drugs, booze, and clubs where the pleasure momentarily eases the pain only to produce a more complex emptiness within. Only *true* love can satisfy. Only the community of the redeemed knows what true love is. Only a loving shepherd can produce a loving community that will rise like a redemptive oasis on a landscape of alienation and despair.

Leaders are the key. A shepherd's love expressed and experienced will ignite the flame of love in the hearts of those who follow.

It's no wonder that Paul included the character quality of love in the list of what is required of a shepherd who will set the example of his obvious belief in the love of Jesus Christ, and as a result build strong relationships that fortify the platform of respect from which he leads. A visible love creates a viable ministry.

But this kind of consistent love from a leader's life will require the undergirding of both faith and purity. In fact, as Paul told Timothy, "The goal of our instruction is love from a pure heart and a good conscience and a sincere faith. For some men, straying from these things, have turned aside" (1 Tim. 1:5-6).

Chapter Eight

A Sense of Solidness

Certainty in a Cynical Culture

Even a casual reading of our culture makes it evident that cynicism is rampant. Due to the public failures of both sacred and secular leaders, people find it hard to trust. Our educational system teaches us to be analytical to the point of suspicion and to critically question every authority and authoritative statement that is posed. The feminist movement has filled our culture with women who look with suspicion upon men, which has given rise to a culture full of men who find it difficult to trust and even understand women. Ours is a culture where *faith* is increasingly an untenable option.

People who exemplify faith in a culture like ours are regarded as somewhat naive. The only faith that is celebrated in our society is faith in ourselves. We are encouraged to place faith in our ability to defend ourselves, build our own kingdoms, advance our own cause, and shape life according to our own dreams and desires. Contemporary faith, because there is so little to trust on the outside, has turned inward, and even then many are finding that their own lives have disappointed them, which begins to dismantle the last outpost of faith.

Faith has taken a beating at church as well. Televangelists who preach the prosperity gospel take innocent faith and render it tragically malformed. These prosperity proponents boast that if a person has enough faith, God will grant health, happiness, and wealth. The downside of that kind of proclamation is that it advances a faith that postures itself to manipulate God to perform according to our wishes and will. We become the puppeteer and the supposed strength of our faith makes God jump to the tune of our physical, material, and emotional desires. Unfortunately, when He doesn't and we don't get what we felt faith would provide, the disappointment points its finger to a God who doesn't keep His promises or to ourselves as the petitioner, as having a faith that is faulted or too weak. Both conclusions damage faith and its future application to life and render believers cynical as well.

Genuine faith is a matter of conforming my life to His will and ways rather than conforming Him to my temporal whims. In fact, faith applied may require me to align myself in obedience to His will in situations that actually diminish wealth, reduce happiness, and may even, in fact, inflict me with physical pain. True faith never conforms God to me but always conforms me to Him.

Yet that kind of faith, authentic faith, has by and large lost its way.

It's in the face of this faithless context that Paul commends faith as a key character trait for spiritual leaders. When faith is applied correctly, effective spiritual leaders rise from the ashes of cynicism like a phoenix, anchoring their faith in the only trustworthy Entity in the universe. A spiritual leader who manifests unstaggering faith in the Word, will, and ways of God will project a consistent focus and strength that will engender the respect of those who are called to follow. This will be particularly true when in the long run the outcomes of that faith are tested and found to be worthy and worthwhile. God never disappoints those who place their faith in Him. When we by faith conform to His Word, will, and ways, the outcomes are ultimately positive.

At the very root of it all, faith is *an unshaken confidence that what we believe about God and His Word is true.* Faith shows itself in actions that are lived out in light of that belief. Faith, more than any other of the five character qualities on this list, is the actualization, the application, of what we say we believe. Faith in God links us to Him in a bond that manages and controls all that we are and do. Yet it is a linkage that is constantly at risk.

In ministry it is tempting to transition our linkage from God and focus our faith on people, which leaves us responding to and playing out our role in ministry based on what people think, expect, and say. Some of us minister from a linkage to our plans. We strategically envision a ministry stretching out before us that is conformed to our dreams and desires, which in turn motivates the movements of our ministry to accomplish our plans. Whereas a ministry driven by a linkage to people will mean that we will be often manipulated and controlled by them, those of us who find ourselves linked to and driven by our own plans will manipulate and manage people to fit into the accomplishment of our dreams.

It's possible as well for a shepherd to link his leadership to prosperity. Whether it be financial prosperity or the prosperity of position, power, and fame, it is easy to minister in order to prosper. When our focus is on prosperity, then all of ministry is viewed through and distorted by that grid.

It is tempting to manage ministry from the perspective of our own safety and security. To do those things that are without risk to guarantee a lack of conflict or opposition. A shepherd whose primary linkage is to a safe and unthreatened environment will not only be unable to do the tough and risky tasks that are often required in a ministry that advances the glory and gain of Christ, but will ultimately create the very insecurity that his focus has tried to avoid. When security and safety are self-manufactured, they are always at risk.

More generally, we readily choose to place faith in our own ways of doing things. We instinctively do what we think we should do in response to our enemies, colleagues, competitors, and general ministry functions. Ignoring Scripture's principles that govern every situation of life and ministry, we live not faithfully but instinctively, like the wayward Children of Israel, of whom it was said that every man did what was right in his own eyes (Jud. 17:6). The chaos that ultimately results when we manage ministry by faith in ourselves and in our own wisdom is hardly worth the end result.

All of these lesser linkages are paths to mediocrity at best and to failure at worst.

It's not a matter of whether or not a shepherd will have faith. It's a matter of where his faith will be focused. Spiritual stability and effectiveness are both accomplished only when our faith is fixed on God. When He is the sole focus of our attention, trust, and the primary impetus for both dreams and direction, there is a sense of both confidence and security that characterizes our ministry. Our sheep will readily respect us when we manage every situation of our ministry in the context of our belief that God is and that His Word, will, and ways are sovereignly supreme and worthy to be surrendered to. That regardless of the outcomes, by faith we will surrender to them. As the writer to the Hebrews defined, faith not only takes that which is unseen and gives it substance, bringing a sense of reality to that which is hoped for, but it is also then an act of application of the unseen, hoped-for realities that God has revealed to us in His Word. Faith characterizes lives that believe and behave unflinchingly according to unseen and inexperienced realities that God has revealed. A faith-motivated shepherd acts as though what God has said has already happened. For instance, when we know that His Word promises to meet the needs of those who generously give to His work, then by faith we go ahead and give as though He has already met our needs. When we are convinced that it is His way to work all things together for good, then we can go through any trial as though His working it together for ultimate good was absolutely certain. Faith is being so convinced of the unflinching reality of His Word that when His Word instructs me to tell the truth regardless, then even when the chips are down I am a truth-teller, trusting that God will work out the details and the outcomes to the satisfaction of His glory and the gain of His kingdom.

Faith enables a spiritual leader to obey God without faltering, even when that obedience leads to that which is uncomfortable and disconcerting. Faith enables a leader to suffer graciously when persecuted. To persevere when nothing spectacular is happening. To forgive when the offender continues to offend.

Faith is belief in action, and it marks the character of the minister as a *true believer.* Faith is the element that aligns life with belief. And it is the lack of faith that permits us to say we believe one thing but to live as though we didn't truly believe.

Faith renders a shepherd as a far less manipulative, controlling, power-playing entity in the ministry. Faith simply believes, then behaves accordingly and lets God manage the outcomes. A faithless shepherd will feel responsible for the outcomes and will often be willing to disobey or compromise a principle in order to guarantee His desired result. Faith, on the other hand, simply conforms a leader to God and lets God bring His results and His outcomes in His time and in His way. At that point the leader can exclaim what a glorious God we serve, since he is not able to take the credit for the outcomes.

There are at least six arenas in which it is particularly critical for the shepherd to exemplify faith as a leadership principle.

PROBLEMS

The toughest arena in which to exemplify unshakable faith is when God walks us into the face of problems. We are quick to hang up our faith and to put on the gloves of self-management when problems arise around us. Shepherds, on the other hand, who exemplify faith remain faithful and steady in the midst of their pain. They are able to forgive those who have caused the pain, believing by faith that God has permitted this intrusion into their life for the purpose of their own growth and as such, these people are a tool in the hand of God to effectively develop character and deepen faith for ministry in the days ahead (James 1:2-5). Shepherds who face problems head-on with an unswerving faith do not become bitter but keep clinging to the fact that ultimately God will work all things together for good (Rom. 8:28). Shepherds who face people problems can continue to love those who hurt them when by faith they believe that God will deal with their enemies in His way, in His time. And since it's God's business to even the score and to bring justice to bear, then they are free to minister even to those who are the source of their problems (12:17-21). When God's will takes us into the face of danger and discomfort, shepherds go there by faith, believing that God can use even the suffering of His people to accomplish eternal goals. Faith endures in physical stress believing that in our weakness He can become strong (2 Cor. 11:7-10).

Faith-focused shepherds, though often tempted, never need to lie to see their way out of a problem. They never find themselves scheming as to how to repay someone who has caused them grief or treated them poorly. Faith-focused shepherds never need to say no when God asks them to do the tough stuff of ministry, because they, with Paul, believe that God ultimately will use everything—even the worst of times—to accomplish the best things. With Job, they are ready to say to those impulses within them that want to curse God and figure out their own way, "Though He slay me, I will hope in Him" (Job 13:15). They believe that ministry is like a marathon that will often face many challenges and pitfalls, yet they have by faith taken hold of the words of the writer to the Hebrews when he says, "Let us run with endurance the race that is set before us, fixing our eyes on Jesus, the Author and Perfecter of our faith" (Heb. 12:1-2).

Recently I stood on that bend in the river where in 1956 five brilliant, savvy, committed men gave their lives to the spears of Auca warriors who dumped their bodies into the Curaray River. I thought of the kind of faith that it took for Nate Saint, Jim Elliot, Pete Fleming, Roger Youderian, and Ed McCully to walk into the jaws of danger, knowing full well that it might be their last trip down that river but knowing as well that their God was the kind of God who could take suffering and loss and transition them to great gain. After all, isn't that what God did through the cross and death of His Son? And, sure enough, those five men died in faith. But like trick candles on a birthday cake, the extinguished torches of their lives soon began to spark, flutter, and flame as hundreds of young people across America gave their lives to missionary work, to go and take their place. And then the killing tribe opened its doors to welcome Nate Saint's sister and Jim Elliot's wife and daughter Valerie into the village to learn the language and tell them of Jesus Christ.

When we landed in the Auca village on our way down to that historical site in the jungle, our plane was met by Indians who came not with spears but smiles on their faces. Most of the villagers today are believers in Jesus Christ. The head of the killing party, now old and a believer himself, was asked what he would do when he gets to heaven and sees Nate Saint, the missionary that he had killed on that day. He responded that when he gets to heaven he will look for Nate Saint, throw his arms around him, and thank him for bringing the good news of the Gospel to his village. And then he said, ". . . and Nate Saint will throw his arms around me and welcome me home."

Not only did those five men not know what would happen to them on the river, but they had no idea how dramatic their deaths would be in terms of worldwide impact toward the spread of the Gospel. Yet they went, not knowing the details, but having faith in the God who manages the details and the outcomes. Faith enabled them to willingly obey in the face of what they knew could be great suffering and loss.

It's not unlike the pastor I met in the former Soviet Union who now pastors five small rural churches in the countryside. As we sat in his tiny home that had not had foreign visitors for over sixty-three years, he told of when he was a young pastor during the days of Stalin and was approached by the KGB to be an informant for them. They promised him a life of prosperity and ease and a bright future if he would only report to them every Monday about what was happening in the church and what the people were doing. He could continue to pastor, and no one would know. It was a particularly difficult choice, knowing that if he said no and obeyed his God, his reward would be a free ride to Siberia. And that's exactly what it was. This pastor's belief in God was bigger and stronger than the lucrative contract he was offered by the government or the intimidating threat of a life of suffering if he refused. By faith he got on the boat with 1,500 other political and religious prisoners. An explosion in the boiler of that boat took 600 lives, and by the time they got to Siberia in that January chill, the 900 who were left were force-marched to prison camps throughout the Siberian wilderness. He was there for ten years before he was released.

I asked him if he was able to fellowship with other Christian prisoners, to which he replied that they gathered on a regular basis for prayer and worship. He then said that during the last few years groups of prisoners were sent out all over Siberia to help build the towns for Stalin's regime. He paused and said with a sense of satisfaction, "Today there are many, many churches all over Siberia that proclaim the Gospel of Jesus Christ—a direct result of those prisoner groups that met in those towns throughout Siberia."

Faith simply obeys and lets God manage the outcomes. That young pastor had no idea what God would do with his obedience, but by faith he obeyed. It's as though God, wondering how the Gospel could be planted in Siberia, said to Stalin, "I want you to send My finest to Siberia. I don't want you to send just anybody. I want only the ones who are fully, by faith, committed to Me regardless of the outcomes. And I want you to pay their transportation costs and support them while they are there. No deputation!"

Faith believes and acts in the face of all odds. Faith permits God to write the last chapter in the journal of our struggles. Faith enables shepherds to cease striving to control every situation and releases them to faithfully serve knowing that God is in control.

PROCLAMATION

Not only does faith play itself out in the arena of problems and uncomfortable obedience, but faith also strengthens a shepherd's confidence in terms of the ministry of proclamation. For thirty to forty minutes on Sunday mornings, we preach the Word of God to a flock that through the week has had its senses titillated with great dining, entertainment, and recreation. Gone are the days when our parishioners looked forward to our Sunday discourses as their primary exposure to outside information and amusement. They are mesmerized by television productions where millions of dollars are spent to produce thirty-minute programs where the scenery is changing every seven to twelve seconds. Buildings explode. Cars drive off cliffs. Keystone Cops and car chases hold us on the edge of our seats, and immodestly clad women flash across the screen. And we on Sunday mornings deliver in a single dimension, without spectacular visual effects, a rather cognitive talk on the Bible and expect it to have life-changing impact.

Add to this difficulty of trying to compete with highly stimulating experiences the fact that we are also trying to pour the Word of God into the hearts of all different kinds of people at one shot. From teenagers to the older folk. From deeply mature saints to those who are just getting started in the pilgrimage. From hard hearts to hungry hearts that anxiously await being fed. How is it possible to preach and satisfy the flock with such a wide variety in terms of needs, openness, and resistance?

If we didn't know better, we would say we're up against impossible odds, and sense that proclamation was futile. In fact, I would give up preaching for good if it weren't for the fact that I have faith in the revealed reality that God's Word is a supernatural power. That it is

God's revelation to us, and that in the hands of the Holy Spirit it has a greater capacity to impact than million-dollar media masterpieces. If we are preaching the truth of the revealed Word of God, then by faith we can be confident that we have a supernatural edge. Faith gives us confidence and courage as we focus not on the impossible but as we focus on the power of the God whom we serve, to take our words about His Word and transition them into life-changing impact.

When the shepherd has his focus fixed not on the impossibility of the task but on the revealed Word of God that His Word will not return void, then he can preach with power and confidence. Though he has no idea how that outcome will be managed by God, he knows that indeed it will be managed and he is not wasting his time in the process. The shepherd can feed the flock with a confidence that, though he is no Chuck Swindoll or Charles Stanley, God will be the one who speaks through a well-prepared, purified shepherd whose life has been so lived that his example supports his exposition. He can count on the fact that God will use even him.

Shepherds who link the focus of their faith on the ofttimes surprising ways of God are encouraged when they consider that periodically people come after a sermon saying, "Pastor, when you said . . . it was just what I needed from God for my life. Thank you, Pastor, for being such a great blessing to me this morning." The interesting thing is that when they quote what they heard in the sermon, we often realize that we never really said that. Does integrity demand that we tell them that that's not really what we said, so scratch the blessing? I don't think so. Rather, we realize that through the faithful proclamation of truth, the Holy Spirit has taken our words and transitioned them through the mind of the hearer and enabled them to land in the lap of their soul in an application form that met their needs.

Faith-focused shepherds are not discouraged when the results of their proclamation seem few and far between. They do not covet the gifts of other proclaimers, but covet rather the clear movement of the Word of God through their lives and gifts. Faith-focused shepherds seek to do better in terms of their communication skills but know that, in the end, the very best that they offer is nothing if God's hand does not guide it to the hearts of the flock. Faith-focused shepherds give God the credit when a sermon is used for supernatural gain in the heart of the hearer.

In God's way and in God's time, He uses the shepherd's proclamation to feed, nourish, and strengthen the flock. When a shepherd claims that outcome by faith, he becomes steady, secure, and confident in his proclamation. He is not easily disheartened when results are not quickly evident. He is careful not to take the credit when sermons work, because he knows full well that preaching in this environment, in our day, is an impossible task unless God prospers the event.

PRINCIPLE

A shepherd's commitment to focusing his faith on God will transition his style of leadership from one of pragmatics to one of principle. A pragmatic leader faces a challenge or opportunity in the road of ministry and tries to figure out what works best for his own desired outcomes. He then applies his plan and is often tempted to compromise righteousness or truth, not necessarily in a blatant way but sometimes in subtle and small ways, to get the job done.

A shepherd whose life is characterized by faith does not start with the design of pragmatic solutions as he faces challenges of ministry, but rather starts with the principles of God's Word. The question of the faith-focused shepherd is, "What principle in the Word of God addresses this situation?" When he finds the answer to that question, he then asks, "What is the most consistent application of this principle at this time?" Then with all of his heart he sticks to it even when the outcomes seem unsure or perhaps even unwelcome in terms of how he'd like to have the scheme finally play out. Faith aligns us with the principles of God's truth. A faith-focused shepherd does not try to squeeze God into the configuration of his own solutions. Often a pragmatic approach to ministry designs the critical path that will be taken and then welcomes God to walk along it. Pragmatic leaders like to tell people that this is "what God wants us to do," when in reality God may be on a path moving in a far different direction. Faith-focused shepherds do what is right and let God take care of the outcomes.

Bob Jones, Sr. used to tell his students, "Do right until the stars fall!" Shepherds who are faith-focused do just that. And they have the strength and the confidence to do it, because they know that any problem or opportunity managed in God's way will turn out for the best.

PLANS

Faith comes into play in terms of our plans. Rarely does a ministry unfold without some plans being a part of the vision of the shepherd. Whether they are programming plans or building plans or ministry plans, shepherds have a way of dreaming about the advance of their ministry. The most strategic point about our plans and dreams is whether or not they are God's plans or our dreams. If they are what

God is envisioning for the ministry, then they will be supported and will prosper. If, however, they are our plans and not His plans—even though they may be good—they will struggle, and if we push them to completion will often bring about negative consequences. The ministries are legion that have been saddled with tremendous financial or programming burdens that, while good on the surface, have sapped and distracted the energy of the flock. Other ministries have been used as platforms from which the shepherd's life and ministry would be launched and have left the flock disillusioned because of an absentee shepherd or disappointed because they feel used for the shepherd's selfish schemes.

Granted, it's a challenge to discern whether or not our dreams are God's dreams, but some of the ways He proves His pleasure or displeasure on our plans is by prospering or withholding financial support, the support of the board, or the support of the flock. If our plan agrees with His plan, He may initiate a flow of circumstances that enable and empower the plans to take place and come to completion. When the resources, support, or necessary ingredients of the plan do not come into place, a shepherd has to be so linked to God that he is willing to open his hands and let the plans go until either they can be done in God's time or until God can structure a new set of plans—His plans—in the heart and mind of the shepherd.

A few years ago a friend of mine who is a gifted visionary was planning with his board a $4 million expansion of their church. The prospect of this kind of expansion would have excited any shepherd and appealed to the ego need of those of us who find personal fulfillment in new buildings and expansions. In particular, this pastor shared with me how critical he felt this building was going to be for the advance of their ministry. They had affirmed together as a church that they would build by cash through a program of promises spread over a three-year period of time. At the end of their capital program, he told me that they had only raised $2.1 million for the project. I asked him what he would do, and he quickly replied that they were not going to build the building. He said, "If God is in this project, then He will amply provide for its completion in His time." That was a faith-focused shepherd. One who was willing to let his plans go until it was clear that his plans and the plans of the church leadership were God's plans as well. They could have pushed the point, cajoled the congregation through guilt or excessive pressure to give, or they could have decided to encumber the ministry with debt. But instead they were more strongly linked to God than they were to their own expectations and dreams. Given that, they were able to let go.

Recently I preached in their Sunday services and had a tour through their new building. They had waited until God supplied before they built. Surprisingly, they announced one Sunday that someone in the church who had sold a business was giving enough to pay for the entire new structure. They went on to ask all who had promised to give to share their gifts with a new fund that had been established to help smaller, strategic ministries that were outside the scope of their own church. Their dream had been the right dream at the wrong time.

God's timing is always best. He wanted to hold the building back until it converged with this parishioner's windfall so that other ministries could profit as well. It took a faith-focused shepherd to patiently build the stage upon which God could display His glory!

In my last pastorate, we had sensed for a long time the need for a pastor to minister to our singles. We processed the decision through every major decision-making and constituent group in the church and felt that it was time to go to the church and ask them to release us to hire an additional staff person for this task. To our surprise, the congregational meeting developed into an extended discussion about the wisdom of such a move and, interestingly enough, even some singles spoke against the proposition. Needless to say, this was a great surprise. As the discussion progressed, it became evident to me that God had not yet prepared the hearts of our people for a move such as this. And while all of us on the staff and the leadership of the church felt that this was an important step for us to take, it seemed that it was no longer wise to press the issue, and that God had obviously not demonstrated a clear path through which to process this decision. I went to the microphone and announced that we needed to defer this decision to a later time, given the obvious discomfort that the concept had created. I communicated that we were willing to wait until God made the way clear for this. The congregation broke out in applause. I had other options and enough leverage to stand tough, to push it through. I'm sure we could have gotten the votes. But I became increasingly sensitive to the fact that what had been our plans obviously were not yet prospered of God since there was so much open hesitation about the position. And so I let go.

In retrospect, God had a better plan. First of all, common sense made it clear that to bring someone into the position with that much opposition to him and his ministry would set him up for less than a good start. In fact, it might sow the seeds for his demise and ruin the possibility of a singles position on our staff for years to come. But more than that, it was several months later that I accepted the call to serve Christ at Moody. If we had just brought on a brand-new staff member before I vacated the senior pastorate, with all of the uncertainties that that means for associate staff, it would have been hardly fair to that individual. In fact, I might not have been able to see my way clear to hear God's call in my life to Moody, given the restraint of having just brought on an additional staff person. A couple of years later one of the men in that church changed ministries and was called to shepherd the singles ministry. He was the perfect choice. He is doing an outstanding job, and that part of the church ministry is prospering under his care. Had we moved at the time that I thought it was right, the ministry would not have been available when God's choice for the position was ready to fill the job.

Faith believes that God's ways are always best and remains sensitive to His leading, to His dreams, to His desires.

Paul himself had his own plans about where he should minister, and in each case God prevented him from going, until the time came for him to hear the Macedonian call. He then went to Philippi where God wanted him to serve and from which his imprisonment would stand as a legendary lesson to Christians who suffer and where a church would be founded that would give to us the classic New Testament epistle, Philippians.

Faith-focused shepherds hold all their plans and dreams loosely and desire His work to prosper in His way and not their own.

PROVISION

Faith-focused shepherds trust God for provision. When called to serve Christ, pay, perks, and prosperity do not factor as a priority in the decision-making process of a shepherd who trusts God to meet his every need.

Martie and I began our ministry in a small church-planting work where our first salary was $6,500 a year. At that time, we became aware of how important it was for us to give regularly and even sacrificially to the Lord's work and trust Him to meet our every need. The history of our family is full of accounts of the abundant provision of the Lord for us. Tires for cars. Clothes for our children. Special additional unwarranted privileges like someone taking us out to a nice dinner or treating us to an evening of entertainment. We were very much aware of the fact that God was sensitive to us and that He really cared for our needs.

I remember one time coming home from the office and having Martie point to a United Parcel box sitting on the table. I noticed in the return address corner that it was from a lady in the church in which I had grown up. Grandma Jensen had always been a generous person, sharing clothes and other things with people in need. I opened the box to find a letter from her saying that her son who lived in Tucson had just sent her these three suits and she wondered if maybe I could use them. Being relatively fussy about the kind of clothes I wear, I immediately suspected that they probably wouldn't be what I'd normally wear, but knew that I would have to buck up and wear what God had given me. To my surprise, all three suits were exactly the kind that I would have picked out if I had gone into the men's store myself. I tried the jackets on, and they fit to a T, and the slacks didn't need to be tailored! I thought back to the passage in the Gospels where Christ taught His disciples not to be anxious for what they would wear, because God knows they have need of these things, but that they should seek first the kingdom of God, lay up treasures in heaven, and that God in turn would supply. It's like a theological version of supply-side economics.

The blessing to shepherds who by faith focus on the providing work of God is that they are freed from hinting, manipulating, controlling, and demanding gain in terms of material wealth for themselves. Not only does that release them from the temporal tension of monetary gain, but it also sets an important example for the flock that struggles as well with putting the things of this soon-to-be-forgotten world above the realities of eternity.

Over the course of time, God placed Martie and me in ministries where the churches were generous and our needs were dramatically reduced. I had to remind myself that this too was God's provision for us. God doesn't just provide and care for those who make less than enough. By faith we accept that God provides and cares for those who make enough and sometimes even more than enough. At those points in our ministry we need to seek to be additionally and more sacrificially involved in sharing provisions back to Him and His work in a generous statement of gratitude for the way He has cared for us. It's important to keep faith intact in good times as well as bad.

PERSEVERANCE

This Godward bond called faith radically alters our view and commitment to this pilgrimage called ministry. It enables us to be what a friend of mine calls "routinely faithful." By that he means living an undaunted ministry life that is regularly faithful to the tasks of ministry, regardless of whether the outcomes are spectacular, average, or seemingly few and far between. Faith believes that ultimately, in God's way and God's time, God will pay adequate dividends on the investments of our gifts, time, talents, and treasures in His work. A faith-focused shepherd realizes that it's not his responsibility to do the task of ministry for the results. If that's the case, we'd all be discouraged. Rather, we should do these tasks for Him. And regardless of whether or not He ever prospers them in our lifetime, we continue to be faithful for His glory and the gain of His kingdom.

It's not unlike the challenge that Abraham and Sarah faced when given marvelous promises concerning what God would do with their lives, only to experience, as Hebrews 11 states, that their lives would end before the promises would be fulfilled. In fact, all God really asked Abraham to do was to be routinely faithful to His call. He didn't even tell Abraham where he was supposed to go, but He asked him to begin the journey. Hebrews 11 summarizes Abraham's life, underscoring the fact that it was lived in faithfulness because of his unwavering trust in God. The account is noticeably marked by the phrase, "by faith." God asked him to move his life into the *unknown.* The unknown is full of unsettling, insecure, distracting, and defeating thoughts of "what if." Yet it's a place where God often asks us to go and to claim by faith that He knows what He's doing to us. God asked Abraham to be faithful in the midst of what was *impossible,* since he and Sarah had passed the age of childbirth when God continued to promise that He would give them a son. He asked them to faithfully persevere in ministry when the *pull of past comforts* sought to seduce them out of the track of God's will back into the comfort zone of the Ur of the Chaldeans. And He asked them to faithfully, routinely persevere in the task with *no instant feedback.* In fact, "all these died in faith, without receiving the promises" (v. 13). But the secret of their success was that they were big-picture people. The text says that their focus was on something beyond this earth, on the eternal city of God. Hence, they were willing to be steadily faithful with little to show for it, because they believed that God would not waste their investment and sacrifice and would, in His time and His way, keep His promises to them even if it was in seasons beyond their lifetime.

I love how the text notes that because they had faith in the bigger picture—faith in God's Word even beyond the span of their lifetime—God was not ashamed to be called their God (v. 16). And think how through the rest of the history of Israel, the nation would rise up and claim, "We worship the God of Abraham, Isaac, and Jacob."

Since it is His business to effect the results of my ministry and it is my business to persevere and be routinely faithful, I wonder if I could manage my life and ministry in such a way that God would not be ashamed to be called my God? This is especially striking in a world where many Christians—and perhaps even some shepherds—are publicly intimidated to clearly and without embarrassment identify themselves with their God.

Some of God's most worthy shepherds have been relegated to small parishes in rural settings where they persevere unnoticed, unheralded, sometimes underpaid, ofttimes underappreciated. But they faithfully stay at the task. Who knows if perhaps the whole purpose of God might not be that they would rear in their family a godly son or daughter whom God would use in great measure in the generation to come? Or if they might not cast a shadow of loyalty and love to Christ over the life of a parent or child within the church, in whom God would use that shepherd's faithful witness to stimulate their lives to greater things for the kingdom? While God does not reveal how He will use our faithfulness, the fact that we have faith in the bigger picture will keep us steady and honored to be a part of His work.

In the 1940s a Bible college graduate left college sensing God's call to an Upper Peninsula logging camp. It was a tough place to minister. In fact, part of that camp was so tough that the local police didn't even patrol the area. He faithfully persevered in planting a church by building a Sunday School. And after having door after door slammed in his face, after being mocked and ridiculed by the rough-hewn loggers in that town, he finally gathered a small group around him to start the church. In that group were two young boys who lived in the roughest part of town. Every Sunday morning the church planter would drive his beat-up station wagon through that area, pick the boys up, bring them to Sunday School, and then take them home. They both accepted Christ and after high school went off to Bible school. One became a pioneer missionary in Bangladesh, cutting a path for the Gospel that has been followed by literally hundreds of other missionaries. The other one became a youth evangelist who touched the lives and hearts of thousands of teenagers across this country and now serves as the president of a Bible college where he supports the training of the next legion of servants of Christ to cover this globe with the Gospel.

Very few people know the name of that Bible college graduate who led these boys to Christ. I doubt that he was asked to speak at major conferences, to be on the radio, or to write. For him it was not fortune nor fame that was important, but a faith-focused perseverance. Routine faithfulness. The kind that just steadily stays at it and trusts God for the outcomes. Servants who are so trustingly bonded to God are wonderfully used by God in His time and His way. And they find that in this perspective, their complaints are few and their covetous comparison to others is but a waste of time.

Martie and I, on our twenty-fifth wedding anniversary, stayed in a tiny, rustic Bed & Breakfast in the North Yorkshire Dales of England. We were there with four other couples, all British, whom we had never met before. After dinner one night, our host took us into the living room around a fireplace where he served us chocolates and coffee. We spent the next three hours just getting to know each other and talking about things in our home countries and hometowns that made for fascinating discussion.

About halfway through the evening, one of them asked me, "What do you do?" Quite frankly, I didn't know how I would answer that question. It seemed to me that no one would know much about what Moody Bible Institute was, let alone what I do. So I began by saying, "I'm with a group of ministries in Chicago known as the Moody Bible Institute." As I was getting ready to explain what that meant, I noticed that the two couples on the couch moved forward with interest and one of them said, "Of Moody-Sankey? That Moody?" I was shocked. How could they have known about Moody and Sankey? I said, "Why, yes!" in amazement. They replied, "We have Sankey hymnals that have been passed down through our families for generations." And then the older couple sitting to our right said, "So do we! Periodically on Sunday nights we gather around the piano and sing from the Sankey hymnal."

Moody and Sankey were in the British Isles over 120 years ago and ministered there for 3 years. The impact of their ministry lingers still. I walked out of that room that night, struck by that conversation and saying to God that I wanted my life to be lived so faithfully that I too would cast long shadows for Him. Shadows far beyond my life. No one would have to remember my name or even remember what I have done. But I asked the Lord to help my life to have long-term impact.

I realize that comes not by planning large, self-manufactured stages upon which to strut the stuff of my ministry, but rather through a faith-focused perseverance, trusting Him to care for the outcomes.

PERSPECTIVE

One mark of a faith-focused shepherd is that his whole life and ministry is managed in light of eternity. What more clear conclusion could be drawn to the Hebrews 11 definition of faith—"Faith is the assurance of things hoped for, the conviction of things not seen" (v. 1)—if among the things the writer is talking about, heaven and eternity are not included? When our lives are lived and our ministries are managed in light of the reality of heaven and eternity, things on this side are dramatically rearranged. Since people are the only entity on this planet that last forever, they become an immediate priority. They are the only eternal commodities that we deal with. A shepherd who by faith has laid a hold on the reality of eternity values people more than anything else in his ministry. The value of people eclipses programs, buildings, position, power, praise, and all the other lesser things that earthbound shepherds live for. Faith in the reality of the other side brings the lostness of man into sharper focus as well. Evangelism thrives when heaven and hell become real through the lens of faith. Believing that Christ is coming to take us to the other side impels us to purity, as John wrote in 1 John 3:3: "Everyone who has this hope fixed on Him purifies himself, just as He is pure." Faith in the world to come creates tenacity and courage in the midst of trouble, since faith teaches us to know that this too shall pass, and that the day is inevitably coming when God will wipe away all tears and eliminate sorrow and death. And upon doing that, He shall usher us into an eternity of unlimited satisfaction, fulfillment, and joy. In fact, that was the context in which Christ spoke to a traumatized group of disciples whose hopes and dreams for the kingdom had evaporated when they heard that their Messiah was going to leave them. Into that troubled moment Christ comforted them, "Let not your heart be troubled; believe in God, believe also in Me. In My Father's house are many dwelling places . . . I go to prepare a place for you. And if I go and prepare a place for you, I will come again, and receive you to Myself; that where I am, there you may be also" (John 14:1-3).

A shepherd who by faith has gotten beyond temporalism to a tenacious commitment to eternalism manages his ministry here in light of the affirmation and rewards that Christ will offer there. Faith-focused shepherds believe that above and beyond all that happens here is the far more compelling thought that over there I might hear Him say, "Well done, thou good and faithful servant." And if that is real, then lack of human affirmation and recognition fades as something that is irrelevant and insignificant in light of the reality of that ultimate divine compliment.

Think of a shepherd who by his faith reflects a sense of solidness in the face of problems, in his proclamation, in principle, in his plans, in his need for provision, who perseveres regardless, and whose perspectives are unshakably grounded in eternity. Think of how a congregation that is caught in a shifting, slippery world where nothing is solid would respond to a leader who is solidly, unmovably aligned with God.

It's easy to have confidence in someone who is believable because they clearly believe. Who provides certainty in the place of cynicism. Who himself is solid. Who has heeded the twist of the phrase, "Don't just do something, stand there."

Chapter Nine

The Preeminence of Purity

Treasure in a Toxic Environment

Nestea Iced Tea used to market their product by means of a TV ad showing a golfer on what is obviously a hot, sticky summer day, walking up the fairway under the weight of his bag, perspiring in obvious discomfort, clothes clinging to him in the clammy humidity. The sound of ice cubes crackling in a glass as liquid is poured over them mesmerizes him. He drops his bag and rushes to the adjoining backyard where a pool party is well underway. As he stands on the edge of the pool, his back to the water, he reaches out his hand and takes a glass. Again frosty ice cubes are bounced into the bottom of the glass and ice tea is poured over them. Sweat begins to run down the side of the glass and the ice cubes crack again under the impact of the liquid. The golfer lifts the glass, swallows the refreshing ice tea, and in a moment of abandon freefalls backward into the pool, disappearing under the swirling, bubbling water. In a moment he reemerges through the surface of the water, shaking the water from his head with a blazing smile across his face. The words at the bottom of the screen invite viewers to "Take the Nestea Plunge!" Just watching the ad made you feel refreshed.

I've often thought that biblical *purity* feels a lot like that. And that those who will be effective shepherds in a shamelessly impure culture will do well to take the purity plunge and live and lead from the power of a clear conscience. Fewer things distort, distract, and disarrange a well-ordered ministry like an impure heart. It leaves us feeling defeated when we have to continue to look victorious to those around us. Our hearts scream the charge, "Hypocrite!" at our soul, and a mind that needs to be committed to redemptive thoughts ends up being distracted by the rationalization that is necessary to quiet the ever-present guilt. Impurity breeds fear and focuses a shepherd's attention on self-protection.

On the other hand, a clear conscience enables the shepherd to both love and lead without hidden agenda or haunting self-delusion. The clearer a shepherd's conscience, the more capable and effective the shepherd will be. And like a focused beam of light through the darkness of night, he will cast a compelling and noticeable image that will not only be respected but will be capable of sending sure and secure signals about sin and sanctification.

Purity becomes increasingly important in contrast to our culture's disinterest in the theme. When nothing is wrong nothing is impure; guilt is unreasonable and pleasure is paramount. Yet deep within there is a hunger for a clutterless life. No matter how much permission our security grants us to dabble in decadence, there is a residual sense of propriety that is more deeply ingrained than external pressure from a fading Judeo-Christian ethic. We are image-bearers, created in His image, and hence have an intrinsic (though often buried or denied) sense that something is right and that our lives ought to be in balance with the rightness within.

While purity will often be castigated, ridiculed, and resisted, a consistently pure life will engender confidence and respect, and will be a drawing force for those who long to be clean and right within. Our lives will be like a treasured diamond in the toxic landfill environment in which we live.

Purity is also a prerequisite for fellowship and intimacy with God. A shepherd who will be empowered with the pleasure and presence of God in his life and ministry keeps the way clean and clear. As the psalmist said,

> Who may ascend into the hill of the Lord? And who may stand in His holy place? He who has clean hands and a pure heart, who has not lifted up his soul to falsehood, and has not sworn deceitfully. He shall receive a blessing from the Lord and righteousness from the God of his salvation (Ps. 24:3-5).

Christ taught, "Blessed are the pure in heart, for they shall see God" (Matt. 5:8). Literally, "for they shall continually be seeing God." Purity is the ongoing key to intimacy. As the hymn writer said, "Nothing between my soul and the Savior, So that His blessed face may be seen; Nothing preventing the least of His favor; Keep the way clear! Let nothing between."[1] Note too that we are talking about purity of heart, internal purity. Lest we be like the Pharisees who had the externals taken care of on the back stroke yet were, as Christ said, defiled within, we must measure purity in heart issues like our dreams, desires, decisions, will, mind, and all that is at the core. My heart is the authentic me. That's where purity begins.

A leader bent on purity becomes a living advocate for a lost but valuable commodity. He draws defiled lives looking for cleansing and shows them the way to enjoy a deepening intimacy with God.

In our culture someone needs to stick up for purity. Spiritual leaders need to lead the charge.

It's no wonder, then, that Paul places purity on his list of personhood qualities that are nonnegotiable if the shepherd is to express his belief in Christ in an exemplary way that will enable him to be respected by those who follow.

Two aspects of purity are particularly vital in terms of spiritual leadership. While most of us would instinctively focus on moral purity, we cannot afford to miss the strategic importance of the purity of our motives as well.

MOTIVES

I don't know of a more difficult aspect of ministry to get a grip on than our motives. It's not always clear why we do what we do. In-depth introspection and long periods of trying to evaluate why we do what we do are usually counterproductive, and those who say, "If you suspect that your motives may be wrong, don't do anything until your motives are right" do not help us in the process. Unless there is a clear signal that our motives are out of line, we need to learn to be faithful to the task regardless and seek to align ourselves with biblical motivations. As we have mentioned, God calls us to routine faithfulness and obedience.

What are the principles that relate to the purity of our motives? The first deals with *why* we are doing what we are doing, and the second with what we are doing ministry *for*. When these two principles of motivational purity are corrupted, our leadership will be defiled and respect will be eroded.

Why

One of the letters to the seven churches in Revelation is fascinating. A reproof is laid at the feet of the church at Ephesus, who, interestingly enough, is celebrated for a long list of accomplishments. In fact, after reading through the list you'd want to vote for them as Church of the Year. Christ says through the pen of John, "I know your deeds and your toil and perseverance, and that you cannot endure evil men, and you put to the test those who call themselves apostles, and they are not, and you found them to be false; and you have perseverance and have endured for My name's sake, and have not grown weary" (Rev. 2:2-3). But after that rather impressive list of accolades, there is a warning. The warning is that if they don't do the right things for the *right reasons,* the lampstand will be removed from their midst. While some commentators dodge the issue of what the lampstand is, Scripture consistently uses light as a metaphor for the power and impact of God's work in this world. It seems to me that the warning is that if they do not repent and remediate their impure motives, God will remove their capacity to have impact through what they are doing. It is as though God is saying, "You want to do the right things for the wrong reasons? Fine. But the power will be gone."

We usually think, "We must be doing something wrong" when what we are doing seems to be ineffective. We should probably ask, "Are we doing the right things for the wrong reasons?"

The motivational problem mentioned in this text is that the Ephesians left their first love for Christ. We should note that the word *first* here is not a matter of first in time, but a matter of first in priority. In other words, they were no longer doing works of ministry because first and foremost they loved Christ, but rather for a host of lesser reasons. The lesser reasons may be that they were doing things because they were the right things to do. Or perhaps these things were what others expected them to do. Perhaps they were doing the work of ministry because it was simply the exercise of a career, a vocational or avocational responsibility. Perhaps it was a matter of the carnal joy of glory, power, and control. Perhaps these works of ministry were performed because there was no one else to do them, and they rose as martyrs in the moment to give their lives on the altar of what no one else was willing to do. Perhaps it was out of sheer duty. A sense of legacy or propriety. Or out of guilt or some other inner psychological compulsion. Perhaps for the praise of men, the affirmation of parents, or the prospect of being written up in *Leadership* or asked to speak at a denominational meeting.

It's often hard to know *why we do* what God has called us to do, but it's not difficult to know *why we should do* the things that God has called us to do. We should do them because we love Him, making our works on His behalf acts of worship that display our sense of gratitude and loyalty to Him as our Lord and Savior to whom we owe everything.

Recently I noticed on a flower shop marquee, "Take some flowers home to your main squeeze." It was a new thought to me. I liked thinking of Martie as my main squeeze, though I should hasten to add that there's no secondary squeeze in my life. The advertisement was calling people to do something nice for the one they loved the most.

Ministry is doing something, everything, for the One we love the most. And when we cultivate ministry as an outworking of an indebted response to Jesus Christ, our motives purify themselves. It's not only a matter of purity; it's a matter of liberation. We become quickly weary when we do ministry for earthly affirmation, recognition, money, responsibility, career call, or even the fear of retribution. If, however, it is done out of a heart that is searching for ways to express its love for Christ, it will thrive and be steady in the face of any ministry environment, because it is not responsive to or dependent on a ministry environment. It is solely a matter of my grateful connectedness to the One who called me to do something on His behalf. Needless to say, ministry done in that context will reflect a steady, undaunted flow that will capture the respect of the flock. The purity of this motivation reminds me of the words to the old chorus, "After all He's done for me; After all He's done for me; How can I do less than give Him my best; But for Him completely; After all He's done for me."

Those of us who serve because of Him and for Him find that, regardless of whether we have the greatest board or the worst board in the world, whether we are affirmed or unaffirmed, encouraged or criticized, paid well or seemingly unrewarded, we continue to give it all we've got because He has given to us all that He has. It will also disengage people's capacity to pull the strings of the leader by manipulative criticism or seductive promises. Those who serve Christ for Christ are free to do what's right, say what's right, and decide that which is right regardless of the outcomes, producing leadership that is stable, trustworthy, and empowered by the Spirit.

Martie and I recently got away for a couple of days at a Christian conference ground in North Carolina where we were the only people on the grounds. Graciously, the conference director insisted, despite our opposition, that their housekeeping staff service our room. It meant that the cleaning lady had to come in and do extra duty, and he assured us that she would want to do that. It was particularly significant since she had to give up part of a holiday weekend to serve us. We had the joy of meeting this delightful person as she came to clean our room, and needless to say, we were effusive in our expression of appreciation for her willingness to be of help. Through the whole conversation, she beamed. And then she revealed her secret. She said: "Oh, don't worry about me coming in to do this. I do this for the Lord."

What a lesson. Can you imagine beaming when required to do some of the tough stuff in ministry and confessing to those who wonder about your unusual attitude that it's your privilege to do this as unto the Lord? At the heart of it all, that's exactly why we do all that we do. The good stuff and the tough stuff. Because He did so much for us.

When Martie wraps gifts to our friends she often gets fancy with the ribbons and takes great care to wrap the gifts in a way that is fully expressive of our appreciation to them for their friendship. In a very real sense, the way we wrap and package our ministry as a presentation to Christ is a reflection of our love for Him. Wrapping our ministry in gratitude instead of grumbling is a worthy statement of love to our Lord.

What For

Purity of motives relates not only to why we do ministry but to what we do ministry for. It's a matter of aligning ourselves with God's objectives. Clearly God has redeemed us that we might glorify Him and bring gain to His kingdom. Unfortunately, we are so prone to drive the energies of ministry toward our own glory and our own gain, ministering for our own significance instead of His. Those who serve for His glory and His gain find their greatest joy not in the affirmation that may come at the door after the sermon, but in a life that over time is functionally changed through the ministry of proclamation. In a life that now brings more glory to God than in days gone by. In a life that gives credit to God—not to us—for what God has done in their lives through us.

This motivational issue is tested in whether or not we are able to rejoice in others' spiritual successes in ministry even when they bypass or eclipse our own. We need to ask ourselves how well we would do in a church where our ministry tended to be more in the background. How well would we do if while we were preaching and managing and envisioning, most of the apparent power-work in ministry was being carried out by others on our staff or lay persons who were exercising their gifts. The purity of our motives is revealed when, as spiritual leaders, we gladly give others the credit for the effective ministry that they are carrying out and celebrate those whose gifts are more apparently and effectively being used. This motive liberates us to rejoice in the success of others, whether it's within the context of our own flock or in regard to those outside, above, and beyond our own.

It is not unusual for us to struggle when we hear how effective, successful, or outstanding a colleague is in ministry. Or to hear that our parish people celebrate the way God has used the gifts of another feeder to enable and strengthen their lives. Why do we feel a sense of creeping negativism when we sit under the ministry of others and realize that what they are doing in the pulpit or in the execution of some plan or program is far and above what we would ever be able to do? Such negativism usually leaks out in some unguarded evaluation of what they are or have done, sounding an awful lot like criticism. Though we veil it, others will hear it as the sound of jealousy. It will make us look small and betray our inappropriate motives and erode the respect factor in our own ministry lives.

On the other hand, if it's the glory of Christ and the gain of His kingdom that our hearts are fixed on, then any time He is glorified we will rise and cheer. And as we do that, the purity of our motives will lead others to rise and cheer as well.

I was standing over the water fountain grabbing a quick drink before the Sunday evening service when I sensed that someone was approaching. I lifted my face and, with water dripping down my chin, noticed one of the leading ladies in our church intensely focused on me. The context of her intensity, I came to find out, was that on this Easter Sunday a church across town had decided to expand its Easter attendance by having it be a "Friends Day" and throwing an Easter egg roll on their front lawn for all the kids who came. To be candid, I had felt a sense of competition with this particular church and had been quietly critical about its philosophical approach to ministry. On this Easter Sunday, my sense of propriety was offended when I realized that many of the friends that their people called to invite to their service were members and attenders of our church. But I was rebuffed by the Spirit through Philippians 1 where Paul said about others who were being spiritually successful even though the motivation for their ministry had been competitive and less than pure, "What then? Only that in every way, whether in pretense or in truth, Christ is proclaimed; and in this I rejoice, yes, and I will rejoice" (v. 18).

As I stood to attention she immediately began to vent her frustration. She said, "Pastor, do you know how many they had at Temple Baptist Church this morning? They had over 1,500 there, and many of them were our own people. I don't think that's either right or fair, do you?" It was a test! A test of my motives. I wish I could always be this on-target, but thankfully the Word remediated any carnal perspectives in my heart, and I found myself saying, "Are you telling me that over 1,500 people in our town heard the Gospel of Jesus Christ this morning? Isn't that the best news you've heard in a long time?" She was stunned and verbally backpedaled to a retiring statement like, "Well . . . well . . . yes, I guess it is."

When our focus is on the glory of Christ and the gain of His kingdom, then it doesn't make a whole lot of difference who is facilitating the goal. When the goal is being accomplished, our hearts rejoice.

To minister out of any other motivation than for His glory and gain will create an environment of jealousy that is critical, conflicting, and divisive. It may even motivate a shepherd to try to hold all of the privileges of ministry for himself, and in the process take on more responsibility than he can handle, heaping undue stress upon his life and withering the flock in terms of exercising their capacities to share in the responsibilities and joys of ministry.

I may have done well at the water fountain but I was to struggle with this motivational challenge again. As I mentioned earlier, when I took the pastorate in the Detroit area, I found that one of the most difficult transitions for me was being placed into a context where my primary functions were few. Basically I was to be an effective teacher of the Word of God in the public services; direct, manage, motivate, and resource the staff; and cast a vision for the future of the ministry. That's not to say that other ministry details didn't end up on my desk, but those were the three fundamental responsibilities. While most of us would delight in moving into such a clearly focused ministry setting, I found that it was unsettling to me, because several of the aspects of ministry that I had found fulfilling and affirming in previous settings were, in this new setting, passed out to others within the church. I had worked in each of my pastorates with young married couples and found great joy, some success, and lots of affirmation in bonding with these individuals in the church. But a lay couple in my new ministry setting had been working with young couples for years and had been doing it with great effectiveness. The younger couples in the church seemed relatively unimpressed that I was their pastor and had a strong heart focus toward this gifted couple. The couples in my age bracket were ministered to by another lay couple in a dynamic, well-taught Sunday School setting. Much of their affection and emotional heart focus was toward this couple. To heap coals of fire on my motives, this couple was not shy about telling others that they were not real excited about my being chosen to serve as their new pastor. I had often found affirmation in my ministry in the hospitals, particularly in times of crisis, but in this church, one of the staff persons had developed a strong and bonded ministry to the flock in this area. In fact, if I as the senior pastor showed up in the hospital, it was traumatic. The patients would think that they were on the edge of death to see the senior pastor show up!

My struggle related directly to a sense of loss in terms of relationships and the fulfillment of some of my ministry needs. But to be honest, I also struggled with sharing the glory and gain of the affirmation and affection of the flock. It was not until I got biblically sane and transitioned my motives that I felt liberated from this sense of loss. Realizing that God was being glorified, not only through work well done but through lives that were being changed through those ministering, and that there was great gain being brought to the kingdom, I was set free to rejoice, affirm, support, resource, and pray with an enthusiastic spirit regarding not only those ministries but also those who were ministering. It brought a surprising sense of joy as well to publicly affirm and encourage their ministries, since I no longer needed to have all of that resound to my glory and gain.

Paul's perspective on this issue is highly instructive. Functioning as the premier apostle, he suddenly had the scope of his ministry dramatically reduced as he found himself incarcerated in house arrest in Rome. Having what had been an expansive and celebrated ministry severely restricted, he didn't let his attitude sour but maintained the primary motivation that had undergirded his ministry all along. In fact, that attitude gave him freedom to lay claim on a new mission field, as several in Caesar's household came to know Christ. And, it enabled him to celebrate even in the face of opposition by Roman believers who were leading many to Christ out of a competitive spirit against him and his gifts. The secret of it all is revealed in Philippians 1:20-21: "According to my earnest expectation and hope, that I shall not be put to shame in anything, but that with all boldness, Christ shall even now, as always, be exalted in my body, whether by life or by death. For to me, to live is Christ, and to die is gain."

Note that the primal motivation of Paul's life was that Christ be magnified. In fact, the whole focus of his life was Jesus Christ, as he noted in the last statement of the passage. Unfortunately, many of us reverse the equation to say, "For me to live is gain, and to die . . . that's when I'll be with Christ." Our motivation needs to resonate with Paul's. His only expectation in life and ministry was that Christ be enhanced and enlarged through his life regardless of his circumstances. And it's clear from this context that it didn't make a whole lot of difference to Paul whom God decided to choose to glorify and advance the cause of His Son.

It would be fascinating to assign a project at the next ministerial meeting for all of the shepherds in attendance to list what their primary expectations are in ministry. My guess is that we'd have a lot of things on the list, and that on very few lists would Paul's expectation to magnify Christ be found, let alone found near the top.

It should not go unnoticed that Paul had only one expectation in ministry. And even though he was in prison experiencing a dramatically reduced ministry environment and a troubling opposition from those that he had loved and served, his heart could still rejoice because his expectation was being fulfilled.

Pure motives in ministry are grounded in shepherds who do what they do because of an unquenchable love for Christ and who desire only to see the glory of God enhanced and His kingdom advanced.

But motives aren't the only point of vulnerability in our souls regarding purity.

MORALS

Increasingly, the society in which we live celebrates sex in terms of a redefined function. In our society, sex is both entertainment and recreation—two commodities that a stress-filled leader's life is usually short on. Yet it is to be enjoyed without restraint, and the only cultural caution is that it be safe. Not safe in terms of enjoying it within the safety of its intended purpose, but rather safe in terms of limiting the consequences as we enjoy its limitless pleasures.

Increasingly, our congregations have less and less sensitivity to the purpose and practice of sanctified sex and are becoming increasingly vulnerable to moral laxity. Like frogs in the proverbial kettle of water whose temperatures slowly raise, dulling their nerve ends so that by the time they're boiling they are cooked without even knowing it, Christians have become increasingly numb to this societal invasion of the sanctity of sex. Captured by soap operas, we end up rooting for someone to have an illicit affair, or we blandly entertain ourselves with nudity on the silver screen, as though these things were in the proper parameters of legitimate permission in our lives. Music lyrics from pop to country to rock entertain us with seductive and suggestive notions about sexuality. MTV celebrates sensuality without boundaries, and magazine covers invite readers to peruse their pages to learn how to enhance their sex lives from a distinctly pagan point of view.

It's in this context that shepherds must be *observably* above reproach, exemplifying a life that is untainted and unsuspected in this arena. And yet in this strategically important task we have to remind ourselves that we are particularly vulnerable. In chapter 6 we discussed our vulnerability given our position since it projects a perception that appeals to the inner needs and desires of most women. We need to be aware of two additional points of vulnerability.

First, that ministry is a prime resource for our ego's need for affirmation. This makes us particularly at risk in counseling. When you track the course of moral failure in shepherds' lives, often it goes back to a relationship that started in counseling. And much of the time, if not most of the time, it is triggered by the ego stroking power of affirmation. The affirming satisfaction of being needed, listened to, celebrated for wisdom, relied upon, and appreciated. It might play out like this.

You promise your wife that you'll be home for supper at 5:30. You probably don't understand this, but she looks forward to that time all day and, unless she is totally inundated with other tasks, that 5:30 hour is the focus of her planning and expectations. Your last counseling appointment begins at 4, and you finally are making some headway with this lady in your church who has been coming to see you on several occasions regarding a significant problem. A problem that not only relates to her own relationship to her husband, but to her past as well. The time flies by, and you notice that it's 5:15. Instead of getting up to go and telling your counselee that you'll pick up from here next time, you continue to track the process of helping her and finally create a window at about 5:45 to begin winding down the session. All the while she sprinkles the session with affirmation about your wisdom, caring spirit, sensitivity, and how greatly you have helped her. Of course, the more she affirms you, the more willing and eager you are to continue to help. At 5:50 you pray with her, and again as she leaves she tells you what a wonderful man and pastor you are and that you are God's gift to her and her problem. She looks at you like she really means it.

You clean up a few things on your desk and walk in the door at home at 6:15.

Your wife curiously asks, "Where have you been?" You victoriously respond that you have been helping Mrs. Smith overcome some of her struggles and that, in fact, the Lord really gave you a depth of wisdom today to really help get her problems into focus.

Under average circumstances, your wife will not be impressed. I doubt if you will hear her say, "Oh, Darling! You are such a marvelous pastor. I so admire your gifts of counseling and help, and it makes me proud of you to see God use you in the lives of other women in the church!" More than likely, affirmation will not flow from the lips of your life partner, but rather, something like, "I thought you said you'd be home at 5:30. I fixed a nice dinner, and now it's cold. You give more time to women in the church than you give to your own wife," or other statements that may be periodically even more brutal than these. And, I have to say, rightly so.

The least we could have done in that important counseling moment would have been to call our wife to relate that we needed to be in the office a few more minutes. In fact, it would have been a marvelous picture of love and loyalty that may have built a fence in Mrs. Smith's heart that she knew she would never be able to climb over. Or an even stronger statement would have been, "We need to stop now, because I promised my wife that I'd be home at 5:30. That's an important commitment for me, so let's resume next week and in the meantime I will be praying that God will help you."

At any rate, the sequence is now in place. Mrs. Smith admires and perhaps even adores you. Your own wife is not impressed and heaps reproving coals upon your head. As Mrs. Smith's heart is drawn to you as her helper and healer, your heart is drawn to her as your admirer and affirmer. Hence, the trap is laid.

It is this trap which we in helping ministries must learn to avoid and protect ourselves against.

The second vulnerability relates to the intense pressure of shepherding work. In my last pastorate, the counselor on our staff shared with me that he was counseling with two area pastors who were struggling with moral failure. He said that he had noticed an interesting pattern that had been affirmed in other settings. The pattern was that the phenomenal stress of pastoral work and the inevitable discouragement and disappointment that it brings to the pastor's soul makes shepherds vulnerable to attacks in the area of morality. Shepherds' lives are filled with heavy doses of responsibility. They are responsible for the transference of the Word of God to people's lives; responsible for church management and administration; responsible to meet the expectations of the flock; responsible to their board; responsible to their own dreams and visions; responsible to their children; responsible to their wives. As we have noted before, our faithfulness to these responsibilities rarely brings the affirmation and satisfaction that we'd like to enjoy. When all of these responsibilities are not managed appropriately, they create a busyness that works against an appropriate intimacy with God, our spouse, children, colleagues, and friends, leaving us hungry for closeness. Sexual opportunities and experiences become easy escapes from a life filled with overwhelming, stressful responsibility. They offer us pleasure in the context of a fantasy world where there seemingly is no responsibility, a fantasy world filled with the pleasure that shepherds often do without. Affirmation from someone who cares about them, who is interested in them, and who will deliver the satisfaction, gratification, and intimacy they are longing for. When the inhibiting thought tracks through the mind of the shepherd on the verge of failure, "If I do this, I'll lose my ministry," the mental response to this overstressed, responsibility-laden pastor is, "So what?" In fact, to exit the ministry through a moral failure is probably more easily justifiable than standing up on a Sunday morning and simply saying, "I've had it with ministry, and I would like to quit and publicly deny God's call in my life." At least if he exits through the window of moral failure, there will be a few people with mercy gifts who will rally to his side, and others who will say, "There go I but for the grace of God," and others who will castigate themselves for not praying enough for their pastor.

Whatever the spin on this kind of a situation, one thing is clear, that when a shepherd's life is not managed well in terms of stress, responsibility, and adequate windows of recreation and legitimate pleasure, he'll be particularly vulnerable to a slow but perhaps steady and inevitable erosion of his commitment to moral purity. And not always with an affair. Satan's playground could be pornography, prostitution, homosexuality, incest, or abuse.

What can we as shepherds do to cultivate and solidify purity in such a volatile and destructive area?

Build fences! Build fences that will not only protect our lives from the encroaching adversary, but also provide arenas in which we can live, play, love, and enjoy both ministry and life with a conscience that is pure from the haunting guilt and fear that moral failure in any configuration will inevitably bring.

What fences can be built to grant safety and success for ourselves? To enable us to enjoy a guilt-free and fulfilling relationship with our wives? To project the attitude that women are safe in our presence, assuring them that we care about them spiritually rather than sensually? As we think of building these walls of protection, let's remember that no one else can build them for us. Moral purity is our personal responsibility. And we should remind each other that these are walls without windows. Let me suggest four fences that the effective shepherd ministering in the midst of a sensual society should build to keep himself pure in relationship to the women in his life.

Recess

Given the observation of my colleague regarding the part that stress and the overload of responsibilities plays in making us vulnerable for moral failure, *recess* becomes a vitally important part of our purity paradigm. Of all the things I loved about kindergarten, recess was no doubt my favorite. It was my favorite part of first grade, second grade, and remains to this day one of the favorite parts of my life. Like the old country western song says, "You've got to know when to hold 'em, know when to fold 'em, know when to walk away, and know when to run." Nothing could be more important than creating within our ministry scheduled spaces to be away from responsibility and pressure. If you don't build your own playground, then you can count on it that Satan will build one for you. Recess is different for different shepherds. For some of us, it may be woodworking in the basement. For others, recreational reading. Golf. Tennis. Scuba diving. Walking. Jogging. Music. Working in the yard. Or any other events that we regularly schedule into our lives where we are free of any responsibility. Events that gratify and satisfy.

It's important as well to schedule some recess time with our wives. Martie and I consistently plan each year times when we get away to be alone. People in the church were always happy to baby-sit, and now that we are emptynesters, we continue the practice. It may be anything from dinner out (not always fancy) to an overnight at a favorite get-away place. Sometimes it's a walk up the lakefront and through the parks of Chicago. But whatever it is, we not only need to take recess alone; we need to take it with our spouse.

It's important to remember the value of vacations. These need to be planned out and protected at all costs. This is when the whole family gets away from the normal routine and responsibilities of life. Now that our children are grown, some of the fondest memories that they talk about are the vacations that we took together. A pastor friend of mine was sharing with another shepherd that he and his family were getting ready to go on vacation, and the other pastor quickly responded, "Vacation? I never take a vacation. Satan doesn't take a vacation, and neither do I!" To which my friend replied, "Well, that's all right. Satan has never been my example." Oh, to be so quick!

In fact, if we're looking for an example, we need to remember that on several occasions the Gospels record that Christ went apart and rested awhile. He knew that it was impossible to continue to give effectively without replenishing His emotional, spiritual, physical, and mental tanks. When we're running on fumes, we are most vulnerable to all kinds of failure and in particular, moral failure. When you look at that gauge of your life and you notice that you're running on "weary," get apart and rest awhile.

No excuses. Just do it.

Your board may say that you need to get away and not burn yourself out, but they will not schedule the time for you to do it. It's something only you can plan. And it probably needs to be said that shepherds who, in terms of the conduct element of personhood, work hard, earn the right for people to appreciate the fact that they take recess. If the perception among the flock is that your ministry is an ongoing recess, then there will be resistance to the time that you take for yourself.

Realism

Before you get to the edge of moral failure, think through the dynamics carefully. A good dose of realism is the second fence to keep strong.

First of all, we need to be realistic about our thought life. Scripture says, "For as he thinks within himself, so he is" (Prov. 23:7). What I do in private in regard to the moral fiber of my life will eventually show in public. If I permit my thought life to wander over the boundary of love and loyalty to my own wife and respect for other women, then eventually it will show in the way I look at women, talk to women, flirt with women, and perceive women. If in the unknown corners of our lives pornography plays a part, or movies, videos, or television drain their swamp water into our souls, then there is no getting around the fact that it will affect our relationships to women. They will increasingly be perceived in our minds as objects of our own gratification. We will look to them for the affirmation, gratification, and pleasure that they can bring to us, instead of perceiving ourselves as shepherds who are given the responsibility to elevate their worth and value as people and keep them safely on the track of Christ's glory and gain in their lives. We should not think that private practices do not create addictions in our lives. Studies show that they do. The more we permit hidden immoral patterns to develop in our lives, the more controlling they will become and ultimately lay the groundwork for defeat.

Second, we need to be realistic about the fact that sin brings consequence. The pity of it is that those of us who think that we can morally compromise our minds, hearts, and habits and get away with it, simply have been self-deceived. As God warns, "For the one who sows to his own flesh shall from the flesh reap corruption" (Gal. 6:8). We will experience consequences as a result of immoral attitudes toward secretaries, staff members, and not only the women in the church but the women in our communities as well. We will erode the sense of confidence and security, to say nothing of the respect, that our congregation has for us, as they notice how we look at women and what segments of the torso we pay attention to as they walk by. And none of us are exempt.

And before we get close to such a failure, we ought to be realistic about the failure itself. Why would any of us want to erode the vital foundations of our children's respect for their dad? Think of the devastating consequence to the heart of a child whose father morally fails, particularly when he was not only Christ's undershepherd to the flock, but God's appointed priest in their home. Think of what that does to a child's perspective of God, faith, Christianity. Think of how it lays fatal cracks in the foundation of their own future and their own relationships with dates and future spouses. Why would we want to destroy the tender, delicate fabric of these precious lives entrusted to our care? Why would we do this to our wives? And why would we want to do harm to the precious flock of God who has been entrusted to our care, to say nothing of the testimony of Christ in the community?

In one of the churches I pastored, a predecessor had morally compromised his life and family with one of the staff members at the church. It was interesting to note that the generation of teenagers that was in the church under his ministry, who are now adults cultivating their own families, was the weakest link in the fabric of the church. Many of them were marginal. Some of them no longer attended church. And the few that did still struggled with the memories of a shepherd who had so deeply disappointed them.

What shall we say, then, of the shadow that a failure like this casts over our successors who will be shrouded with the suspicion of our failure, discounting their capacity to have full and unblemished impact?

We need to be realistic about the consequences! And when we are, we will ask ourselves, "Would I really trade that for a moment's pleasure? A bowl of porridge?" It's a matter of values.

We also need to be realistic about the dynamics of an illicit relationship. Track it. While it is true that a man will have a hard time keeping an illicit affair covered, women almost always eventually tell. Not because they want to make trouble, but because they move into an immoral relationship for far different reasons. Men can carry on an affair interminably because their need is usually not much more than affirmation and gratification. A woman seeks something deeper in terms of security and a deepening intimacy of relationship. When she finally wakes up to the fact that there's little more in the tryst for her than periodically having him all to herself, she will feel less than fulfilled and increasingly guilt will weigh on her heart relative to her own character. Her self-perception as a mistress or a loose woman will either move her to a counselor where ultimately the information will leak, or will lead her to make trouble for the shepherd in terms of spilling the information to a few key friends, or to his wife, hoping to break up the marriage so that she can have him totally for herself. It's important to have a realistic perspective about what that other woman really wants and needs, and how ultimately this dynamic may very well poke a hole in the dike of the secret.

Be realistic!

Relationships

The third fence that needs to be constructed is a commitment to the development of growing, satisfying, appropriate relationships.

The story of Joseph is without a doubt one of the most compelling stories in Scripture for me. How could a young man in the prime of life, with all of his drives running in high gear, be able to resist a woman who no doubt was one of the most beautiful in the land given the fact that she was married to a high-level bureaucrat? In a land where sensuality was celebrated, and in a time of his life when he seemingly had been deserted by both family and God?

When she sought to seduce him day after day, he finally said to her, "[Your husband] has withheld nothing from me except you, because you are his wife. How then could I do this great evil, and sin against God?" (Gen. 39:9) There are two key relationships that Joseph had both cultivated and secured at the core of his being. His relationship to his God, and his relationship to those to whom he was responsible. To go to bed with Potiphar's wife, though no doubt it was an alluring option, would be to take a step into a relationship that would directly violate the two relationships that had become far more important to him.

Taking the time to cultivate key relationships in our own lives is not only the right thing for us to do, but helps build ironclad defenses against the intrusion of moral laxity. A consistent walk with God that is deepening in terms of its intimacy and love will say with Joseph, *How could I do this great evil and sin against my God?* A shepherd who has taken the time to cultivate an increasingly enjoyable and satisfying relationship with his wife will out of sheer loyalty not let an immoral thought linger long and will find himself saying, *How could I do this to my wife?* Spending time with our children and getting to know them, understand them, and build bonds of love with them will inhibit disloyalty to them on the moral front. We'll find ourselves saying, *How could I do this to my kids?* And even our presence with and cultivation of good relationships with those in our flock will help deter impulses toward moral failure. When we are building productive relationships with the men in the church, teenagers, and others in the various constituencies of the ministry, there will be a much deeper realization that to fail in this arena would not only violate their trust and betray their expectations, but cause them deep pain and disillusionment. And, most troubling, the disillusionment will often have long-range consequences on their trust in and walk with God. The more time I spend with our students on the Moody campus, the more I am aware that major failure in any aspect of my ministry, let alone morals, could be a devastating and disillusioning distraction in their own walk with and commitment to Jesus Christ.

Loving, well-cultivated relationships create leashes that keep us out of trouble.

The danger for a spiritual leader who distances himself from others and does not make attempts to build bonded relationships is that the distance perceptually discounts the impact of moral failure and leaves him far more susceptible to naively assume that he can sin without impact.

Responsibility

The fourth fence is a commitment to be a responsible person. Joseph's statement to Potiphar's wife reveals as well that his life was characterized by an important sense of responsibility to the tasks that were given to him. Although our culture often works against responsible behavior in favor of self-gratification, we must realize that one of the key defenses against moral failure is, if nothing more, simply a sense of being a responsible person. Even if there weren't a deep sense of intimacy and loyalty cultivated in my relationships, I have a responsibility as a husband, father, and shepherd which I must fulfill. Moral failure is, at the core, tragically irresponsible. A betrayal of a basic trust.

Those who are busy about the fulfillment of their responsibilities have little time to morally fail. Cultivating relationships outside the boundaries of what is right takes time, and its emotional focus distracts us from the capacity to be focused on maximizing our ministry. We spend time plotting, planning, dreaming, protecting, and hiding the patterns of our actions rather than pouring our best into the ministry. It's interesting, isn't it, that David, when he failed with Bathsheba, was supposed to be at the front line of battle with his troops? It was when he neglected to focus on his responsibilities that he became particularly vulnerable to failure.

These four fences provide barriers in our lives that enable us to prevent our tendency toward impurity to become a reality. And prevention really is the name of the game. The British system of medical care is somewhat different than our American system in that it focuses on remedial health care, whereas our system tends to focus more on preventive health care. There is no doubt that an effective shepherd needs to stay in the prevention mode.

The Jews of Christ's day had an interesting practice that enabled them to avoid even incidental contact with impurity. At feast times they would whitewash sepulchers to clearly point out the places and sources of ceremonial defilement. This whitewashing of the graves called attention to that which was impure and enabled people to avoid defiling contact. It would be well if we as shepherds would whitewash the sepulchers in our lives and mark them clearly, that we might avoid them at all costs. Flirting with impurity will inevitably lead to casualty. The only way to prevent impurity is to mark it and avoid it.

I'm convinced that pastors should have windows in their study doors. That we should never counsel members of the opposite sex when our secretaries or staff members are not in close proximity. That we should not stay after hours alone in the building while working with anyone of the opposite sex. That we should avoid explicit sexual talk with women and refuse to go into sexual details in our counseling. That we should immediately mark our feelings when we are in the least bit drawn to another woman and mark the moment lest we seek to cultivate it. We need to constantly monitor our physical, emotional, and spiritual gauges, and when we start running on fumes, mark the problem and replenish our reserves through recreation or rest lest we run our ministry into the ditch. We need to whitewash the kinds of movies, videos, and other mediums that stimulate our sensuality out of bounds and purpose not to participate. We need to mark when and where we are vulnerable and avoid those times and places. We need to be accountable and honest not only with those we are accountable to, but with ourselves, that we might prevent any measure of disqualification of our ministries through slippage, no matter how small it might be, in the area of our purity. May God help us to say with Job, "I have made a covenant with my eyes, how then could I gaze on a virgin?" (Job 31:1)

Of the heroes in my life, I find myself looking to my grandfather and father. Both served their entire lifetime with a depth of character and the resolve to remain pure. Both finished well. I look at them and others in the generation that went before me and have determined that with God's help I too will be among those who finish well.

In the ancient Greek Olympiad, there was a race called the torch race in which runners ran with torches raised above their heads. The interesting thing about this race is that it was not the one who finished first that won the race. It was the one who finished first with his torch still lit who was the victor. I want to finish with my torch still lit.

CHARACTER IS A PROCESS

Character development is a lifelong process that is never fully attained, but rather an intentional growth experience toward an ever-deepening, enriched quality of life. Paul's short list of the importance of cultivating speech, conduct, love, faith, and purity that exemplify our belief in Christ creates the targets toward which we must continually aim. Developing these traits requires a heart that is willing to nurture the process of character development. It requires that we refuse to compare ourselves to others, particularly our weaker brothers, and set our sights on Christ who is our true pacesetter. There are several elements to the successful development of character in our lives. Needless to say, our walk with, exposure to, and *submission to Christ* is the most vital focus that makes progress both measurable and possible. You can't spend time being exposed to Christ through the indwelling Spirit without being reminded of weakness and stimulated toward remediation and growth in His likeness.

Character development depends as well on *accountability* to others who share your goals. In fact, it would be especially beneficial if shepherds who were mutually committed to both the visibility and viability of their ministry could establish an effective means whereby they could encourage, counsel, and hold one another accountable in these five areas that Paul required of Timothy.

Openness to our critics is another important aspect of growing character. Those who oppose us have a wonderful way of quickly noting the weaknesses in our lives. And even though their criticisms are often unbalanced, unfair, and without compassion, they most often have a point about an area of our lives that could improve.

Encouraging and welcoming the honest evaluation of our wives and children may be the clearest input we have in regard to character.

There are few things like *failure* to remind us of how far we still have to go. Failures mark the potholes in our lives and provide a stage upon which to reconfigure our actions, responses, and perspectives to fortify ourselves for success in the future where we have failed in the past.

And last but not least, we need to remember that God will use *trials* to not only reveal our weaknesses, but to complete us in terms of our capacity to have the character to deal with life even in its rawest forms in the context of faith, confidence, and courage (James 1:1-5).

Character development takes time.

A lifetime.

It is indispensable to transformational leadership. A shepherd whose heart is fixed on developing the kind of character that will make him respectably effective will have his heart open to all the influences that God brings into his life to enable him to hit the target of becoming an exemplary believer. Those who preach well from both life and lip will find that their exemplary visibility gives their preaching viability. And as their lives become more and more exemplary, their proclamation ministry will take on a depth of meaning and transformational power, because their transformed lives will support what they preach. What does it mean then to be an effective transformational proclaimer?

Section Three

PROCLAMATION: *Transformational Preaching*

"The pulpit calls those anointed to it as the sea calls its sailors; and like the sea, it batters and bruises, and does not rest. . . . To preach, to really preach, is to die naked a little at a time and to know each time you do it that you must do it again."

—Bruce Thieleman

CHAPTER TEN

Preaching for a Change

Empowering the Proclaimer

In an unusual moment of candor, the preacher's wife said that while she had kept no secrets from him, there was just one thing that she had kept to herself and hoped he would never discover. She went on to say that through all their years together she had kept a box hidden away, and she simply asked her husband that if he ever found the box he would never look inside.

That evening she went out and, overcome with curiosity, he began a frantic search of the house to see if he could find the box. There, under the bed, was the box that she had been hiding for so many years. He pulled it out and lifted the lid, and to his surprise there were three eggs and $2,000 inside. Immediately, he was distraught with guilt for breaking this confidence with his wife. He replaced the lid and slid the box under the bed exactly where he had found it.

When she came home, he confessed and begged her forgiveness. In the process he couldn't resist expressing his curiosity and said, "But I don't understand; what are the eggs for?" She replied, "Honey, every time you preached a bad sermon, I put an egg in the box." He reflected that they had been married for several years and felt encouraged by the fact that there were only three eggs in the box. He asked, "Then what's the $2,000 for?" to which she replied, "Every time I got a dozen, I sold them."

A crushing thought to all of us who preach for a living!

Those of us who are called to preach aspire to do it well. Our problem is not that we desire to do it well; it's that most of us want to be great preachers. And while we shouldn't feel guilty for desiring to maximize our success, we do need to know that very few of us will ever be truly *great* preachers. There have only been a few through history, and in our generation there are a mere handful of individuals whom God has, for reasons best known to Him, sovereignly gifted and lifted to a place of stellar impact. Our aspirations to greatness are complicated by the fact that technology has brought these few gifted communicators into the cars, homes, and hearts of our congregation, victimizing our hopes that our people will revel in our gifts and vote for us as "Preacher of the Year."

It would be far more productive for us to target something that is realistically attainable in terms of our preaching. If it can't be greatness, then it certainly can be *effectiveness.* All of us can be effective in terms of transformational proclamation. Effectiveness is our calling. Greatness is God's business. Greatness, when sought for on our own, focuses the process on us and tends toward pride, self-enhancement, self-promoting, and self-affirmation. Nothing could be more deadly to the effectiveness of proclamation. Effectiveness, on the other hand, focuses on the intended results of preaching. I am effective not when I feel that I am great, but when God's intention in the course of my preaching is indeed being accomplished.

What, then, is God's intended outcome of preaching that measures and defines our effectiveness?

As we will note in more detail later in this chapter, the intention of God's Word proclaimed is to transform lives. To transform persons to think more clearly about Him and who He is. To think more clearly about who we really are. And to transition lives that are prone to sin to lives prone to sanctification that increasingly bring glory to Christ and are dedicated to the gain of His kingdom.

Effective preaching is *transformational preaching.* Preachers and sermons can be funny, entertaining, enthralling, intriguing, intellectually stimulating, controversial, full of impressive theological and doctrinal footpaths, or authoritative. But if *ultimately* the outcome does not result in a changed life because of an encounter with truth, then it has not been what God intended preaching to be.

What then would it take to be effective? To be a transformational proclaimer?

There are hundreds of books that have been, are being, and will be written about the techniques of becoming an effective preacher. I don't pretend to be a highly tuned technician, nor am I qualified to write an extensive treatise on the task of preaching. The focus of this chapter is to create a target with definable goals, helps, and hints that enable us to track our preaching toward a ministry that can be used of God to effectively transform lives for His glory.

Paul wrote these words to Timothy on the heels of his call for Timothy to focus on his personhood, "Until I come, give attention to the public reading of Scripture, to exhortation and teaching. Do not neglect the spiritual gift within you, which was bestowed upon you through prophetic utterance with the laying on of hands with the presbytery. Take pains with these things; be absorbed in them, so that your progress may be evident to all. Pay close attention to yourself and to your teaching; persevere in these things; for as you do this you will insure salvation both for yourself and for those who hear you" (1 Tim. 4:13-16).

FOUR ELEMENTS OF TRANSFORMATIONAL PROCLAMATION

Four elements relate directly to being an effective transformational feeder: the preacher, the text, the context, and clarity. A good understanding of each of these will put the shepherd on the right track.

Before we deal with these four strategic elements, it might be good for us to place them in the context of Paul's exhortation. Undergirding the platform of respect are the issues of personhood, which we have studied, and now proclamation. If we are to build the platform of respect, then both the quality of our life and the quality of our preaching need to be balanced. Together they are the focus of our ministry.

These two elements that are fundamental to our success as respected shepherds are almost constantly under siege. If we gathered an arena full of preachers and had them write down what they spend most of their time on, my guess is that they would admit to spending too much time on the urgency of lesser things. If we were to ask them what frustrates them most about their ministry, they would probably say that they have too little time to cultivate their personal walk with the Lord and find it difficult to give adequate time to prepare to effectively preach.

In an attempt to find the pulse of pastors in this area, I conducted an informal survey of pastors and their wives. Mark Johnson, senior pastor of Independent Bible Church, states that his greatest challenge in ministry is "having enough time for the Word, prayer, and my family. There is always more to do than I can do. A pastor is never 'done.' I work hard at keeping major blocks of time each week for study and for family. Even so, the press of many other 'worthy' things constantly erodes into these time blocks."

Larry Messer of Battlecreek Bible Church notes that he finds it challenging "to maintain a vital walk with the Lord (meaningful prayer, meditation in Scripture, taking the time to listen to the Lord), and faithfully carry out my responsibilities as a pastor. It is easy to be so busy ministering to others and neglect fellowship with God."

With our two brothers all of us say, "Amen and amen!"

Though it may be our constant struggle, it must always be our all-consuming goal to prioritize these two preeminent ingredients—our growth as persons and our growth as proclaimers. In fact, most of us will need to learn the delicate art of saying no to lesser stuff and yes to this twofold focus.

In the previous section we studied the particulars and process of the development of personhood. In these next two chapters we will bring the issue of proclamation to the fore. The first of the four elements in transformational proclamation is the *preacher* himself.

THE PREACHER

We should not miss the inference that 1 Timothy 4:13-16 is written to a preacher about preaching. As in any trade, the sharpness and adeptness of the tool is critically important in terms of being used effectively by the master craftsman. Dull, unsuited tools inhibit the process of transformation. There are four issues to which we must yield ourselves as sharpened scalpels in the hand of the divine Surgeon-Healer. An effective transformational proclaimer understands the importance of the *quality of his life;* sees beyond his profession as a proclaimer to the *purpose* of his proclamation; accepts with a good dose of *reality* not only the pleasure but the pain of his calling; and grants the process sufficient *time* and attention.

Quality of Life

We cannot ignore the sequence in 1 Timothy 4:12-13. Personhood precedes proclamation. Proclamation that is able to transform a life is undergirded by a life that is observably growing in its consistency to the truths that are proclaimed. There are fewer things that damage transformational proclamation more quickly than a proclaimer who is consistently flawed.

As we have noted, our living leads. Preaching fills out our exampleship by giving it content, establishing the foundation, and articulating the process of transformation for the listener. People are observers first and listeners second. When they observe us, respect us, and want to grow to where we are, the sermon serves to tell them how. To show them the way. And when, for some reason in some fallen moment, we contradict what we seek to articulate, humble repentance and steps to rectify the flaw are the only things that can restore power to our preaching. The proclaimer who is growing in Christ-motivated character that is reflected in his speech, conduct, love, faith, and purity, will be a proclaimer who gains the ready attention of his hearers and opens the door of their desire to change and grow.

It's no wonder Paul told Timothy to "pay close attention to yourself" before he exhorted him to pay close attention "to your teaching" (v. 16).

Purpose

If the proclaimer is to pay close attention to himself as a prerequisite to effectiveness, he must constantly measure the perspective that he brings to proclamation. Perspectives in terms of preaching are built on two distinctly different platforms: one that perceives preaching in terms of profession as opposed to the other that focuses on purpose. One deals with the form, and the other with the function. The professional asks, "How am I doing?" The purpose-oriented proclaimer asks, "How are my listeners doing, and how well is Christ able to effect His transformational power through me?" The platform of profession focuses on performance. The platform of purpose focuses on power, and instead of urging us to become a celebrity reminds us that we are but a conduit of the power of God to His people.

There are three important purposes that an effective transformational proclaimer must always keep in mind. The first is that we are speaking God's Word on His behalf to His people. Christ made a profound statement in John 7 when, speaking of His own proclamation ministry He said, "My teaching is not Mine, but His who sent Me. . . . He who speaks from himself seeks his own glory; but He who is seeking the glory of the one who sent Him, He is true, and there is no unrighteousness in Him" (vv. 16, 18). Note that the purpose of Christ's proclamation was not only to transfer God's Word but also to transfer words that would bring glory to God. How prone we are to seek to speak His words to glorify ourselves. This misspent motivation leads to a lack of trueness and an increase in pride in the proclaimer's life. Hence Christ notes that when we speak His words for His glory, we remain true and there is no unrighteousness found in us.

The quickest way to wear ourselves out in the ministry of proclamation and to want to ditch the whole assignment, is to do it for our own glory and gain. Preaching is too tough, too long-term in terms of outcomes, too fickle in terms of people's responses, to be a source of sufficient glory and reward to the preacher. But shepherds who remember that they speak His words to His people for His glory and His gain see themselves as instruments through which God will do His work and their sermons as lunches placed in His hand that He will break to feed the masses on the hillside.

When we do this with clarity and consistency, listeners will be bonded not to the proclaimer but to Christ and His Word, which is the second purpose of transformational proclamation. The ultimate purpose of our preaching is not to develop a relationship between the parishioner and the preacher, but to facilitate a deepening relationship between the parishioner and his Lord. The successful proclaimer bonds the audience to God and His Word and builds a sense of accountability to God and His Word as well.

As a little boy I could never quite understand why, nailed to the back of the pulpit from which my dad preached, was a sign that only those on the platform could see that read, "Sirs, we would see Jesus." Every time my dad walked from his center chair to the pulpit, he was reminded afresh that the task of the proclaimer was to show the flock to Christ and not himself.

I was reminded of the importance of this when, speaking at a recent conference, a colleague of mine embraced me and said, "You are a great communicator." While I appreciated that moment of encouragement, I have to tell you that left me disappointed in my heart. My heart's desire is that people see Him and not me.

In my first pastorate, one of the deacons used to pray every Sunday in our pre-service prayer time that God would "hide our pastor behind the cross." It was his wonderfully simple way of saying that they wanted to see Christ instead of me.

I recently visited a church where the pastor has national recognition. I deeply admire his gifts as a communicator. It was a midweek service in which people were sharing testimonies about the Easter Sunday services. During the course of the evening, a man stood up and said to the pastor, "Bill, ten minutes into the sermon you disappeared, and I began to hear the voice of God in my life."

I want to preach like that.

The purpose of the proclaimer is to be a conduit, not a celebrity, and to show people the greatness of his God, not the greatness of his gift.

Which leads to the third purpose of the proclaimer, and that is, as we have already noted, to effect change; to be an instrument of transformation in people's lives. It is our purpose to bring people to a place of maturity where they have developed truth grids in their minds and hearts through which all of life passes. Grids that reject automatically that which is wrong and give entrance to all of that which is true and good. Our purpose is to produce people who reflect the measure of maturity that the writer to the Hebrews noted when he wrote, "But solid food is for the mature, who because of practice have their senses trained to discern good and evil" (Heb. 5:14).

Our purpose is to speak His words to His glory, to bond people to Him, that they might be transformed into His likeness and live lives that effect glory to His name and gain to His kingdom. If I hear that someone is a great preacher, then I want to see his people. I want to see if they love Christ more and live more like Christ today than they did a year ago. The effect of great preaching is building a church of people whose lives continue to be effectively transformed and who show the transformation in the midst of the daily grind in their homes, marketplace, relationships, and ministry within the church. People who through their good works create compelling stories through transformed lives that cannot be ignored by a watching world.

Sometimes we as pastors become so weary in the well-doing of preaching that we feel that we wouldn't care if we ever preached another sermon again. For us, preaching has become a task. A ritualistic fulfillment of a calling that we long ago became tired of. When we get to that stage, we know that we have slipped back into performance and have forgotten the purpose.

It's the purpose, the ultimate outcomes of preaching, that will provide continuing motivation and glad perseverance in the cause.

The vast majority of pastors who responded to my survey mentioned that their primary joy of ministry was to see the hand of God working in lives to effect change and growth. Interestingly, a large percentage of the wives agreed. They echo the heart of the Apostle John who wrote, "I have no greater joy than this, to hear of my children walking in the truth" (3 John 4).

Bob Dow of the Liberty Bible Church expresses his sense of joy in the ministry as "seeing people who were lost in a sea of darkness come on line and become committed, knowledgeable—livers and proclaimers and reproducers of the light." And, he mentions that his greatest challenge in ministry is "convincing people that following Jesus Christ in devotion—biblical expertise, accurate lifestyle, and a soul-saving mentality (home and abroad) is worthy of [their] time."

Rex Beresford of the Firth Community Church writes that his greatest joy is "being given a part in people's growth in the Lord... watching the light go on." He goes on to say that he also enjoys getting paid to study, preach, and teach the Word of God. Could it be because he understands the purpose and has learned to love the process of preaching for the joy of transforming people's lives?

Those of us who focus on the ultimate triumph rather than the daily task will find sufficient motivation to prioritize the issues of personhood and preparation for proclamation. This is where the faith factor has to kick in, because some of the triumph will never be noted in our lifetime, and some of the triumph will only be revealed when we get to the other side. The real measure of the effectiveness of our proclamation will not be fully known until the books are opened and we come to understand all the things that God accomplished through His Word through us to their hearts, lived out in the quietness of their lives in public arenas.

Jay Jentink, pastor of Calvary Baptist Church, writes that his greatest joy is "seeing God change people! There is something so incredible about watching a person who moves from a disinterest in God to intense commitment. The joy comes from knowing it is a privilege to have a place in God's plan for that person."

Dennis Huebner of Hilltop Church of God notes that his greatest joys are "those times that I know I have connected with another; I have truly communicated. When someone finally gets it. They understand the Gospel; they catch the vision; they hear the voice of God."

An onlooker walked up to a construction site and asked a bricklayer what he was doing. The bricklayer pointed to the pile of bricks and said, "I'm laying these bricks." The onlooker asked the next bricklayer what he was doing, and that bricklayer pointed to his work, and said, "I'm building this wall." He went to the next bricklayer and asked the same question, to which the last bricklayer enthusiastically replied with a sense of pride in his mission, "I'm building a cathedral!"

Proclaimers are like bricklayers. We're either merely laying the bricks of preaching sermons, building the wall of our professional expertise, or we're making a contribution to the development of the grand, glorious, and eternal cathedral known as the body of Christ.

Reality

The preacher who is committed to the quality of his life and embraces the purposes of preaching also needs to be realistic regarding not only the pleasure of preaching but its pain as well. If we expect that we can tune our proclamation to be solely a source of pleasure, then we will be disappointed.

I've come to realize that preaching is the sweetest agony in all the world. Sweet because it's being about the business of a supernatural transition from the pages of revealed truth to the transformation of hearts toward the glory of Christ. Can there be a better calling, a more rewarding experience, than to be a channel of God's life-changing power? But there is a certain agony as well. Bruce Thieleman wrote, "There is no special honor in being called to the preaching ministry. There is only special pain." And while I believe that there indeed is a special honor to proclamation, I would have to also say that I have regularly felt the pain.

Although I have never had the experience, it seems to me that the process of preaching is like having a baby. The text germinates within our soul, develops cell upon cell, thought upon thought, insight upon insight, until it begins to take form and shape within the depths of our being. The labor pains begin on Saturday, and we wake up Sunday morning needing to deliver this internal mass of energized truth with which we have become so intimately engaged. Whether we are ready or not, it's countdown to delivery. I think I know why C.H. Spurgeon was nauseous and sometimes vomited before he preached. Inevitably, then, the moment comes when we deliver the sermon, laying it out there for all to look at and inspect. And like parents who want onlookers to admire their baby, the weaker side of us hopes that there will indeed be a measure of admiration and affirmation. Besides those people who say something nice every Sunday, even when they've slept through major portions of the sermon, there usually are less than we would hope of those who interact with the power of the proclamation, at least in terms of their feedback to us.

Next is the pain of the meltdown stage which is not unlike postpartum depression. During my meltdown I rewind and replay portions of the sermon that I felt were strategic and try to measure whether or not I had said it the way I wanted to say it. Like someone who has been to the Grand Canyon at sunset, awestruck with the beauty and grandeur, who drives back to New Jersey and tries to explain to someone else what they have seen, so the preacher feels inadequate to have expressed what he has sensed, felt, and experienced in the text during the week. It's that foreboding sense of failure at the end of the message—a sense that has often been used of God to motivate me to begin preparation for next week as soon as possible, lest I fail again. This postpartum season of review and reevaluation finds us often involved in self-flagellation for not spending more time. For not having said it the way we had planned. For forgetting that key illustration. For not measuring up to our own expectations.

My meltdown stage usually focuses on my wife's response. If Martie affirms that God used a message in her life, even if no one else is affirming, I feel like it has been a proclamation that was well worth all that was involved in its preparation and delivery. And while there are Sundays when the sermon, for one reason or another, is not necessarily compelling to Martie and does seem to connect with others, even then my assessment of its effectiveness usually rises and falls on her honest feedback. If Martie says to me, "God fed me through you this morning," then I am fully satisfied.

Donna Jentink wrote that one of her greatest joys was hearing her husband preach, "and feeling like I'm going to burst with pride because he has been so used of the Holy Spirit." There could be no earthly joy greater to a preacher than to know that he has fed his wife. And by the way, that's probably not going to happen, regardless of how good the sermon is, if there hasn't been a ministry through the quality of his life at home that has already opened his wife's heart to his pulpit proclamation.

In addition to the preparation, delivery, and postpartum experience, preaching can be painful because it is so public. So one-way. There is little opportunity to explain what you meant when you are misunderstood, and the only dialogue that usually takes place about the sermon, unfortunately, is not with us but among our parishioners over Sunday lunch.

There is a certain agony as well when we realize that the perception of our capabilities as a preacher is so locked into the present. If we're struggling, from a human standpoint, through a series of sermons that are not communicating the way we want them to, don't count on the fact that your people will understand and say to each other, "This series isn't really very good, but remember when we were wonderfully fed through the series he preached a year ago at this time." Unfortunately, that's rarely the case.

Frank Tanana, who helped pitch the Detroit Tigers to a divisional championship by throwing a two-hitter against the Toronto Blue Jays, days later struggled in his appearance on the mound in the American League playoff series. When I asked him how he felt about being criticized for his struggle so soon after there had been much affirmation for his earlier victory, he remarked, "I learned a long time ago that fans are fickle. They have short memories, and the only thing that really counts in their minds is, 'What have you done for me lately?' "

As a preacher, I could relate to that. To many in the pews, the issue is, "How effectively is he feeding me today?"

While the pleasures of preaching abound, we have all felt its pain. And, while we all have different pain thresholds, just like having a baby, when we remember the ultimate impact, the pain is worth the gain.

Time

The last aspect that the preacher needs to keep in focus is the matter of time. The time that it takes to get ready to preach. The time that it takes to preach. And the time that it takes for preaching to work.

Periodically people ask me how long it takes me to prepare my sermons. My somewhat flippant answer often is, "A lifetime." It's true that we pour into our sermons the molding, making, shaping, and forming influences that have happened throughout our entire lives. Very few of my insights and/or observations are new to me. I often wonder if my insights aren't merely something that I heard my dad say, or something I learned from a mentor or a professor or someone else whom I admire as a preacher. Having logged it in my memory bank, it pops to the surface without reference to whence it came. My sermons are forged out of a lifetime of experiences, successes, and failures.

But we need more than just a lifetime to get ready to preach. We need time during the week in order to do it well. And while some sermons are quickly evident in certain passages and come together with more speed, others are like walking through dark caves in which there is no light. We feel discouraged as we make our way along the dark, cold, exegetical wall of the text, looking somewhere for light and deliverance. Those passages take extra time and require an extra dose of discipline.

And discipline is critical. I struggle with staying in my seat for long periods of time. Quite frankly, it's not always that I'm pressed by other duties, though the duties are there. Sometimes I just find myself getting up and walking away. It's then that I have to say, "Stowell, sit down. Keep your seat in your seat until the job is done."

It's important as well to remember that He is with us and that, given enough time and preparation, His message will crystallize through us.

John Stott laments that in his lifetime he has noticed that the name of the place where pastors work on their sermons has been changed from "the study" to "the office." He insightfully wonders if it's not a reflection of the change of the mind-set of the modern shepherd. There's no doubt about the fact that, given the press and demands of this rapidly changing culture, the job of the preacher has taken on additional baggage in terms of administration, management, and oversight. But in spite of those pressures, in the midst of a changing environment the effective shepherd must stake out a significant claim in the territory of taking the necessary time to be all that he can be in terms of his preaching ministry. The proclamation of the Word of God supported by personhood and bathed in prayer is the most important tool we have to transform our parishioners' lives for the glory of God.

Programs, books by other people, tapes, videos, seminars, workshops, counseling, and all the other things that we do that are good and meaningful do not compare in priority with hearing God's healing, helping, sometimes convicting, sometimes comforting Word. And so it is this, God's Word through His servant, that is of utmost importance in the busy agenda of the shepherd.

Speaking of time, do we need to mention how important it is that we begin early in the week? Sermons need time to find illustrations. To be lived out in our own lives, that they might be tested by reality. Time to be nurtured, formed, and reformed not only in our minds but in our souls. While a few of us are disciplined enough to be working on sermons weeks ahead of time, the rest of us find that we end up doing it one week at a time. If that's the case for you, then the crack of the starter's gun goes off on Monday.

In thinking about the importance of the effective preacher's preparation time, we must also consider the actual sermon time. Most of us are far more enthralled with our sermons than our hearers are, and we must somehow realize that time is not only our window in which to preach, but a precious commodity to them. It takes more work to preach a good sermon in less time than it does to preach a poor sermon in a longer amount of time. And everyone's time expectation is different. Some churches expect their pastors to be done in thirty minutes. Others in forty. Some in fifty. A good preacher understands the maximum time that he has in which to be effective from the perspective of the hearers. One of the best pieces of advice I ever received was when a deacon in my first church told me, "Pastor, remember that the mind can only absorb what the seat can endure."

And then there is the time it takes for God to do His work. We are called to be faithful in proclamation. It is His task to be faithful in bringing the results. As we lay claim by faith that His Word will not return void, we also by faith permit Him to do His work in His time. As Dr. Litfin, president of Wheaton College, has often reminded me, "Joe, rarely does one sermon dramatically change a life. It's faithful preaching over the long haul, week after week, text upon text, and principle upon principle that finally effects change."

We should mention as well the importance of a sense of timing. Some sermons and some series are appropriate at certain times and would be highly inappropriate at others. When it comes to selection of topics and themes, timing is everything. If a congregation thinks that a certain sermon or a certain series has been selected to beat them over the head about a particular congregational problem, then there will probably be more resistance than receptivity. It would be better to have an all-church meeting where the problem was addressed from a biblical point of view by a patient, caring, yet firm shepherd, than it would be to use the pulpit to whip everybody into shape according to the shepherd's expectations. One nice thing about series that move through a book of the Bible is that timing cannot be blamed on the pastor if there is a point of reference to a particular congregational problem. As long as the text *clearly* speaks to the problem at hand, because twisted applications create more consternation than consecration. Let it be said as well that when we preach through one book for two to three years, it is difficult to remain effective. It takes a particularly gifted teacher to keep the material fresh and enable people to understand the fullness of the theme of the book, without getting lost in a myriad of its details and its rabbit trails throughout the rest of Scripture.

THE TEXT

The second element that is critical to transformational proclamation is the *text.* Once a preacher has aligned himself with the purposes of preaching, created a realistic perspective on the pain of preaching, and wrestled with issues of time all of which is supported by the quality of his life, he needs to understand the indispensably strategic place that the text plays in his sermon.

It is clear that Paul grounds both exhortation and teaching in the text of Scripture, as he instructed Timothy to "give attention to the public reading of Scripture, to exhortation and teaching." The text must be preeminent in our preparation, and preeminent in our presentation. Sermons that deal only lightly and/or obscurely with the text cannot achieve the purpose of bonding people to God and His Word. Nor do they carry the long-term power that is needed to effect life-changing proclamation. Power is not in the clever creations of the communicator but rather in the intrinsic truth of the Word of God through him.

It should concern us that increasingly, preaching in America today is being postured as more of a self-help values lecture with periodic tips of the hat to Scripture references than it is to a clear exposition of the truth of the authoritative Word of God. This is not to say that there aren't some times when our communication is geared to certain audiences of seekers or secularists where a detailed exposition of the Word of God may not be an appropriate entrance into their hearts. It is to say, however, that when the church gathers as the body of Christ, it needs to be taught the Word of God. For in that is the only real power of transformational growth and development to the glory of Christ.

Given the illiteracy of the New Testament culture and the scarcity of copies of biblical texts, the early church regularly read Scripture to the congregation, as Paul instructed Timothy to do. It was an important part of the service. The New Testament church did not resemble our churches a few decades ago, when people would stream in with Bibles clutched under their arms to hear a sermon with their Bibles open before them. New Testament churches heard the Word read and then listened as the Word was expounded. Some of us may have noticed that the church of today is looking more and more like the church of the New Testament. As I travel to speak in different churches I am surprised that increasingly there are fewer people who bring their Bibles to church and follow along in their own text as the sermon is preached. The public reading of Scripture is becoming more important in our culture as time goes on.

And we should not discount the power of the Word read. I grew up as a boy in a church where one of the important elements of the morning worship service was the time that the congregation would stand in honor to God and His Word and then read aloud in unison a portion of Scripture. We were able to do this because we all carried the same version of the text. To do that today would sound more like a charismatic renewal without an interpreter. The use of pew Bibles for public reading, Scripture printed in the bulletin, responsive readings in the back of the hymnal, or passages projected on a screen are helpful toward the end of repositioning the public importance of Scripture. Still, I can't help but think that we have lost something in terms of people holding their own copy of the Word and hearing it affirmed through a mutual and massive congregational statement of its value and worth.

I recently visited a church in which, as a part of the worship service, individuals were welcomed to microphones to read without commentary, passages of Scripture that were important to them. I was amazed at the powerful impact of hearing God's Word read, with nothing else being said. As time went on, the momentum of the Spirit's influence grew as the simple recitation of the words of God brought comfort, conviction, and encouragement toward growth.

Christians in the early church had been saved out of blatant paganism and had no orientation to the truth. Every word that was read fell on the deep curiosity of hungry hearts who wanted to know what this faith in Christ was all about. Many of us, particularly those of us who have been hanging around the kingdom for a lifetime, have grown accustomed to the words of God, and our curiosity has been buried under layers of exposure. Yet the more secular and pagan the culture becomes, the more hungry new adherents to Christianity will be to hear the Word of God.

When the focus of public worship and proclamation are not built on the Word but rather on self-help and experiential paradigms, the lost who are drawn to temporal help find that they are not bonded to the Word of God but rather to therapeutic presentations within the context of the church. And while we desperately need to meet people where they are, we must ultimately bring them to the only source of authority and healing in our lives, and that is the Word of God. It's time to focus on bonding our people to Christ through a bonding of their hearts to Scripture. One of the ways that can be done is through the elevation of the Word and its centrality in both worship and proclamation.

Paul adds that Timothy should not only give attention to the reading of the text, but to *exhortation* and *teaching*—two critically important words. Exhortation involves applying the Word of God to a person's real-life situation with the goal of transforming that life toward the glory of God and the gain of His kingdom. It deals with the function of the truth applied to life. Teaching involves the clear communication of scriptural fact and biblical data in its appropriate theological context. It lays a foundation for the exhortation which moves us toward application. The end result of an effective presentation of the Word of God must go beyond what it says on the page, beyond the factual and contextual analysis of the text, to the functional application of the text that will lead to a transformed life.

As preachers committed to a ministry of transformation, it is critical that we remember the worth of what we are proclaiming. Paul reminds us in 2 Timothy 3:16 that all Scripture is the very breath of God. It comes from the core of God's being, and therefore it is not only consistent with all that He is but carries the full weight of His authority. Statements are verified by the credibility of the source. If we cast a statement in the context of "C.S. Lewis says . . ." or "Packer writes . . ." it carries far more weight than a statement by someone who is either unknown or not credible. If the source is credible, we pay attention and take it to heart. We as proclaimers can never give anyone the impression that the source of our proclamation is anything less than a word from the Almighty God of the universe. It is His name that brings credibility and worth to our presentation.

The *presentation* of the text as the foundation for the *teaching* that leads to the kind of *exhortation* that appropriately calls the listeners to consider the implications of the text on their lives. Diminishing any three of these elements discounts the power.

As we work toward integrating these elements of the text into our proclamation, it is critical that we do so understanding the *dynamics* of the text of Scripture. Paul lists four transformational dynamics that make God's Word profitable. First, it is useful for *teaching.* Teaching transitions listeners from the ignorance of the fallen context in which their minds have been trained before redemption into a clear mental grip on kingdom truth. It takes them from the ignorance of their false views of God to a true view of God; from false views of people to God's view of people; from false views of success, wealth, happiness, and the instinctive drives of life itself to true perspectives about critical areas of living.

The second dynamic is *reproof.* This highly transformational profit-margin of Scripture is the confrontational work of God's Word, revealing the shortfall and shortcomings of our lives, measuring us to righteous standards, convicting us, and calling us to a life that repents and grows toward conformity to the truth and righteous living. For some of our listeners the Word proclaimed should expose the hidden faults and shameful secrets of their inner lives. They should at times feel the discomfort of sensing that all the lights have gone off and that a spotlight has come on, shining directly on them as though a voice were calling out, "Thou art the one." God's Word will do that. And it will do that all by itself. We don't need to point our biblical bazooka at anyone. We simply need to effectively communicate the principles with clear yet gentle applications.

The third transformational dynamic rooted in 2 Timothy 3:16 is *correction.* This is the quiet, careful nudging of the Word of God to keep us on the pilgrim path of what is right. While reproof deals confrontally with those willful sin patterns of our lives, correction is a more subtle influence on our spiritual walk, given the fact that in the normal course of events, as the hymn writer so well noted, we are "prone to wander." It is somewhat unsettling to discover that once a plane takes off, the pilots sit back and put the plane on instrument control. Flying by "automatic pilot," the radar guides the plane to its intended destination by interacting with tracking stations on the ground that keep it oriented to its path. Imperceptibly, the plane is corrected all along the journey to make sure it gets where it was intended to go. The Word of God does exactly that for us. It touches our lives at places where we may be, even unknowingly, beginning to veer aside and corrects the course of our living.

The fourth transformational dynamic of the Word of God is that it trains us in *righteousness.* Like a parent rears a child in what is right, so the Scripture rears us through a maturing process to live our lives according to the righteous standards of God. The Word "righteousness" in Scripture, particularly in the Old Testament, means "the correct standard." In a culture where standards are always on the move, given to societal whim and fancy, the standards of God remain the same. These bedrock benchmarks of conduct are the measurements of Christian growth. The Word of God in its changeless form stands firm in the shifting sands of our society. The Word effectively proclaimed will transform meandering lives into well-directed righteous patterns of maturity. As Paul says, "that the man of God may be adequate, equipped for every good work" (2 Tim. 3:17).

It's interesting to note that when Scripture speaks of itself, it often speaks in metaphors. Most of these self-describing metaphors point to the power of the Word to accomplish transformation. Hebrews 4:12 says that the Word is like a two-edged sword that goes past the externals of a person's life, divides him asunder, and speaks directly to the thoughts, intents, and motives of his or her heart. Proclaiming God's Word is like a Spirit-empowered moment of divine surgery, and the Word will dig more deeply into lives than we could ever even hope to do, given the fact that we really don't fully understand what's happening at the core of our parishioners' lives.

Christ said that the Word was like a seed. Dry, wrinkly, hard—like a lot of our sermons—but when the seed falls on receptive soil, while there are elements and distractions that threaten to take the seed away, there will be, as Luke recorded, good and noble hearts that will hear, retain it, and from it bear the fruits of righteousness (Luke 8:11-15).

Scripture also notes that the Word of God is like a mirror in that it focuses us to see ourselves for what we really are. Every morning when I get up I see myself in the reality of my sad, disheveled state. My first impulse is to take some transformational steps to become socially presentable. The Word of God is a mirror which stimulates us to make ourselves spiritually presentable (James 1:23-24).

Since these are the divine intentions of the text, transformational proclaimers need to keep these intentions at the forefront of their minds as they prepare to communicate God's words to the hearers. Throughout the study of the text and the preparation of the sermon, an effective preacher keeps asking himself, "What are the teaching elements in this text? What is there in this text that would serve as a reproof? How would this correct a wandering life? What are the righteous standards that are raised on the landscape of this text? How could I enable and empower people to conform to them? In what way would this text bring me to a place of adequacy in my Christian walk? What good works would come out of a passage like this if it were truly practiced in my life?" A transformational communicator of the Word will align his prayer life during times of preparation and presentation with the purposes of the text. He will ask the Lord to perform the surgery, plant the seed, and erect the mirror so that lives can be moved toward His glory through good works. As these questions and this prayer focus are present throughout the process of preparation, the development of the sermon begins to cooperate with the divine intentions of the text. The closer the alignment, the more powerful the proclamation.

When the proclaimer is convinced of both the worth of the Word of God, its fourfold transformational dynamics, and its profitable outcomes, he comes to the pulpit with a sense of boldness and perseverance as a proclaimer. Paul commanded Timothy, based on the presence of God and His Son with us and the unavoidable reality of the coming judgment of God, to be committed to "preach the Word" (2 Tim. 4:1-2). It is highly instructive to note that the word for "preach" in this text is the New Testament word for "herald." In New Testament times, when the king made a proclamation, the subjects of his land could not hear it over national television or by manuscript printed in the newspaper the next morning. When the king made a proclamation, heralds were the ones who carried his words to all of the villages throughout the land. They communicated the message with clarity and the authority of the king himself to those who lived under the dominion of the king. The herald would not bring it as an option or a possibility or something that should be considered in discussion groups, but was called to proclaim it as the king's words and to call the subjects of the land to respond to with cooperative submission.

I find it interesting that today shepherds often mount their pulpits seemingly intimidated by both the crowd and the culture. It's so much easier to preach in the spirit of pluralism, couching our proclamation in phrases like, "It seems to me . . ." or "I believe . . ." or "Wouldn't it be good if . . ." or "We should think about . . ." or "What would you think . . ." instead of simply underscoring the truth with a clear sense of "Thus saith the Lord," to which the subjects of God will be held accountable. Needless to say, if we are expressing a personal opinion or preference we dare not give it the weight of the King's words. It's important to keep the difference clear.

Having confidence in the intended purpose of the Word of God gives us the courage and boldness to minister as heralds of God, not in strident, but compassionate yet clear, unintimidated tones.

Paul then goes on to encourage Timothy in regard to his proclamation, that both in season and out of season he be faithful to the task in reproof, rebuke, and exhortation, and that he do it with a spirit of *patience* and a desire to build up his flock through instruction.

Attitude is everything!

Any pastor who exercises his proclamation ministry with patience can be used by the Spirit of God as an instrument of transformation in the lives of His people. It's when we are impatient, angry, demanding, demeaning, or self-serving in our proclamation that we build barriers between the text we are proclaiming and the hearts of those who hear.

As proclaimers who are focused on transformation, we need to be careful that we do not emphasize the product of a transformed life without giving people the biblical process in the text that enables them to arrive at a biblical destination. Hence Paul told Timothy to do all of this with a commitment to patient *instruction* (2 Tim. 4:2).

Studying Pauline literature makes it clear that he was committed to instructing the readers of his epistles in the processes that led to the product of sanctification in their lives. Romans 6–8 are laden with biblical processes for the attainment of sanctification. The pattern is reflected over and over in Paul's letters. For instance, in Philippians 1, instead of demanding that they make excellent choices in their lives and live lives that are fruitful and glorifying to God, he instructed them first in the process that would effect the result by saying that it was his prayer for them that they would have a growing *love* in the context of *knowledge* that was expressed in *discernment.* If they lived out these three processes well, they would automatically choose that which is excellent, reflect the fruits of righteousness, and bring glory and praise to Christ in their lives.

I remember being in northern New York state talking with a retired gentleman as we sat on a small beach on a beautiful Adirondack Lake. He said that he had retired from the aerospace industry and was now a consultant in quality control. Since I was a pastor at the time and considered pastoral ministry to be somewhat a matter of quality control, I asked him about the basic principles of quality control. He responded that the most important thing about quality control was not the product. That statement almost blew me out of my beach chair since I had always figured that quality control people focused on the product and if it wasn't right sent it back to get it fixed. Rather, he said, "In quality control, we're more concerned about the process. If the process is right the product will be guaranteed." How profound!

Projecting product-oriented exhortations will only lead our people to frustration. Crafting process-friendly presentations will enable and empower our people to grow. Process-oriented proclaimers ask the question as they study the text, "What does this text say about how I can achieve the spiritual goal in this text?" Sometimes the answer lies in the broader context of the paragraph we are preaching, in the broader context of the book that we are preaching; sometimes it is expounded in parallel passages in Scripture that call for the same outcome but give greater detail about how to arrive at the desired end.

Transformational proclamation places a high value on *instructing* believers in biblical process.

A transformational feeder constantly works to move the development of his sermons toward an alignment with the general transformational intent of God's Word. It is important as well that we as preachers align ourselves with the specific intent of the text that we are dealing with. When we keep ourselves aligned with the fundamental idea of the text, we will be enabled to be a conduit of the power of the text. Every passage has a point that the author intended to make to his audience. The most powerful sermons are those that clarify, communicate, and stay consistently in the context of the author's intended communication. Using a text as a springboard to proclaim our own intentions deletes the power of our proclamation and tempts us to pervert the Word of God to our own ends, for our own purposes.

The author's intent is best understood when we study the historical, grammatical, literary, and cultural elements of the text in light of the immediate and extended context. Needless to say, this takes more time and more work, but it is fundamental to the empowerment of transformational proclamation. Every text has one major point. If our text carries more than one, we would do well to split it into as many messages as there are ideas. Sermons are far more effective when they are like a pistol shot instead of a scattering of buckshot. When the listener leaves, one major challenge should be beating in his heart. The applications to different listeners will be varied, but the principle for all will be the same.

This kind of consistently focused alignment with the transformational intentions of Scripture in general and the specific intentions of the text produces preaching that is effective in changing lives.

As Paul told Timothy, the divinely intended outcome of the Word proclaimed is lives that are prepared to do good works. God will use His Word to produce a community of lives so well lived that our society will find it hard to ignore. When they come and ask us what it is that makes the story of our lives so different, we will have the joy of answering, "We thought you'd never ask! Let me tell you about Christ."

The highest sense of satisfaction for shepherd-feeders is to know that God has used His Word through us to produce the kind of lives that are adequately equipped for every good work.

Once we have a sense of direction in regard to ourselves and the broad ramifications of the text that we proclaim, it then becomes critically important to realize that the context into which it is proclaimed must be clearly understood as well.

CHAPTER ELEVEN

Preaching with Precision and Clarity

Enabling the Listener

When *Forbes* magazine celebrated its seventy-fifth anniversary it did so with a special issue that focused on the theme "Why Do We Feel So Bad When We Have It So Good?" *Forbes* invited nine authors, philosophers, psychologists, and poets to write a response to that rather probing question. Peggy Noonan, former CBS correspondent with Dan Rather and speech writer for Presidents Reagan and Bush, was asked to be one of the contributors. In her article that she entitled, "You'd Cry Too," she made a stunning observation regarding our culture. An observation that goes to the heart of the dilemma we face in a society that has shifted far from its moorings.

She wrote, "I think we have lost the old knowledge that happiness is overrated—that, in a way, life is overrated. We have lost, somehow, a sense of mystery—about us, our purpose, our meaning, our role." She went on to observe,

> Our ancestors believed in two worlds, and understood this to be the solitary, poor, nasty, brutish, and short one. We are the first generation of man that actually expected to find happiness here on earth, and our search for it has caused much unhappiness. The reason: if you do not believe in another, higher world, if you believe only in the flat material world around you and if you believe that this is your only chance at happiness—if that is what

> you believe, then you are not disappointed when the world does not give you a good measure of its riches. You are despairing.[1]

Peggy Noonan stands as a compelling model for transformational proclaimers. She has obviously taken the time to thoughtfully and accurately understand the context of the culture into which she writes, and then with penetrating precision she brings the truth to bear on the culture's dilemma.

Effectiveness demands that we as preachers not only come to grips with ourselves and the text, but that we learn to *precisely* go beyond the text to the context of the culture and our congregation and then craft a vehicle for truth that is marked by *clarity*. If a sermon is to be transformational, these are vitally important parts of the process. It is the point where the preacher moves the tested, changeless Word of God with clarity into the arena of the real life of the contemporary parishioner who is himself being tested by the pressures and seductions of the changing world around him. Coming to grips with the context of the congregation means that we ask the penetrating questions, "Who are they? In what kind of world do they live? and What difference can this text realistically make in their lives?"

In order to answer these questions accurately, we must be willing to know something about the lives of the congregation; to be sensitive to and to grow in our understanding of the context in which the congregation lives. Every listener . . . every candidate for transformation . . . has three distinct contexts: personal, local, and universal. All three of these contexts play into the attitudes, perceptions, and points of view in the congregation. These three contexts create grids through which all the pulpit information is passed. These contexts have distinct codes and languages, doors and windows, and barriers, and create a variety of passageways into the parishioners' hearts. John Stott has insightfully noted that the effective preacher must not only exegete the text, but he must exegete his audience as well.

PERSONAL CONTEXTS

The shepherd-feeder has to relate in his proclamation to a variety of people. Single. Happily married. Sadly married. Single parents. Divorcees. Widows. Widowers. Those who carry the secret of being abused and abusing. Those who come from horrendous backgrounds. Others who have happy, positive legacies through past generations. Some are struggling with their lusts. Involved in illicit affairs. Cheating at the office. Disappointed with life and carrying deep-seated questions about

God. Some are successful, complacent, and self-sufficient. Some are proud; others are going through humbling experiences. It wouldn't be a bad idea, over a period of time, to list the various personal contexts that sit in our congregation Sunday after Sunday.

As we prepare the applicational portion of our sermons, it is imperative to keep in mind the variety of backgrounds and life situations that people bring to church. This becomes especially important when sermons begin to take direct application in terms of abortion, divorce, fathering, mothering, success, wealth, failure, and other specific applications of truth. When standing against abortion, we need to know that there probably are some in the congregation who have had abortions, and if we do not carefully craft the application, we will compound their guilt and despair, when what they really need to hear from us as we proclaim the value of life is that God values their life and will forgive, forget, and grant a second chance. But even that needs to be done without creating an environment where those contemplating an abortion will feel free to do so and then claim the grace of God to forgive them. In the process of that applicational moment, it would be well to note in a compassionate way the consequences that inevitably come. It may even be wise to call on those who have been through it to join you as silent prayer partners on behalf of those who face the temptation, to be a constructive part of building a stronger wall of righteousness in the congregation.

When we do a family series, those from broken homes will suffer through the whole sermon if we don't put in a disclaimer that wraps them in hope and understanding. Sermons on parenting often create undue grief for parents who already feel that they have failed or lost their children. Some note of biblical encouragement and perspective must be shared with them in the course of the application.

Illustrations are often open to offending personal contexts if they are not handled carefully. I used to use a killer illustration of an elementary school child who wrote a paper about his grandparents moving to Florida. In the paper this child innocently referred to his grandparents not as being retired but as being "retarded" and their retirement as their "retardment." It was a real crowd pleaser, a laugh-a-minute story. But on more than one occasion I got notes from people in the audience who said that while they understood that this story was funny, it compounded their suffering since God had given them a child who was mentally challenged. Needless to say, that offense to the personal context of a few made it less than wise to use the story.

I have an illustration that I use about taking our children out for Halloween. Recognizing that some of my listeners would be horrified to think that our children went trick-or-treating, I used to throw in a disclaimer in the course of the illustration. Something like, "Now I know how many of us feel about Halloween, so don't send me any letters." And then I would do a little aside about those who wreck our holidays by doing historical research on them. It always engendered understanding laughter and permitted me to go on with the illustration. Recently I got a three-page handwritten letter from a woman who started out by saying, "I know you said you didn't want any letters, and I know you don't like those who research the meanings of holidays, but I felt compelled to write to you anyway." She went on to tell of her childhood—growing up in a home where Satan was worshiped and how year after year on Halloween her family participated in satanic rituals where child sacrifice took place. She said, "For me, Halloween is not a joke, but a horrible memory that I struggle with to this day." You can count on the fact that I'll craft the articulation of that illustration differently the next time I use it.

Effective transformational proclaimers are sensitive to the wide variety of personal contexts into which we preach. And while we cannot be paranoid about or overmanipulated by the less significant nuances of them, we must be aware of them and pattern our preaching in such a way as to demonstrate that we are an understanding, sensitive, helping, healing shepherd. As the outcomes of our increasingly pagan society become more desperate and despairing, sensitivity regarding the personal situations of our flock will need to be increasingly sharp.

Haddon Robinson says that as he is working on the application side of his sermon he mentally invites representatives of various contexts in his church to sit across the desk and interact with the text. He envisions a divorcee, a teenager, an older charter member, a successful businessperson, or any number of other persons and listens to what they would ask and to how they would view the text. A tactic like Robinson's forces the transformational proclaimer into personal contexts, sharpens his sensitivities, and enables him to fine-tune his illustrations and applications accordingly.

LOCAL CONTEXT

Local contexts are broader than personal contexts and relate specifically to the environmental implications of particular communities and regions of the country in which our people live. These local contexts deal with race, class, gender, politics, local history, and general civic environments. And while all of these diverse local elements filter down in terms of their ramifications to personal contexts, they do exist as important categories in and of themselves. If you minister in Grand Rapids, Michigan, for instance, your local context will be far different than if you are ministering in Los Angeles or San Diego. Ministry in Massachusetts is a far different context than ministry in Dallas, Texas. More liberal constituencies demand a far different perspective in terms of applicational preaching than do conservative contexts. The emphasis of transformational proclamation in the liberal context would lean far more toward righteousness and sensitivity to sin, while ministry in a highly conservative context would need to lean more toward applications that deal with compassion, justice, and freedom. Contexts in which there is racial diversity will require specific applications that call for greater sensitivity toward others, that cry out against the barriers of racial prejudice, and call people's attention to the unifying factor of our mutual allegiance to the cross and the cause of Christ. Rural towns and urban settings call for different applications in our sermons. Blue-collar areas are far different than professional areas. The teens bring their own local culture, as do the elderly, as do the baby boomers and the baby busters. A good shepherd stays up to speed on the environment into which he proclaims.

The challenge to every shepherd is to escape his own local context lest he impose his context onto the context of others and appear to be either insensitive or irrelevant. A good shepherd-feeder works hard to become an astute student of the variety of local contexts in which his people live.

Local contexts involve civic and regional pride. It would be well when we move into a new area to begin with an appreciation for the citizens' local pride toward their hometown. Speaking disparagingly of or belittling unusual practices in the local culture rarely provides an openness of heart in the congregation. It's important to honor the place and its past. Civic and regional pride relate to specific identities that have marked a community's success. Their sports teams become important commodities for a proclaimer to embrace, from the high school team, to colleges and universities, to the professional teams that they enthusiastically embrace. It would be a mistake for someone to come to Chicago and not at least speak well of the Chicago Cubs—and a drastic mistake to try to be cute by rooting for the New York Knicks instead of the Chicago Bulls.

Local contexts may have ethnic twists or certain socioeconomic dynamics. I recall in my second pastorate referring on occasion to *The Wall Street Journal* in my sermon when it seemed germane. To my surprise, some in our congregation, including a staff member, expressed a measure of consternation that I would refer to the *Journal* in my sermons. While we had a scattering of professionals, many in the congregation were blue-collar workers and farmers. To them it was a reference to something totally out of their context and a reference, in fact, that in their perception made me appear to be uppity. These references removed a measure of effectiveness in my proclamation. I came to discover that quoting from The *Journal* was a tool that was not made for the shaping and making of that particular congregation. It violated their local context.

Few of us would ever consider supporting a missionary who went to a field and did not minister into the context of the local language and customary cultural patterns of those he or she ministered to. We dare not ignore the importance of learning the languages of our people and becoming students of the ever-changing environment of our culture that has dramatically affected the mind-set, life patterns, and response mechanisms of those who hear.

UNIVERSAL CONTEXT

There are several elements to this broadest of all contexts in which our people live. Regardless of the diversities that are represented in the personal and local contexts of our people, there are some elements that are universally experienced by all in the flock. Everyone wrestles with greed, hate, guilt, anger, prejudice, impatience, lust, procrastination, self-indulgence, and a propensity to be obsessed with the enhancement and maintenance of significance or the loss of it. Students of literature tell us the reason that the classics remain great throughout generations is because they deal with the fundamental themes that transcend culture, race, and creed. Effective sermons ultimately deal with these universal issues.

It's interesting to note as well that it is these issues to which Scripture most specifically speaks. A shepherd who is confused about feeding a widely diverse flock needs to draw from the text the most pointed common denominator to which the text speaks and articulate it in a clearly formed principle. Its applications will move in a variety of ways in the skillful hands of a sensitive shepherd-feeder. Everybody in the congregation wrestles with some aspect of the fundamental needs and drives that are universally shared by all of humanity.

Our American culture is also an important part of the universal context. It used to be that you could segment the American culture by region and count on the fact that rural areas would be more innocent and naive, while urban areas would be far more exposed to the impulses of their fallen nature, and more sophisticated in their acquaintance with and expression of it. Television, music, movies, and videos have changed all of that. More and more, the American society that used to be broad and expansive in terms of its diversities has become like a national village, where secular values counteract spiritual development and are universally felt and sometimes accepted by even those within the Christian community. A clear understanding of the context of this universal culture may be the most important context for a transformational proclaimer to understand and effectively deal with.

Of the several ramifications of this universal cultural context is an increasing sensitivity to appropriate words, phrases, and attitudes toward a variety of constituent groups within the culture. Not only is it a violation of the dignity of all mankind, but in our present cultural climate, words, statements, or innuendos that can be construed as demeaning toward different races, genders, classes, or a variety of other particular groups need to be avoided. The more we can stay abreast of appropriate terms, the broader influence our proclamation will have. What makes this challenging is that nomenclature is forever changing. As we mentioned earlier, people who serve on planes are no longer "stewardesses" or "stewards"; they are now appropriately called "flight attendants." People who are handicapped are "physically challenged," and the mentally retarded are "mentally challenged." Racial groups prefer particular identities: Hispanic, African-American, Anglo, Native American. Political slurs and cynical innuendos focused on particular politicians or parties are bound to narrow the proclaimer's influence with those on the other side of the political spectrum. Our audiences are bound to include some who are sympathetic toward those who have been perceptually maligned. Insensitive remarks about singles, the elderly, women, or teens become equally inappropriate for the proclaimer who wishes to keep as many heart doors open as possible and to communicate that he is a caring shepherd to all the flock.

Some time ago, I was asked to speak at a downtown lunch that was specifically focused on career persons, many of whom would have a secular orientation. As I prepared my introduction, I chose to use an illustration from the musical *Music Man.* Its classic song refers to the problems in River City. According to the lines of the song, the trouble with River City "starts with T and rhymes with P, and that stands for pool!" Pool is the problem in River City; it's what was happening in the pool halls that was the source of the problems. Since I was addressing the problems of our cities, that "pool hall" line from *Music Man* provided a common point of reference with this mostly secular audience. I decided, unadvisedly so, to say that it was the environment of booze, brawls, and broads that had created the trouble in pool halls of River City. In retrospect, using the word "broads" was inadvisable for many reasons. While I was trying to contextualize to a more secular audience, it was not fitting terminology for a proclaimer of the Good News of Jesus Christ. But beyond that, it wasn't fit for my audience. I received a kind but clear letter from a woman who mentioned that she had always been blessed by my teaching and had been delighted to hear that I would be at the lunch. But she had been so disappointed to hear me use that word, since for professional women it was a demeaning reference to womanhood. I had to write her a note and apologize for my insensitivity and chalk it up to one important lesson well-learned in the process of trying to become a more effective relational, transformational proclaimer in terms of understanding *content.*

One of the most powerful influences in this universal context has been the influence of television. It has had not only a dramatic influence on how people perceive and listen to communication, but also has had an impact on how we as communicators must approach the applicational formations of our sermons. While we can bemoan the fact that television is style over substance, we cannot discount the fact that it has set a high standard in terms of image and has projected a level of excellence that people have come to expect. Pastors today need to keep in mind that throughout the week their people are under the influence of communicators who are well-dressed, well-coordinated, well-groomed, and clearly and carefully articulate in terms of choices of words as well as grammatical correctness. Presentations on television are well-packaged, crisp, clear, concise, and interesting. A disheveled communicator in terms of appearance who brings a sloppy presentation that is uninteresting, unorganized, and factually flawed begins way behind the eight ball in terms of being an effective tool in the hand of God toward reaching this TV-sated generation.

Television has raised the level of the pool in which we communicators swim. And while we don't have to be just like Tom Brokaw or David Letterman, we need to present and represent our Lord's truth in a way that would not bring Him shame.

Increasingly, the effective proclaimer must also realize that we live in the context of a story oriented culture. This presses us to learn to be an effective storyteller in both the crafting and delivery of our sermons. The increasing illiteracy of the populace calls for greater attention to the value of compelling stories. The fact that television, movies, and music are all story-related increases the value of the story in our society. As such, story-telling becomes one of the proclaimer's important commodities. The evening news is a compilation of stories of what happened during the day. Newspapers are stories in print. Great movies are extended stories. Even athletic contests are sprinkled with interviews with leading athletes that create stories behind the game.

Some of the clearest moments in Christ's communication were times when He told dramatic stories to illuminate a point. In Luke 15, instead of preaching a long, cognitive discourse on the importance of having compassion on the lost, He told three stories that capably proved His point. These stories stand today as outstanding moments in Christ's ministry and remain stories with which we are all familiar. The story of the prodigal son in particular stands as a classic example of a great short story, even in secular circles. And while a proclaimer must never let sermon time become little more than story time, stories powerfully serve to illuminate, clarify, and drive the biblical point home. They are becoming increasingly more important.

The most critical element of today's universal context has to do with *values.* Values are what shape us, mold us, drive us, and define us. The dramatic shift in values in America challenges the proclaimer to stay up to speed lest his communication seem irrelevant. Not because of his biblical material but because of the language of these changing values. If we are not sensitive here we will lose touch and put our people in jeopardy of being sucked into the vortex of this new set of rules by which the general culture lives.

What are the values of our societal system that have become so influential?

As we noted earlier, our culture has moved away from its Judeo-Christian roots where even those who were unchurched basically gave mental assent to biblical values. Today biblical values are not only out of mode but are often considered to be bigoted and restrictive. The trashing of the historic value system of the American culture did not give rise to a valueless culture, but instead opened the door to a host of secular values that have filled the vacuum that was created when we dismissed God from our land. These values are primarily a reflection of the instinctive desires and directions of persons without God, and they have no sense of moral responsibility or accountability to God. We have refused to heed the warning of G.K. Chesterton who said, "Before we remove the fences we should find out why they were put there in the first place," and have deserved the critique of Toynbee who laments that we are the first generation of man to try to build a society without a moral reference point.

Our contemporary reference points are now amoral or immoral, yet they hold the upper hand in terms of influence. An effective proclaimer understands what they are . . . the power brokers in the hearts, minds, and behavioral patterns of our populace at large and a threat to our parishioners. He understands as well the biblical values that counteract the influence of these destructive societal standards, addresses the contrast, and sets the distance by calling his sheep to unintimidated allegiance to the values of Scripture that will keep us safe, stable, and sanctified.

There are at least ten cultural values that permeate the universal context. These values must be placed in the transforming light of a biblical perspective as we feed God's flock.

Temporalism

We live in a society that places all of its value on the here and now. The bumper sticker that says "He who dies with the most toys wins" is no joke. That's what our culture believes. We are a society that has long forgotten the reality of the world to come. And if anything after death is considered at all, it's that human recycling project known as reincarnation, which, quite frankly, puzzles me since I wonder why anyone would want to go through life on this planet again. There is no thought of meeting God after death, or of the reality of a heaven as the reward of redemption, or hell as the consequence of rejecting Christ. The vast majority in our culture live, behave, and respond as though the only thing that really counts is this moment in life, and in living this moment to its fullest with no thought of the consequences of tomorrow or of jeopardy in eternity.

In Luke 12, Christ made a dramatic point regarding temporalism when He spoke about the pagan man who was phenomenally successful. So successful that he had to tear down barns and build new ones, but tragically unsuccessful in terms of his view of eternity. To this macro-mover in the marketplace who would have been heralded as the ultimate success in our culture, God said, "You fool! This very night your soul is required of you; and now who will own what you have prepared?" (v. 20) The reproof was not focused on his stuff, but that he lived as though eternity didn't exist. His fault was not materialism but rather temporalism.

Peggy Noonan was right: we are the first generation of man to forget that there are two worlds; to believe only in the flat, material world around us which, as she noted, has brought us such despair.

How many of our parishioners measure their life, success, and possessions in terms of a temporal perspective rather than an eternal perspective? As proclaimers we need to remediate this fallen part of our cultural value system by transitioning the hearts and minds of our people to eternalism, to weaving into messages applications that force the perspectives of our hearers beyond the temporary to that which is eternal.

To prove that none of us are exempt from this failure, God designed the 73rd Psalm which tells us of Asaph. Though a man of God, Asaph found that his feet had almost slipped when he envied the prosperity of the wicked. And this envy of those who had so much while they were so godless was only remediated when, in verse 17, he entered the sanctuary of the Lord and saw the wicked from God's point of view. Asaph said, "It was troublesome in my sight until I came into the sanctuary of God; then I perceived their end." Before he transitioned to God's eternal perspective, temporalism had skewed his perspective and put him on slippery ground spiritually. But when he became an eternalist he in essence concluded, what difference does it make to have a big inning and lose the whole game? Or, as Christ said, "For what is a man profited if he gains the whole world, and loses or forfeits himself?" (Luke 9:25)

It was to a distracted band of disciples who had become anxious about temporal things that Christ said, "Your Heavenly Father knows that you need all these things. But seek first His kingdom and His righteousness; and all these things shall be added to you" (Matt. 6:32-33). "Sell your possessions and give to charity; make yourselves purses which do not wear out, an unfailing treasure in heaven, where no thief comes near, nor moth destroys" (Luke 12:33).

A consistent pointing of people's hearts toward the reality of the world to come will be an important step in remediating the influence of the societal value of temporalism.

When we really believe in the other side, everything on this side is radically, wonderfully changed. Our flock needs to come to believe as Malcolm Muggeridge did that "The only ultimate tragedy in life is to feel at home here."

Materialism

Having eliminated the preeminent value of eternal pursuits in our culture, we have dumbed ourselves into the assumption that fulfillment and satisfaction in life can be found in what we can gain, keep, and accumulate in terms of the material order. We need to be careful here that we don't impose false guilt on those who, for reason of honest, astute business practices and the sovereign bestowal of God, have gained much in this world. The real point of materialism is not how much we have, but what has us. It's not what we hold, but how tightly we hold it. Not what we have but how we got it. The test of materialism is whether our goods have made us proud or grateful, self-sufficient or God-sufficient. Scripture teaches that things are to be used as mechanisms through which we can perform good works. They are things that we can use to share with those who are in need. The things we have are resources that can be transitioned into the advance of the kingdom (1 Tim. 6:17-18).

Scripture also teaches us to accumulate treasures for ourselves in heaven rather than here on earth, and to find our fulfillment, satisfaction, security, and sufficiency in our relationship to Jesus Christ and not our relationship to earthly treasures. When this happens we are released, as Paul told Timothy, to enjoy the things that God has given to us, but not to trust in them or count them as a source of our security and sufficiency.

Proclamation in this secular age must continue to point our people to the values of godliness over gain, of personal piety over property, and of people over the stockpiles of our things.

While visiting dear friends in Tennessee, I got up early one morning before anyone else and made my way to the kitchen to get a cup of coffee. On the way I inadvertently knocked over one of their treasures, and it fell to the floor and broke. I was embarrassed to tell them, but when everyone else got up I admitted to breaking the very thing that last night they had said was so special to them. My friend looked at me and, without skipping a beat, said, "That's all right, Joe. In our home people are more important than things." What a refreshing moment . . . a Christian who had escaped the clutches of materialism and risen to the values that are important to God.

Tolerance

There is no doubt that the most celebrated value of our pagan society is tolerance. Given the conclusion of relativism that there are no absolutes, and of pluralism which states that everyone is entitled to affirm and activate their own conclusions about life, the natural outgrowth is that we must therefore be tolerant of others' ideas about life and the ways in which they express and actualize their conclusions about living. The opposite of tolerance in the culture's eyes is bigotry. As a result, our culture has little stomach for dogmatic statements about right and wrong and even less patience with those who claim that particular activities are not only wrong but sinful and will be judged of God. In light of our culture's embrace of pluralism, to be effectively modern one must be tolerant.

Alan Bloom makes an astute observation about our modern mind-set. Speaking of today's students, he says, "The danger they have been taught to fear from absolutism is not error but intolerance. Relativism is necessary to openness; and this is the virtue, the only virtue, which all primary education for more than fifty years has dedicated itself to inculcating. Openness—and the relativism that makes it the only plausible stance in the face of various claims to truth and various ways of life and kinds of human beings—is the great insight of our times. The true believer is the real danger. . . . The point is not to correct the mistakes and really be right; rather it is not to think you are right at all."[2]

It's fascinating that the only people the culture is not tolerant of are those of us who are Christians. We're fair game for everyone's slander and fair game for their slapstick sitcoms. The reason that we can be rejected is because we have rejected the fundamental value of our culture, and that is tolerance. The culture refuses to tolerate anyone who is intolerant. Since authentic Christianity cannot tolerate sin or false systems of dogma, then Christians are out of step with this god of our age.

Unfortunately, many Christians have been influenced by this predominant value and have little stomach themselves for specific applications of truth or for scrutinizing false belief systems by the authority of the Word. Christians are prone today to segment their beliefs by saying, "It's wrong for me but I can't say that for everyone." Many get real nervous if we get close to saying that other systems of beliefs are wrong—especially if we name them.

In order to counteract this in our proclamation, we must go all the way back to our belief in God. We believe that God is true and that all that He is and says is absolute truth. Given that, He becomes the standard of what is true and what is untrue. What is right and what is wrong. When we accept by faith that God is and that He is true, we automatically project a righteous intolerance of sin and all that contradicts His truth, and as such we are unable to tolerate false philosophies, behavior, and systems of belief, if we are to be faithful to our Lord.

An effective transformational proclaimer continually underscores belief in a God who is true. This leads the flock to a gracious, compassionate yet firm sense of right and wrong which stands even in the face of a culture that seeks to intimidate and threatens to reject anyone who refuses to tolerate the secular drift.

Sensualism

Ours is a society that places a high value on the stimulation of our senses, whether it be through thrill-a-minute horror and violence in the media, or by sexual satisfaction in any context and to any extent. Standing in bold contrast is the biblical encouragement toward self-control, where we are to stimulate our senses with the presence of the indwelling Spirit and turn our impulses and passions toward loving what God loves and finding our fulfillment in doing His will.

Hedonism

Hedonism fans the flame of sensualism since it dedicates itself to the pursuit of pleasure regardless of the cost. It minimizes the consequences, seeks to erase the guilt, and invites people to *enjoy.* However, God calls His people to find their pleasure in bringing pleasure to Him. In fact, that's how we're built. Just as a child finds his greatest pleasure in pleasing his parents, so we are to focus our attention not on pleasing ourselves, but on pleasing God and others on His behalf. This is the true source of pleasure.

Narcissism

Narcissus is a mythological character who one day, walking by a still pool of water, looked in and saw his face, and immediately fell in love with himself. He became preoccupied with himself and found himself often wanting to go to the pond to see himself again. Our culture fans the flames of this preoccupation with self by preaching the importance of self-advancement, self-enhancement, and self-fulfillment. It's the old "Look Out for #1" syndrome, which has led our culture to clamor for personal rights, privileges, and recognition.

Scripture lifts the biblical value of servanthood as the antidote to the values of a narcissistic world. The best thing, according to Jesus Christ, is to give the treasure of self totally to God, and then in turn as an expression of our love to God, give it to others (Matt. 22:34-40). True fulfillment and satisfaction come not by heaping all of life upon self, but rather giving self away. By serving, not by being served.

Cynicism

Since we have had such massive disappointments from political and spiritual leaders as well as from parents, teachers, and others in authority, society has come to value cynicism—approaching all of life with a calculated mistrust. Needless to say, this is counter to the value of faith which plays such a strategic role in the actualizing of our Christianity. The transformational preacher must work biblically to divorce hearts from cynicism toward God by convincing them biblically and experientially that His character, Word, and will is worthy of their undaunted trust.

Individualism

Our nation has been built on encouraging people to stand alone and make it on their own. Needless to say, this societal value works against the sense of community that the New Testament church reflects. Christians are not rugged individualists but community-minded brothers and sisters in Christ. As Christians we are anchored in biblical values, willing to give ourselves for the benefit of the community as a whole, to submit ourselves to communal accountability and discipline when necessary, and to seek the best for the body of Christ as opposed to seeking the best for ourselves. Proclamation needs to aid this values transition.

Pragmatism

Since our world has eliminated absolutes and a clear sense of right and wrong, the prevailing cultural guiding ethic is pragmatism . . . if it works, do it, regardless of whether it is right or wrong. The values of the kingdom are quite opposite. The kingdom of Christ is driven not by pragmatics but by principle. Christians live their lives doing what is *right* even if it doesn't seem like it will work; even if it's not pleasant or convenient. Our society lives to do what works even if it seems that it isn't right.

Violence

The devaluation of the worth and dignity of life has given rise to random violence in our dorms, in our homes, on our streets, and in the marketplace. Society has placed value on violence by using it as a means for entertainment and enjoyment. It values the violence of abortion and encourages violence through pornography. We have come to tolerate violence as standard fare in a free society. Those of us who accept the values of Christ's kingdom realize that violence against the created order is violence against the handiwork of God, hence violence against God Himself. Biblical values affirm violence of any kind toward another individual or toward our environment as an offense toward God. Violence not only harms another; it harms what God has made for the purpose of bringing glory and praise to His name. It is no doubt the ultimate stroke of the adversary to turn the tables of the instruments of God's glory and make them instruments of shame. And then, strangely, to have the world look toward God and blame Him for the mess that we're in. It's interesting to note that the sin of Nineveh that caused God to send the warning of severe judgment was the sin of violence. God's Word instructs us to care for His creation, to value it, and to use it for His glory and the gain of His kingdom.

Those of us who are dedicated to transforming lives through the proclamation of the Word of God need to keep these ten value conflicts clearly in mind as we study the text, prepare our sermons, and seek to transition our people from the fallen destructive values of the society in which they live. It is our task to enable our people to know and understand the biblical values that replace these secular rules; values bring safety, stability, and satisfaction. Over the stretch of many Sundays our people should be regularly pressed out of their cultural context. Maturing believers need to be taught to identify false values, trained to reject their messages, and project authentic biblical values in their lives.

It would be well to prepare each text with these questions in mind:

1. What biblical value is taught in this text?
2. What is the counter value that our culture promotes?
3. How will this message:

a. define, articulate, and illustrate this biblical value.

b. address the counter value?

c. encourage and enable Christians to transition from one to the other?

A chart like the one on the following page may be helpful to the process.

Vandals broke into the local hardware store and for several hours in the early predawn morning did their work. The doors opened the next morning at 7:30 A.M. as usual and surprisingly everything seemed to be in good order. No one knew that the vandals had been there. Until they went to purchase their goods. The intruders had switched all the price tags. Hammers were $.07 apiece, and bolts were $6.95. Screwdrivers were $139.95 and small televisions were $2.95. While everything basically looked the same, all the values had been changed. When it was discovered, chaos resulted. For years in our culture, most things continued to look the same. What we didn't know was that the fundamental

VALUES SHIFT

Cultural Value	Core Struggle	Biblical Value
Temporalism	Living in the Context of the Immediate	Eternalism
Tolerance	Unlimited Freedom	Righteousness
Materialism	Greed Significance	Priority of the Spiritual
Sensualism	Lust Passion	Self-control
Hedonism	Love of Pleasure	Pleasing God
Narcissism	Self-centeredness	Servanthood
Cynicism	Self-trust	Faith
Individualism	Self-autonomy	Community
Pragmatism	Self-management	Principles
Violence	Pride Vengeance	Stewards of Created Order

PROCLAIMER'S TASK ——▶ TRANSITION – TRANSFORMATION

When isolating the cultural values, here are some questions for the proclaimer to ask as he prepares his message.	*When identifying the biblical values, here are some questions for the proclaimer to ask as he prepares his message.*
1. Where is this value most readily evident? Most effectively communicated and taught? 2. What groups in our culture are most vulnerable? 3. In what ways do Christians reflect these values? 4. What are the short-term and long-term consequences of these values? 5. Which of these values work together to support and encourage each other?	1. What passages best teach and/or illustrate this value? 2. What are the practical problems in applying this value? 3. What problems might one face if he lives in a consistent commitment to this value? 4. What are the good works that result from these values? 5. How might these works impact family, friends, enemies, ministry, church, marketplace, etc.?

values, the price tags of our culture, were being switched. We are just now waking up to the resultant chaos of the change.

A transformational proclaimer is in the business of redoing the price tags of his people's lives. Of taking them biblically through a transition from secular rules to biblical rules for life and existence. It may very well be the most important aspect of the universal context into which the shepherd-feeder communicates.

If we are to be effective preachers, we must come to grips with ourselves, the text, and contexts in which our congregation lives. Effectiveness also demands *clarity.* As we form our sermons to be instruments of change, if they are not clear in their presentation, transformation will be inhibited. The most discouraging compliment I ever hear is, "Thank you for that sermon. It was really deep." They usually mean that they couldn't understand it.

CLARITY

No proclaimer can hope to effectively transform lives unless his presentation is clear. It's surprising to discover that when we think our presentation is clear, in reality it may not be clear at all to those who are listening. We need to work hard to make sure people clearly understand our sermons in two important dimensions. The first dimension is that they clearly understand what the text is saying; and secondly, that they clearly understand what the text is saying to their lives. The first relates to *information;* the second to *application.*

Sermon preparation is both a science and an art. The *science* side of preaching deals with the exegesis of the text. The scientific process mines accurate information from the text based on historical, grammatical, and cultural research. It creates a base from which we can clearly share information with our listeners and reveal to them our discovery of the author's intent for the use of the text.

The *art* of preaching relates to transitioning this information into applicational packages that enable the listener to effectively infuse the intent of the text into the context of his or her own life. The most powerful sermon applications are those that remain consistent with the intent of the text. At this point the science and art of the process must be unalienable partners. Applications clearly grounded in the text ring truest in the hearts of believers as they look at the text, hear our applicational exhortation, and in their heart say, "Aha! I can see that! This indeed is what God is saying in this passage."

Given the importance of the functions of information and application, our preparation process needs to be built around them. The science side of it comes first as we execute our exegesis by studying the full context of the text so that we can create a clear exegetical outline that reflects the flow of the thoughts and information in the text.

Unfortunately, most of us begin to stall out in the process at this point. Once we feel like we have come to understand the information we shortchange the art side of the process—the creativity that yields good forms of application.

Preparing a sermon is like preparing a meal. You get the recipe out, shop for the necessary ingredients, and bring home bags full of all the right stuff. At that point, having set the ingredients on the counter, you are not at the end of the process. You don't ask your guests to grab a can of tomatoes and a little cream and make soup for themselves. But quite frankly, that's what happens in many of our sermons when we stop at the end of our exegesis and then lay the message out in its informational form having little or no relationship to the reality and the context of their lives. If we are to be effective transformational preachers, we will take the preparation of the meal into the next phase with a dedicated commitment to preparing a meal that is palatable, digestible, nourishing, and enticing to those who pull their chairs up to our table. The more effectively and creatively prepared, the more prepared our people will be to ingest it. Even the "eat it anyway; it's good for you" portions of the meal.

Like meals, messages have a sense of presentation about them. A message can develop welcoming aromas and be like a table beautifully set with flowers, matched linens, and the warmth of an hospitable host. In message presentation, these elements are in the form of word choice, timing of thoughts, pace of proclamation, appropriateness of illustrations, and the attitude of the presenter who communicates both a sense of passion about the particular passage and a compassion in his heart toward the listener's context and needs. A good proclamational meal is clear in regard to the text and its application. It provides comfort when necessary, conviction when necessary, healing when necessary, and proves to be contemporary in terms of facing real issues in the real-life contexts in which our people live. And finally, the dessert—the closing moments of the message where both the idea and its application are summarized, and the hearer is brought to a crossroads where a decision can be made for repentance, growth, transition, or transformation, whichever may be appropriate.

Clarity is grounded in both clear information about the text and clear, carefully crafted applications from the text.

The challenge to every sermon-preparer is the challenge of making an accurate transition from the exegesis stage to the applicational stage, from the scientific work to the artistry of the sermon. The transition takes place when we restate the exegetical outline in terms of the real-life situations of the listener. For instance, an exegetical point gleaned from Philippians 1:12 and following might be, "Paul relates his personal perspective in the midst of great difficulty." While this is good information, it lacks assistance in terms of its application to contemporary life settings. Instead we need to transition this same piece of information into an applicational concept, a statement that results from the artistic side of the process, something like, "When our perspective is right, we can sense delight in the midst of difficulty." Note that applicational outlines have personal pronouns that relate to the listener rather than the author ("we" instead of "Paul"; "our" instead of "his"), focusing the text toward the experience of the listener as opposed to the experience of the author. A good applicational point in the outline turns the listener toward a personal goal rather than a piece of information and is best stated in a general principle rather than an explicit application. The subpoints and illustrations will come later to serve as explanatory and support material. The more concise and more memorable the applicational outline the better.

The outline needs to include enough material to adequately support the thesis and enable the listener to arrive at the applicational point, but not so much that it seems cumbersome or distracting.

There are several elements that enable a shepherd-feeder to structure a sermon that is clear in terms of its applicational impact on the listener.

Codes or Principles

An applicational preacher needs to decide whether or not to apply the theme of the text in *specific codes* or *general principles.* By specific codes, we mean focusing our application on specific situations. For instance, if we are dealing with applications regarding biblical purity, we might, after elucidating the accurate exegetical information in the text, jump immediately to specific references to movies, music, pornography, or mental fantasies. We might even list the types of music that render us impure or the kinds of movies that endanger our purity, or refer to the dangers of pornography. These are certainly valid applications, but we need to remember that there will be many within earshot of our sermon who will feel exempt from the proclamation since none of the applications particularly pertained to them.

It is better to precede the articulation of specific codes with the articulation of the general principle found in the text. A clear principle will provide an overarching statement that everyone can use to measure and evaluate their own lives in regard to purity. For instance, in teaching

Matthew 5:8 we might say, "A pure life measures its actions and reactions by the standards of a pure God." Everyone can find an application at this point. The person not hooked on pornography is no longer off the hook. They may, according to this principle, be impure in their business practices. An applicational principle is effective when it points to a target big enough to include everyone. Application may then move to the next level, taking the reader into broad arenas of application.

In regard to purity, we may speak of the need to measure our motives, morals, management of relationships, and life in the marketplace to the standards of God instead of the standards of society. Then we can move to a delineation of particulars that relate to certain codes or behaviors. We may introduce it by saying, "For some of us, this principle may mean that we move from living for our own significance through self-centeredness, greed, and pride. Or for others of us, our challenge may be in the arena of our morals in relationship to music, magazines, videos, or even our thought life. For others it may involve conforming to God's standards in terms of the contracts we write and the deals we strike. . . ."

But we must remember it is the biblical principle that people need to take home. Principles form the targets and the reasons. Codes form the rules. Codes without principles foster rules without reasons and often leave our people helpless when the code doesn't fit the situation they find themselves in.

In light of this it's important to rearticulate the principle toward the close of the sermon. It might be formed like this: "Regardless of the specific applications to our individual lives, all of us are called by our Lord to be pure by conforming our lives to the standards of a pure God regardless of the situation we find ourselves in." Then it is helpful to fold in the data that has been taught about purity. "When we make progress in inner purity we will know the joy of intimacy with Him, and the blessedness of a clear conscience." Stating the textual outcomes of living by the applicational principle provides our flock legitimate biblical motivation and encouragement to apply the proclamation to their lives.

Applicational Transitions

As we move through the sermon from applicational point to applicational point, transitions help to clarify the progress as they reflect on what has been previously taught and whet the appetite for that which is to come. An applicational transition might sound something like this: "Since purity promises us blessedness, in what ways can we expect to be blessed according to this text?"

Applicational Illustrations

More and more, given the fact that we live in a story-oriented culture, the effective preacher must hone his skills as a storyteller. This brings us to the role of illustrations. Needless to say, the best illustrations are illustrations that everyone can clearly identify with. Illustrations out of our weekly newspapers, out of family life, and the proclaimer's personal experiences are often very effective if they are done carefully and in the right context. If the illustrations are from our own family or personal experience, particularly if they reflect positively on our lives, we need to be careful that we don't set ourselves up as being unrealistic examples of spiritual success. Sometimes a disclaimer like, "I wish I were always this successful in my walk with Christ" might be appropriate in front of a story that talks about our personal spiritual victories and stories that share our faults should be clearly formed to not be so specific that they erode the congregation's respect and confidence in us. We don't need to tell in vivid detail all of our struggles. At the same time, it is important that the congregation knows that we struggle with the same kinds of things with which they struggle.

Stories that come from our experience at home can never reflect badly on our children or our wife. In fact, it is helpful for our kids and our spouse to grant us general permission to have them play a part in our sermons. If done well, our children will enjoy the exposure, and while our wife will probably never feel fully comfortable with having her name dropped from the pulpit, if the story doesn't degrade her she will probably be willing for the sake of the ministry to play her part.

If the supporting material is a quote, we will need to be careful that it not be too long. People have a hard time staying with several paragraphs of someone else's material being read by the preacher. In long quotes it is helpful to periodically insert, "the author continues by saying," or "he points out that . . . " etc. And, we must always give credit if we are using someone else's supporting material.

Illustrations from common experiences like television advertisements, popular songs, books, or movies can be powerful if they speak directly to the points, as long as the reference doesn't stand as an endorsement of something less than wholesome.

The most important thing to remember about illustrations is that they must clearly focus on the point we are making. Periodically we get a killer illustration that we try to force into our message, whether it really fits or not. And while it is great to have a smashing story, it will be readily evident to our listeners that it doesn't fit with where we are going and will serve as a distraction to the flow of the text.

We must be careful as well that the weight of the story matches the weight of the point of the message that we are illustrating. When we place our most powerful illustration to support a minor point in the sermon, it will exaggerate that point in people's minds and will be what they carry away from the sermon. As a result, they may miss the full impact of the main point of the text. Main points should be supported by our main illustrations.

The best illustrations never need to be explained. When at the end of an illustration we have to explain, "What that means is . . ." then it probably has not been a good illustration.

When we tell stories that relate to the text, we don't always have to tell the whole story, but only the part of the story that will serve to bring home the application of the text. To tell how a situation concludes or finally unfolds may distract our listeners and diffuse the impact of the point we are trying to make. In fact, a story not fully told will often keep their curiosity. Many times I've had people come up to me after sermons and ask me to tell them the rest of the story.

Some stories can even be broken into pieces, with the first part being told in the introduction to whet the curiosity, and the remainder in the conclusion of the sermon to drive the point home.

Applicational Introductions

When a feeder-proclaimer has prepared his meal through a clear exegetical outline and clear applicational principles, supported by clarifying transitions and illustrations, he is then ready to develop an introduction that whets the appetite of his listener to want to listen to the sermon. Good introductions do three things. They capture the interest of people; create a sense of need in the listener by indicating the relevance of what is to come; and help orient the listener's attention toward the message. Which means that we can't write a good introduction until we have finished preparing the body of the sermon so that we know what it is that we are introducing. Introductions should be compelling and concise and, as one homiletician says, "reach out and grab the listener by the jugular vein."

Applicational Conclusions

Like the introduction, the conclusion is among the last things that a transformational preacher works on. A good conclusion re-articulates the theme of the text and repositions the basic principles of the text. A good applicational conclusion moves the listeners toward a resolve for transformation in their lives and suggests ways in which they can apply the text in the coming hours or days. It may cast suggestions in terms of the parishioners' various arenas of life, like home life, thought life, the marketplace, or key relationships. A good conclusion may include questions like, "Since we have learned what it means to be pure, what difference will this truth make in your relationship to your boss tomorrow morning?" It's important at that point to give them a mental moment to interact as they begin to form their own plan of action. He might encourage their interaction by saying, "Before you go to work tomorrow morning, why don't you write down one way in which this biblical principle will change your attitude toward those you work with?" A good applicational conclusion summarizes the truth of the text, focuses on the fundamental principles of the text, and launches applicational plans by which the listener can effectively transform his or her life into greater conformity with the will and glory of God.

Applicational Programming

A good transformational preacher searches for programmatic ways in which the applications of a text can have an expanding influence on the listener's life. One way might be through a bulletin insert that focuses on take-home applications. Or perhaps through a sermon follow-up program. If the configuration of your Sunday worship service permits, a special elective after the sermon for people interested in reviewing the principles and discussing personal applications can provide interesting and productive interaction for many in the congregation. If you have a Sunday evening service, it can be effective to use that time to deal with specific applications in greater depth or consider other portions of Scripture that speak to the theme. A panel of lay persons could effectively discuss ways in which the sermon could be effectively implemented in their own lives, and in turn help others to glean new insights and applications. This panel can be selected from different constituent groups in the church, depending on the particular focus of the text. Sometimes it would be fitting for older people to participate, or business persons, young people, parents, or a mix of these. As people discuss their own life perspectives and struggles in relation to the text, it can be a tremendous time of raising the sensitivities of others in the congregation to what their brothers and sisters deal with in life, which in turn will create a deeper bond of care and concern.

If we are involved in a series of sermons around a particular theme, testimonies might be used as a part of the worship service to focus on victories and/or challenges that people in the church are experiencing as a result of seeking to apply the themes to their lives.

A proclaimer cannot do enough to enable his messages to land in the mind and heart of the listener. God's Word, as we have noted, is intended to be a tool of transformation, to take our people's lives from living according to the values and impulses of the domain of darkness to promoting and propagating lives that reflect the brilliant light of the likeness of Jesus Christ.

CONCLUDING THOUGHTS

The most powerful sermons are forged out of a preacher who has sought to live out the principle of the text in the week or weeks prior to its presentation. Sermons forged in life smack of the reality of life and will find easy transition into the heart of the listener. Sermons formed in the mind of the preacher with little effort to filter them into the challenging arenas of his own life will probably affect little more than the mind of the listener. We must remember that God gave us His Word not just to make us smart, but to transform our lives into the powerful likeness of Jesus Christ.

We can never forget that the *ministry* of the message is up to the Holy Spirit. It is He who will finally and ultimately take it all home and do His work of convicting, comforting, healing, helping, encouraging, motivating, and transforming. We have simply been the conduit. He will be the enablement. He calls us to do our best to create an unobstructed channel.

And where will a sermon be that is not bathed in prayer? A pastor friend of mine regularly goes into the sanctuary on Sunday mornings long before the people arrive and thinks about the lives of those who will be coming. He then prays for them, most of whom will sit in their familiar places Sunday after Sunday. He prays for the unsaved who may come and for the visitors who will attend. We need to remember that the effectual fervent prayer of a righteous man availeth much.

It's a good plan to save a season of time early Sunday morning to pray through every point and illustration and transition of your message. It will not only give it back to God for His empowerment, but will also help to familiarize you with the material and anchor it in your heart so that it can be expressed more deeply as a passion than as a presentation. I have often found as I have done this that God brings additional insights and sometimes even a reorganization of the final form of the message as a result of my spending time with Him.

The target for effective proclamation is that we be preachers who understand ourselves and our role, who have come to grips with the text in terms of the real-life contexts of our people, and have formed a transformational instrument that the Spirit of God can use to glorify God through changed lives and bring gain to His kingdom.

Could there be a higher privilege in all of life than to be a herald on behalf of the King of kings?

Section Four

PROFICIENCY:
Finishing Well

"Be on guard for yourselves and for all the flock, among which the Holy Spirit has made you overseers, to shepherd the church of God which He purchased with His own blood."

—St. Paul
Acts 20:28

Chapter Twelve

Maximizing Ministry

Proficiency, Progress, Perseverance

Periodically I'm asked what my greatest challenge is at Moody. It's not a hard question to answer. The answer does not relate to finances, personnel, management, or even the busyness of my schedule. My greatest challenge at Moody is me. When I'm keeping myself spiritually, emotionally, and physically fit, I have a far greater capacity to deal with the problems at the office. More specifically, when I keep myself functioning in the context of my gifts and sense that I am growing as a person and am committed to staying at it, even on the tough days, that's when I do my best on behalf of the Lord who called me to serve Him at MBI. Like the old spiritual says, "It's not my brother, nor my sister, but it's me, O Lord, standing in the need of prayer."

Paul concludes our text with an intense challenge to Timothy,

> Do not neglect the spiritual gift within you, which was bestowed upon you through prophetic utterance with the laying on of hands by the presbytery. Take pains with these things; be absorbed in them, so that your progress may be evident to all. Pay close attention to yourself and to your teaching; persevere in these things; for as you do this you will insure salvation both for yourself and for those who hear you (1 Tim. 4:14-16).

It's clear that the primary focus of Paul's paradigm for Timothy's success is Timothy himself. In fact, the text indicates that his leadership will rise and fall on how well he manages his personhood, his proclamation, and how well he proficiently makes progress in his ministry—not perfection, but progress. Paul urges Timothy to take pains with these things, pay attention to these things, and persevere, that he and his flock might spiritually prosper.

Pastor Larry Potts of the Cairo Baptist Church understands the importance of keeping himself fit and focused for ministry when he writes that his greatest challenges are "to stay fresh and enthused; to be interested so that I will be interesting; to work with what is and not wish for what isn't; to remember that no place is obscure and no moment unimportant."

PROFICIENCY

A shepherd whose work is proficient will be admired and respected by the flock for his capabilities and consistent fruitfulness. This outcome depends largely on whether or not the shepherd-leader has learned to function in and through the spiritual enablement that God has given to him. Known as spiritual gifts, these divine empowerments for ministry have been given to each of us as shepherds, although not all of us share the same gift. To be proficient, we must discern what our gift or gifts are, and then do all of our ministry through the motivation and energy of that gift. When we are not functioning in the context of our gift, we end up being frustrated, drained, and stressed beyond our capacity to cope. This soon shows and people get the distinct impression that we are not thriving in or energized for our service to them. They may even draw the conclusion that we are actually not fit to be a shepherd. Fewer things are more discouraging to the flock than a shepherd who is not energized and fruitful in his ministry on their behalf. When caring for the sheep is a chore, the heart of ministry evaporates.

We have already looked at the gifts to the church in Ephesians 4, so let's focus at this point on the list of ministry gifts given to us in Romans 12. In that text Paul records seven spiritual gifts that God has given for the enablement of ministry. They are:

- Prophecy: the capacity to have a clear view of right and wrong and of God's truth in relationship to it.
- Serving: the ability to spontaneously desire to be of help, with no thought of personal gain or acclaim.
- Teaching: the capacity to understand, clarify, and communicate truth related to biblical facts and systems of theology.
- Exhortation: the instinctive ability to relate truth to life and to stimulate others to spiritual growth through the application of that truth.
- Giving: the capacity to gain resources and the energy and interest to give resources away.

- Leading: the ability to envision, organize, and oversee a task with a desire to see it brought to completion.
- Mercy: an innate capacity to feel deeply with others, particularly those who hurt or who have experienced loss.

A friend of mine envisions the networking of ministry gifts in a hospital setting. The first pastor walks in, pulls up the chair, sits by your bedside, opens his Bible, and reminds you that often in Scripture sickness is related to sin in a person's life. After pointing out particular passages of Scripture, he queries whether or not there is anything in your life for which you need to repent. He clearly has the gift of prophecy.

The next pastor to walk in the room straightens the sheets and the covers, fluffs the pillow, and asks with sincerity, "Is there anything else I can do to help?" He has the gift of serving.

The next pastor enters, pulls up a chair, opens his Bible, and begins to expound the scriptural teaching regarding illness, tracking it back to the fall of man, the consequences of original sin, and urges you to take comfort in what God teaches about sickness. He has the gift of teaching.

Not long after he's gone, the next cleric enters the room, pulls up the same chair, opens the Bible, and begins to trace patterns in Scripture where sickness and trouble are used by God to stimulate growth and development in our lives. He talks about getting excited about what God is going to do in your life through this time, and envisions patterns of character development and a deepening empathy in your life that will enable you to more effectively minister to others in their times of need. He has brought you the gift of exhortation.

The next pastor comes and, after a few pleasantries, asks concerning your financial needs. He wonders whether you have enough insurance, or whether your employer is caring for you during this time of your absence from work. He mentions that he knows several people in the church who have the gift of giving who would love to help out, and not only will he contact them, but he and his wife will be happy to help as well. He has the gift of giving.

Not long after this giving-focused pastor has left, the next representative of the clergy enters, walks by the bed, and immediately starts straightening up the cards, straightening the flowers, making sure the room is well organized to accomplish the task of your recovery. He checks your water glass, makes sure that things are easily accessible to you, well within reach. He has performed ministries of the gift of leading.

And then last, but certainly not least, another pastor enters the room, pulls up that now well-used chair, takes you by the hand, and just looks at you with a sense of understanding and empathy. A tear may come to his eye as he sweetly and softly asks, "How are you doing? I've been praying for you." He doesn't do anything. He just emotes, and while you feel better now that he has come, you end up wondering why he feels so badly about you. He has demonstrated the gift of mercy.

Obviously, the setting is slightly exaggerated for emphasis. Nevertheless, it demonstrates how we tend to minister in the context of and from the strengths of our own gifts. We are the most proficient when we are functioning in the context of our gifts. When we use our gifts to do our ministry, we are functioning the way God has built us to function.

How then can we as shepherds succeed at maximizing the potential of our gift?

First, we should strive to, as soon as possible, discern what our gifts are. We have already noted that there are four helpful measures in discerning our gifts. When we are functioning in our gift there will be a sense of joy in the work, we will have energy for the task, there will be fruitfulness, and others will affirm us. When we are not sure what our gift is, we should get busy in the Lord's work and by process of elimination keep searching for the ministries that match how we've been equipped.

Second, upon discovery of our gift we should fulfill our pastoral duties from the vantage point of that gift. Not every pastoral task will be a welcome part of our schedule of events. In fact, many of the jobs we must do, quite frankly, we would rather not do. But when a prophet is driven to lead people to righteousness and away from evil, he realizes that acts of mercy, serving, and giving will often create an environment in which he can clearly call people away from wrong to do what is right. Those of us who have the gift of mercy must realize that one of the ways we extend mercy toward people can be through teaching the Word of God to them. Exhorting the flock to grow can be done from the motivation of mercy particularly if it will help soothe spirits, calm souls, and bring to them the peace and joy that only Christ can give. Those of us with the gift of giving can see the ministry and even those tasks that are tough for us to do as ways in which we give to the flock what they need to receive. Exhorters teach biblical facts, good theology, and foundational doctrine so that they can have a platform from which to exhort people to grow. And teachers need to do the hard work of exhortation and application so that people will be interested enough to come back and hear their teaching the next time. An effective shepherd ends up looking at all of his ministry through the joy and fulfillment that he gets in the exercise of his giftedness.

Which means, third, that all of us are called to be routinely faithful to each one of the ministries that the gifts reflect. In fact, the New Testament commands us to fulfill each one of these ministry responsibilities. Routine faithfulness to all seven of these ministries helps make us a complete shepherd. But the routine faithfulness of each one is energized when we exercise them through the motivation and strength of our own gift.

Fourth, it's important that we recognize the inherent weaknesses that come with each of these gifts, so that we do not destroy the potential of the gift by letting the weaknesses overshadow the effectiveness of our ministry. Prophets, if they do not implement the other responsibilities along with their gift, tend to be harsh, discompassionate, intolerant, and unable to see applicational nuances. Servers become easily overcommitted and end up struggling with priorities and even resenting the commitments that they have made. Teachers tend to shortchange their ministries by rejoicing in facts without application or focus on growth. Exhorters often rush to the application without keeping it consistent with biblical fact, theology, doctrine, and/or revealed truth. This tends to ground their "six ways to become a better father" in their own opinion instead of clear exegesis of the text. Givers tend to give on impulse and can be indiscriminate in terms of who they give to or how much they give to immediate felt needs. Those with the gift of leading are oftentimes more focused on the task than they are on the people who help get the tasks done, showing insensitivity to the weaknesses and failures of others. They often struggle with delegating duties as well. Those with the gift of mercy tend to be more sensitive to the person than to the problem and have a tendency to overlook sin, simply excusing the problem to help make the individual feel better. The result is that the person in pain is not urged to face the reality of his or her part in the problem, and therefore is shortchanged in terms of repentance, remediation, and growth.

Given the inherent weaknesses in our gifts, an effective shepherd learns to welcome others to his side to help him shore up his weaknesses so that he can maximize his strengths. Teachers need to welcome exhorters to their side and rejoice in the ways in which this gift complements his gift of teaching, instead of being jealous and coveting the applause of the crowd that normally goes toward the exhorter. Prophets need to welcome those with the gift of mercy, who put Band-Aids on the flock after he has done his prophetical surgery. And the one with the gift of mercy desperately needs the prophet there to remind people of the part that sin has played in bringing about pain.

Early on in my ministry, there always seemed to be someone who, after I would announce an idea about how to advance the ministry, would ask the irritating question, "How will we get this done?" and then go on with a list of questions that dealt with the details. These individuals were a phenomenal irritation to me until I finally realized how desperately I needed them to fill out the picture of the accomplishment of the dreams that God had given to my heart. The programs needed more than a goal; they needed a detailed planning track along which they could be brought to completion. I have learned to rejoice in the gifts of others who complement my strengths and minimize my weaknesses. This kind of mind-set is important when we build a staff, select deacons and elders, and welcome others to the table of ministry with us. Gifts were not meant to compete, but rather to complement. Or, as Paul said, "What if the whole body were an eye?" A graphic metaphor when you think about a huge eyeball rolling down the street with no hands, legs, mouth, brain, etc. to fill out its function.

I have a friend in ministry who, I am convinced, has the gift of prophecy. It troubles me that periodically he speaks disparagingly toward our colleagues in the work who have different gifts of ministry, exhortation, mercy, or serving. I get the impression that he values only those who minister through the same gift that God has given to him. I think all of us need to learn to accept, respect, value, and rejoice when others exercise complementing gifts of ministry.

It would be helpful as well for us to communicate with one another what we feel our gifts are so that people will understand our approach to ministry better and know how they can come alongside to enable, resource, and complement our ministry. The more we understand one another's gifts, the more we understand why we do things the way we do them.

And last, to be a shepherd who is proving to be proficient in his ministry by the use of his gift, we must work to sharpen the gift that God has given to us. Most of us spend large amounts of mental energy worrying about our weaknesses and trying to eliminate them or make them a strength. If the weaknesses are inherent, then most likely they will never be our strength and may never be eliminated. We can learn something from my friend who spent much of the focus of his life trying to shore up his weaknesses, and in the course of that failed to work on maximizing his gift. Paul exhorts Timothy to not neglect his spiritual gift but to stir it up.

Those of us who serve through our giftedness will find that we serve proficiently, with joy. We will have energy for the work, be fruitful in the work, and affirmed in the work. As the flock observes our proficient and productive service they will be stimulated to feelings of respect and gratitude.

MAKING PROGRESS

Paul concludes his exhortation to build the platform of respect through the development of his personhood, proclamation, and the proficient use of his gift by saying, "take pains with these things so that your progress may be evident to all." Successful shepherds give themselves diligently to the fundamentals of successful ministry. And once again we can be thankful that God has given us a short list. If someone were to ask you what you're working on in your ministry, if you were fulfilling the scriptural exhortation to spiritual leaders you would simply reply, "my personhood, my proclamation, and proficiency in my work." Great targets for those who aspire to be effective shepherd-leaders. And what Paul urges Timothy to do is not to aspire to perfection, but to simply be making progress. The further we go, the better we should become. Effective shepherds keep checking their pulse to see if they're stimulated or stagnated. There is a refreshing crispness about a shepherd's life that is going someplace. They stand in sharp contrast to algae-bound, stagnant ponds that simply provide homes for eels, frogs, and scavenger fish. An effective shepherd asks himself, "Am I stronger in these areas today than I was six months ago? A year ago? Five years ago?"

Paul indicates that progress is observable. I love to hear people talk about their pastors. They often say things like, "He's a better preacher now than when he came," or "He has really grown as a person since he came here to be with us," or "His ministry is more effective today than it has ever been before." Progress not only begets respect but catches people up in the flow as well. When you're going somewhere, there will always be some who want to go there with you.

How does a shepherd stay in the progressing mode? First, as Paul has mentioned to Timothy, he concentrates with an intense focus on these three areas of his ministry life. He "takes pains" to develop them in his life. Over the years, I have found that these can be developed by not only focusing on clear targets, but not giving myself too many targets to shoot at. These three targets are all that a shepherd really needs. I've also found that it's important to not only set goals, but to share goals with others who will hold me accountable for movement in my life toward the accomplishment of the objectives. I've found that it's important to set these goals in a realistic context in terms of my own capabilities and capacities. Setting goals by comparing ourselves to others, particularly those who are stellarly capable, only sets us up for failures. Our spouses can be a great help to us in keeping our goals realistic. We need to keep asking ourselves and our trusted points of accountability, "How's my personhood, proclamation, and proficiency in ministry?"

Second, we make progress when we listen to our critics. Most of the time they have discovered a chink in our armor. And while we don't like to give them the satisfaction of knowing that they have helped us through their criticism, we need to learn to welcome what is true about what they have said about us and work on growing out of the fault.

Third, we should take advice from well-meaning friends who want to help us progress in our ministry. Over the years I have received a lot of good advice. In fact, I have kept a mental list of the most important pieces of advice that have helped me to progress. Here are a few of the "suggestions" on my list: (1) Stay close to your wife and children and keep them the priority relationship of your life; they will be with you long after each of your ministries is done and after your last ministry is finished; (2) Choose your issues carefully; very few battlefields are worth dying on; (3) Time and truth walk hand in hand. This is particularly helpful when a barrage of criticism comes; (4) The mind can only absorb what the seat can endure; (5) Don't hang the hay too high for the goats.

Good advice is fertile soil in which you can grow.

Progress also demands that we are realistic about the gifts that God has given us and who we can become. We shouldn't over-expect.

Progress often requires going through difficult times. James assures us that troubles, when handled and responded to correctly, deepen our faith and make us complete, lacking nothing.

PAYING ATTENTION

I'd like to have a dollar bill for every time my mother said to me as I was growing up, "Joe, pay attention to what you're doing." We're so easily distracted and sometimes disoriented in the busyness of all that we're doing that we move to accomplish some task and in the process spill the milk of our ministry. The last thing we can afford to do is be careless with ourselves. When Paul exhorts Timothy to pay attention to himself and to his teaching, he no doubt is referring to the issues of both personhood and proclamation. He's asking Timothy to make these the major targets in his ministry upon which he will stay intently focused. Part of paying attention involves removing the distractions from our lives. Let's deal briefly with two things that distract and disable us in terms of our continuing focus.

Overcommitment

Most of us who have pastoral gifts desire to help those in need. And maybe it's because we want to do well and be affirmed as a good pastor that we say yes to everything coming down the pike. Unfortunately, when we become overcommitted we get busy doing everything but paying attention to our personhood, proclamation, and the proficient use of our gifts. Rarely does anyone ask us to grow in Christ, spend more time in preparation, or focus more singularly in the area of our gifts. Nearly every need that arises around us is a need that distracts us from these targets. Every shepherd has different measures of capacity to do tasks over and above these three priority issues of his ministry. Some have the capacity to do much more without sacrificing core commitments, while others can do far less. So it's important, first of all, that we know ourselves. That we know the limits of our capacities and we clearly mark the boundaries. And once the boundaries are marked, we never go out of bounds lest we become exhausted and possibly disqualified.

We know we're overcommitted when there is little or no joy in doing the things that used to bring us joy. When we resent doing the assignment we've committed ourselves to. When we are rude and grumpy with those who are near to us. When the three core targets of our ministry suffer as a result of other commitments.

A successful shepherd learns to say no. I'm a classic over-committer and have often contemplated starting an Overcommitters Anonymous. I bet there would be a lot of us in the therapy sessions. We would sit around and say no. We'd say no in mad, happy, slow, and fast ways; in French, Russian, German, Japanese, Spanish, and Creole. We'd applaud and cheer when someone finally got up the courage to say no for the first time in his life, and we'd hold each other accountable. Want to join?

Learning to say no may need some assistance. First of all, we have to get over the fear of offending people. The best way to get over that fear is to have a greater fear of neglecting the core responsibilities of ministry that God has deemed to bless in our lives. It's also helpful to have somebody else to blame it on. Most boards will desire to build some protection for their shepherd, and if you ask them to help you mark the boundaries of your life and ministry, they will be glad to ask you not to do as much as you've been doing. That way you can simply say that the board has asked you not to take on these kinds of assignments but they have selected "Fred Smith" to help. It's important to have alternative ways to permit the needs to be covered if you're going to survive the levels of disappointment among the flock because you can't be there.

Many of the things people bring to you are simply whims of a moment's thought or a distant dream that they have conjured up. The vast majority of things you are asked to do either don't need to be done or in the long run can be more effectively done by someone else.

When people come to me with an idea and ask that the idea be implemented, I have learned that the best response is to tell them I think it is a good idea (if I do) and ask them to write up a proposal and to be sure to include whether or not they would be willing to lead in the implementation and follow-through of the program. It's interesting how few proposals ever come to my desk.

I have often thought that when Satan fell, he fell into our schedules. I have proven time and again that I am not capable of scheduling myself by myself. So recently I got together everyone who is victimized by my schedule—my wife, my assistant, and my secretary—and every other month we sit down and go through ministry opportunities that I have been asked to participate in. Together we decide which ones best fit our priorities and our specific calling in ministry. This has been a tremendous help. It gives me accountability and also grants ownership of my schedule to everyone who is affected by it.

As we mentioned before it's important as well to leave space for the unexpected. In my pastoral work, no one ever called me to ask if I had time to do a funeral on Friday before they passed away. Nor did people who had car accidents or major emergency surgery seem to be very considerate of the other things that were going on in my life. Leave space for the unexpected. And don't forget to make a few commitments to yourself. Recess continues to be very important in a shepherd's schedule.

In addition to overcommitment and often as a result of it is the debilitating impact of stress.

Stress

The greatest danger for those who don't pay close attention to themselves is that the stress factor soon mounts to levels that begin to disintegrate and dissipate their energy, emotions, will, and spirit. Few things pull the plug on our resolve to do well like stress. And forget any notions that you can design a stress-free ministry. That only happens in our dreams. There will always be stress. You can take that to the bank.

My second year in seminary was a year stacked with two-hour courses taught by professors who gave us work like they were three-hour courses. Many of us were married and had jobs in addition to our academic work, and we all thought that the high level of stress was not only unfair but unbearable as well. We sent a delegation to the academic dean to file a protest and an appeal to see if the load could be lifted. It seemed like a callous response at the time but, quite frankly, his wisdom has been affirmed in my ministry experience. He said, "Stress? It's designed into the curriculum. Ministry is full of stress, and part of our task in equipping you for ministry is to give you enough stress to enable you to learn to deal with it successfully." Appeal rejected.

The issue is not whether or not there will be stress, but how we will manage it. Successful management of the stress of ministry focuses on two important lists: a list of those things that are causing our stress and a list of the resources that we have to balance out the stress. We are overstressed when the stress list outweighs the resource list. At that point we need to step back, minimize the items on the stress side, and maximize the resources. The stress list may house items like schedule, a wayward child, financial trouble, not enough time, critics, feelings of inadequacy, ill health, unfulfilled dreams, and other items that sap our strength and weigh heavily on our heart and mind. On the resource side are things like friends, spouse, counsel, time, money, rest, prayer, time with the Lord, time in the Word, others to do a task, medical care, realistic assessment of dreams and plans, the willingness to say no, etc. Some items may move back and forth. Our spouse could be a cause or a resource. Lack of time could be a cause, or well-scheduled time could be a resource.

Stress comes back into focus and becomes bearable and manageable when we reevaluate that which is causing us stress and revitalize the resources creatively to support the stress. This can sometimes be a complicated process, but it is a process that will bring first hope and then ultimately relief. Once the stress and resource scale is back in balance, a wise shepherd works on keeping it that way.

And by the way, it's not unspiritual to work at stress relief. J.I. Packer relaxes with traditional jazz. Oswald Chambers used to go fly fishing in the North Yorkshire Dales. Swindoll rides a Harley. R.C. Sproul is a scratch golfer. Bill Hybels races sailboats.

Overcommitment and stress are major contributors to distracting the shepherd from a clear focus on the three biblical commitments to character, communication, and capability in the ministry. As we pay close attention to ourselves, we'll manage them carefully.

Measure your life honestly and realistically. Do you still enjoy your ministry? Do you have at least two evenings at home this week where you have nothing to do but read, work on your hobby, watch a good ball game on TV, or talk with your wife? Have you taken a season of recess in this last month? An afternoon? A Saturday? Have you spent in-depth time with your wife alone in the last month? Do you have meaningful seasons of time in the Word and prayer? Did you laugh with and open your heart honestly to a trusted friend within the last month?

Answering these kinds of questions will be a good barometer of whether or not you've been paying close attention to yourself or whether or not you are a good candidate for a stress fracture.

PERSEVERANCE

As we are serving within the context of the supernatural energies of our gift, making progress that is observable, and paying attention to ourselves, we should be capable of "persevering in these things," as Paul concludes in his exhortation to Timothy.

On June 4, 1940, Winston Churchill made one of his great speeches in Parliament. In this short but historic rallying call, he said, "We are told that . . . Hitler has a plan for invading the British Isles. . . . We shall fight on the beaches, we shall fight on the land and grounds, we shall fight in the fields and in the streets, we shall fight in the hills; we shall never surrender. . . ."

This is the same victory spirit that needs to fill the heart of an effective shepherd who faces one of the greatest invasions by the adversary in the history of the American church. America is no longer safe, nor are our churches or our flocks. And while our government will probably not close our doors, the invasion is far more subtle and severe than that. If it were overt we would go underground, purify ourselves, and be stronger than ever. But the fact is that it has been a subtle invasion of the minds and hearts of God's people. Effective shepherds must be willing to persevere, doing the best things even in these worst times. We must be committed to leading from the platform of respect that is attainable in any culture by exemplary personhood, by empowered transformational preaching, and by the proficient practice of our gifts in the outworking of our ministry. And we must never surrender. In perhaps Churchill's most famous speech, he simply stood before the troops and shouted in his gravelly voice, with a depth of conviction, "Never give up! Never give up! Never give up!"

We are tempted to forget that the victory has already been won. And though our adversary is still a formidable foe, he is in his death throes.

As God promised, the day is coming when, because of Christ's historically completed death on the cross and the Resurrection, the end will come "when He delivers up the kingdom to the God and Father, when He has abolished all rule and all authority and all power. For He must reign until He has put all His enemies under His feet. The last enemy that will be abolished is death" (1 Cor. 15:24-26). And on that day, as Paul writes to the church at Philippi, God will give Him "the name which is above every name, that at the name of Jesus every knee should bow . . . and that every tongue should confess that Jesus Christ is Lord, to the glory of God the Father" (Phil. 2:9-11).

I am reminded that ministry is not a sprint but a marathon. Paul often uses the metaphor of a race to describe the work of Christ through us. In fact, in Hebrews 12:1 we are commanded to run this marathon called ministry with *patience.* The Greek word for patience is graphic and has descriptive power. It is the word *hupomeno,* comprised of two Greek words, *hupo,* meaning under, and *meno,* meaning remain. The picture is that we are to remain under the pressure imposed on us by the race. Our problem is that we so often do not wish to persevere, but rather to escape.

Our family discovered years ago that when we would eat watermelon at the picnic table in the backyard, if wet seeds fell on the table we could place our thumb on a wet seed and, with enough pressure, shoot the seeds. Our kids became adept at making missiles out of seeds, targeting their siblings.

God's call in our lives is that when the pressure comes we remain under it so that the task might be adequately finished, and that the pressure might do its work to form and fashion us to be capable for the days ahead. The exhortation in Hebrews is preceded by the requirement that we set aside any distraction that takes our focus off the race. Distractions like wealth, fame, women, leisure, position, and desire for personal gain, and a host of other seductions that alluringly beckon to us from the edge of the track.

And what is that sin that besets us? Disbelief? Fear? Or some impetuous or obsessive habit that minimizes and discounts our capacity for Christ?

The remedy against our discouragement and weariness is found in verse 2 where we are urged to fix our eyes on Jesus, the Author and Perfecter of faith. What is important is that it goes on to say, "Who for the joy set before Him endured the cross, despising the shame, and has sat down at the right hand of the throne of God. For consider Him who has endured such hostility by sinners against Himself, so that you may not grow weary and lose heart. You have not yet resisted to the point of shedding blood in your striving against sin" (vv. 2-4). The pattern is set. Christ was willing to suffer for the glory and gain of His Father, not because He enjoyed the pain. He endured the pain for the pleasure of the gain at the end of the process. It was for the *joy that was set before Him* that Christ endured the difficulty of ministry.

And so it is with us. Shepherding the church into the twenty-first century requires a fixed focus on creating a ministry worthy of respect through paying close attention to ourselves, and demonstrating observable progress in our personhood, the effectiveness of our preaching, and the proficiency of our work through the exercise and maximizing of our gifts.

I'm reminded of the little phrase that often guided our forefathers through ministry: "Only one life, 'twill soon be past; only what's done for Christ will last." I think of stepping across the threshold, having finished well—having not been perfect but having done my best—looking into His eyes, and feeling His hand on my shoulder as He says, "Well done, good and faithful servant."

I want to finish well.

I could hope that it would be said of me as it was of Sir Robert Shirley, "In the year of 1653, when all things sacred were throughout the nation destroyed or profaned, this church was built to the glory of God by Sir Robert Shirley, whose singular praise it was to have done the best things in the worst times."

May God help us to be known as sons of Sir Robert Shirley. May it be said of us that we built our ministries to the glory of God by having done the best things in the worst times.

Now to the King eternal, immortal, invisible,
the only God, be honor
and glory forever and ever. Amen.
(1 Tim. 1:17)

Notes

Chapter One

1. George Barna, *Today's Pastors* (Ventura, Calif.: Regal Books), 1993, 48–49. Barna's data to support these assumptions is based on his organization's July 1992 poll. Further data is given in "False Promises: The Assumptions that Hinder Ministry," *Currents* magazine, Barna Research Group, October–December 1992, 1–4.
2. Jeffery L. Sheler, "Spiritual America," *U.S. News & World Report,* 4 April 1994, 53.
3. Josh McDowell, *Right from Wrong* (Dallas: Word, 1994), 11.
4. Alan Bloom, *The Closing of the American Mind* (New York: Simon & Schuster, 1987, All rights reserved), 25.
5. Ibid., 50, 53.
6. Stephen L. Carter, *The Culture of Disbelief* (New York: Basic Books, 1993), 29.
7. Will Durant, *Caesar and Christ* (New York: Simon & Schuster, 1944), 602.

Chapter Two

1. Os Guinness, *Dining with the Devil* (Grand Rapids: Baker, 1993), 26.
2. Kent Hughes, "The Foundation of Our Vision" in *Vision 2000* (publication of College Church in Wheaton, Illinois), January 9, 1994.
3. Gene Edward Veith, *Postmodern Times* (Wheaton, Ill.: Crossway Books, 1994), 15.
4. *The Wall Street Journal*, June 30, 1994, Editorial, "Those Troublesome Christians."
5. John Leo, *U.S. News and World Report,* 21 March 1994, 22.
6. John MacArthur, *Ashamed of the Gospel* (Wheaton, Ill.: Crossway Books, 1993), xviii.
7. Raymond C. Ortlund, Jr., *A Passion for God* (Wheaton, Ill.: Crossway Books, 1994), 205–8.
8. Gary B. Trudeau, *Doonesbury.* Universal Press Syndicate, ©1993.

Chapter Four

1. Kenneth Scott Latourette, *A History of Christianity* (New York: Harper and Row, 1953), 224.
2. Ibid., 228.
3. William Hendricksen, *A New Testament Commentary of 1 & 2 Timothy, Titus* (Grand Rapids: Baker, 1957), 157.
4. J.I. Packer, "Despise." *New International Dictionary of New Testament Theology,* Vol. 1 (Grand Rapids: Zondervan, 1978), 461.
5. Donald Guthrie, "1 Timothy," *Tyndale New Testament Commentary,* Vol. 14; 97.
6. James L. Fisher, *Power of the Presidency* (New York: Macmillan, 1984), 1.

Chapter Five

1. H. Müller, "Type, Pattern." *New International Dictionary of New Testament Theology,* Vol. 3 (Grand Rapids: Zondervan, 1978), 904.
2. O. Michel, "Faith." *New International Dictionary of New Testament Theology,* Vol. 1 (Grand Rapids: Zondervan, 1978), 594.
3. William Hendricksen, *A New Testament Commentary of 1 & 2 Timothy, Titus* (Grand Rapids: Baker, 1957), 158.

Chapter Six

1. David McCullough, *Truman* (New York: Touchstone, 1992), 992.
2. James N. Kouzes and Barry Z. Possner, *Credibility: How Leaders Gain and Lose It, Why People Demand It* (San Francisco: Jossey-Bass, 1993), 1.

Chapter Seven

1. James N. Kouzes and Barry Z. Posner, *Credibility: How Leaders Gain and Lose It, Why People Demand It* (San Francisco: Jossey-Bass, 1993), 22.
2. Ibid., 1.

Chapter Nine

1. "Nothing Between," Charles A. Tindley, Singspiration, Inc., 1968.

Chapter Eleven

1. *Forbes,* 14 September 1992, 65.
2. Alan Bloom, *The Closing of the American Mind* (New York: Simon & Schuster, 1987), 26.